THE
SAVE[R]S
&
INVESTORS
GUIDE

1995-96

This up-to-date
edition is crammed with facts
and information for savers
and investors

WISEBUY PUBLICATIONS

November 1995 Budget Update There will be a Budget in November 1995 before the next edition of this book. Changes which affect the advice or information given here for the 1995-96 and 1996-97 tax years will he available in a free update. Send an ordinary stamped self-addressed envelope to:

UPDATE 1995-96
Wisebuy Publications
25 West Cottages
London NW6 1RJ

THE
SAVERS
&
INVESTORS
GUIDE

1995-96

David Lewis

WISEBUY PUBLICATIONS

David Lewis's Guide was published in annual editions from 1982 to 1986 as MONEY MAIL SAVERS' GUIDE. This Guide has no connection with the Daily Mail or Money Mail.

First published 1982
Eleventh edition 1995

While great care has been taken to ensure that the information in this book was correct at the time of publication, the author and publishers cannot accept legal liability for any loss incurred by anyone relying solely on the information contained in this book. Neither can they accept responsibility with regard to the standing of any organisation mentioned in the text although at the time of publication all companies mentioned were believed to be sound.

This book provides information on all types of investments. If you require investment advice you should consult an independent financial adviser as explained in Chapter 2.

Further copies of THE SAVERS & INVESTORS GUIDE can be obtained from most book shops. In case of difficulty copies can be obtained from Dept SG95, Wisebuy Publications, 25 West Cottages, London NW6 IRJ, price £6.50 plus 70p p&p (UK) ie £7.20. If you order for dispatch abroad, please add £1.70 instead for overseas airmail postage.

British Library Cataloguing in Publication Data
The Savers & investors guide.
　1995-96
　1. Investments. Great Britain
　332.6'0941

ISBN 0-9514595-4-6

Printed by The Guernsey Press Co. Ltd, Guernsey, CI.

Contents

PART 2

Foreword

A new feature of this latest edition of The Savers & Investors Guide is the rosette award ❀ for investments which are the best value of their type. Eighteen of the 98 separate investment entries in part 2 of the book have been designated with a rosette. Most of these investments have some tax concession associated with them which raises the return to taxpayers.

As usual a great deal of detail has changed since the last edition, so study the book avidly. Look up the pages for investments you already have. Are they still the best for you and your tax rate? Are you invested with a recommended company? Look at the alternative investments which are suggested under the heading 'How worthwhile'. Look at the investments designated with a rosette which you haven't already got. Then assess whether to leave things as they are or to swop your investments around. Also read the explanatory Chapters in Part 1. They have all been checked and brought up to date.

We are continuing to offer a free update service between editions, showing the major tax and other changes which might affect investment decisions. Just send a stamped self-addressed envelope to Update 1995-96, Wisebuy Publications, 25 West Cottages London NW6 1RJ.

It's pleasing to hear that there is a loyal following of readers who buy new editions year after year. Because this book is published by a small independent publisher owned by the author, we rely on word of mouth recommendation. If you find this book useful, please recommend it to your friends - or buy them a copy as a gift. Copies can be obtained through any book shop, and are stocked by WH Smith, Dillons and Waterstones. If you have difficulty you can get copies direct from us.

How to use this book

The Savers & Investors Guide is in two parts. Part 1 explains how your tax rate determines the type of investment you need to consider. But tax is not everything. Almost as important is the length of time you wish to hold your investments. That depends on what you eventually want to do with the money you have invested. Part 2 lists all the different types of investments to consider. The important points of each investment are detailed on its individual page. An explanation of what the headings mean is given on page 90.

How the companies are chosen

Many pages list the names of individual companies for you to choose from. These have been selected according to individual criteria which vary depending on the particular investment. Building societies, for instance, are those which at the time of going to press, offer the best rate for the particular type of account for the level of investment indicated; where a large society has the same terms as a small one, the small one is not mentioned. These pages also tell you where to get up to date information on the current best building societies and other companies when interest rates change.

In many cases eg pensions, life insurance, unit trusts, personal equity plans, offshore funds only companies with below average charges are included. In some cases eg School Fees Insurance Plan, all companies which offer this type of investment are listed.

Past performance, although widely quoted, is not usually a good indicator for choosing an investment. An exception can be in the very short term when a top performing unit trust or fund in a fashionable sector or market often continues to perform strongly if the market continues to rise.

New entries and changes

New entries in Part 2 this year are *Building Society Escalator Bond, Investment Trust Warrants, National Savings Pensioners Income Bond* and *Stock Personal Equity Plan*. Two new types of investment will appear later during 1995. The first, called *Shares Open Ended Investment Fund*, is a mixture of a unit trust and an investment trust. The second, *Shares Venture Capital Trust*, is more risky but gives a measure of tax relief. *Shares Enterprise Investment Scheme* replaces the similar Shares Business Expansion Fund. Property Business Expansion Fund, National Savings Yearly Plan and Building Society SAYE are no longer available to new investors and have been deleted from the book. There are also some name changes. *Pension Free Standing Top Up Plan* and *Pension In-House Top Up Plan* are the new names given to Pension Free Standing Additional Voluntary Contributions and Pension Additional Voluntary Contributions.

Acknowledgements

My thanks go to Susan Lewis for editing and verifying. Also many thanks to the companies named in the text of this book for checking information on the pages on which they are mentioned.

David Lewis   March 1995

1

Your Investment and Savings Strategy

The key to successful and profitable savings and investment is to keep up to date with investment opportunities. If you are in the know, you can take advantage of them. This book describes all the best ways to save and invest and several which you are warned to avoid.

All savings and investments should be reviewed at least once a year. The best time to make a major review of your investments is from March to May which coincides with the time when new editions of this book are published. This is because by then you will know about proposed tax changes made the previous November which become effective from 6 April. You also have time to dispose of investment by 5 April in a previous tax year if this is to your advantage.

Some types of investment, however, should be reviewed more frequently. For instance you should check the interest rate on your bank and building society savings every time there is a change in interest rates. They don't all go up and down by the same amount - and even if you are notified of a new rate, you won't be told if it has gone down by more than their competitors'.

The same applies to risk investments - **especially if you are investing in shares. You constantly have to keep an eye on what they are doing and make rational decisions about when to buy and sell**. A good investment can quickly become a bad one through neglect.

Financial commentators often remain preoccupied with short-term changes and forecasts. Interest rate changes and anticipation of changes hit the headlines frequently. For weeks and sometimes months there is huge pressure for interest rates to go down - which they eventually do in dribs and drabs. Then there is a 'crisis', usually to do with the money supply or the value of the £ abroad and they rise again, usually much more speedily than when they fell. In 1994 and early 1995 the trend changed and interest rates started to go up by small amounts. Whether this trend will continue remains to be seen.

Share prices on the stock exchange also fluctuate up and down. In the short term they may go up and then go down, even if the underlying trend for all shares (although not individual ones) is usually upwards.

Some people say forget about these short term fluctuations. They say invest long term. **In practice you have to take both a short and long term view about your savings and investments. There is no best investment for all time.**

Savings or investments

What is the difference between savings and investments? The answer is, nowadays, not a lot. Financial institutions which used to specialise are increasingly becoming more alike - and so are the savings and investments which they offer.

Saving is what you do with the money from your income which you don't spend. 'Savings' is a description of the amount you have accumulated. 'Investment' is what you do with your savings. The word 'Savings' has another meaning - it usually refers to a simple place for your money, like a bank or building society account. It sometimes also implies you do it regularly, say each month or year. 'Investment' usually refers to something more sophisticated. But the two words can often be interchanged - and generally for the rest of this book the word investment refers to both savings and investment.

What is your money for?

You may want to accumulate as much money as possible. Everyone feels more secure with more money. But you should really work out what you want your money for.
● Is it to increase your income so that you have more to spend now?
● Is it to pay for obligations you will have in the future like the cost of private education or for supporting a student in higher education?
● Is it to give you a higher income when you retire?
● Do you want the money to pay for a holiday?
● Do you want the money to pay for repairs and maintenance to your home - like exterior decorations or a new roof.
● Do you want the money for major home improvements like a new bathroom, kitchen or an extension?

● Do you want to accumulate a lump sum to give you the opportunity to make a large purchase like a new car, a first or larger home or even a yacht or a holiday home?

● Do you need your money to finance your own business? Or have you plans for setting up on your own?

● Will you want to give some of your money away to your children or grandchildren as well as leaving money in your will?

Your time scale

Think about when you will want to use your money. If you want to boost your current income, you will want your money now. If you want to replace your car in five years' time, you will need your money then. If you want to raise your income when you retire, work out how long it will be from now to your planned retirement date, say in 15 years' time.

How much you need to accumulate

Now we will see whether you are being realistic or dreaming. Write down how much you expect your objective to cost today. For instance if you want to buy a car in five years' time and you think you need £10,000, write that down. If you want to boost your retirement income by £3,000 a year, write down '£3,000 a year'.

Although inflation has fallen from 1991 to 1994 after rising quite sharply from 1988 to 1990, it still can have an effect on the value of money. **Over long periods of time inflation can have quite a big effect, even at a relatively low rate like 4% a year**. At the time of writing inflation was running at around 2.9% a year but in the following examples, I'm going to be slightly more pessimistic and assume an average rate of 4% a year. You can measure the effect of inflation at different dates by looking at the four tables in *Appendix 4 How Money Grows and Falls in Value*.

Suppose you **want to buy a car in five years' time** which would cost you £10,000 today. Assume that car prices will rise by 4% a year over the next five years. Look up *Appendix 4* for the figures in *Table 1 How Lump Sums Grow*. At 4% a year and over five years you find £1,000 has become £1,217. To find out how much £10,000 will grow to, multiply by ten and you get £12,170 which is how much you will need to buy that car in five years' time.

Now what about that £3,000 a year extra income **to boost your pension when you retire in 15 years time**. What will be the average increase in the Retail Prices Index over the next 15 years? Over the past 15 years price rises (inflation) have averaged 6% a year. Over the past five years they have only averaged 4.2% a year. Over the past 10 years, the rise has averaged 4.9% a year.

Take a look at the same Table 1 again. Look what happens to £1,000 if price rises average 4% a year over 15 years - the answer is £1,801. So in 15 years' time with prices in general rising by 4% a year, an extra income of £3,000 a year in today's money, would have to be three times £1,801 a year which is £5,403 a year, to have the same purchasing power as £3,000 today.

But if inflation is 10% a year, £1,000 becomes £4,177 after 15 years. So the same income has to be £12,531 a year to be equivalent to £3,000 a year now.

How much do you need to invest to get that sort of money? Let's look at the car first. Suppose you want to invest regularly for the new car. Look at *Appendix 4* again. This time turn to *Table 4 How Much You Need to Invest Each Year*. You first have to decide how much interest or growth you will get on your money - suppose you decide to invest in a building society and expect 5% a year after tax. Look up the figure for five years and 5% and you get the answer £172.36. So if you have to invest about £172 a year to accumulate £1,000 after five years, then you have to invest about 12 times £172 which is £2,064 a year to invest for the £12,170 which you will need to buy the car.

For your retirement income, assuming that inflation will average 4% a year, you will need £5,403 a year income in 15 years time which is worth £3,000 a year in today's money. Assume you can buy a Life Insurance Annuity yielding 10% after tax at the time you retire - that means you need a lump sum in 15 years' time of about £54,000 to give you an income of £5,400 a year then.

For a long term investment through a Pension you can expect to get a return of, say, 7% a year (probably more) as there is no tax to pay and you get tax relief on your contributions (for more details see Chapter 9). You can calculate how to arrive at the figure by turning to *Appendix 4* and *Table 3 How Much You Need Now to Accumulate for the Future*. Over 15 years at a return of 7% a year to get £1,000, the table will tell you, you need to invest a lump sum of £362 now. So to get £54,000 you have to have 54 times £362 which is £19,548.

Don't worry if you haven't got the lump sum now - you can invest towards your retirement income instead. Use another table from *Appendix 4, Table 4 How Much You Need to Invest Each Year*. At 7% growth and over 15 years to accumulate £1,000 you need to invest £37.19 a year. So to invest £54,000 you multiply £37.19 by 54 which means you have to invest just over £2,000 a year. To work it out monthly you divide by 12 which comes to about £167 a month. If you are eligible to invest through a pension scheme, you get tax relief at 20%, 25 % or 40% on your contributions, so the actual cost is that much less, that is only £134, £125 or £100 a month respectively.

A rising income

It's all very well working out what you need as an income in today's money when you retire. But what about the value of that income year by year after you retire? Unfortunately inflation will eat into that just as surely as it eats into your investments before retirement. At age 65 a man can expect to live for another 14 years to age 79, a woman 19 years to age 84. Many people live even longer, into their late eighties and nineties.

However if you want a rising income to compensate for, say, 4% a year inflation, a *Life Insurance Annuity* instead of costing £54,000, would cost around 38% more for a man age 65, that's around £75,000, to have the same starting income of £5,400. For a woman the cost is even higher - 45% more for a woman of the same age, or £78,300.

There is another, and probably better, way of investing for a rising income. Instead of allowing your investments to mature at one fixed date, you arrange for enough to mature to keep you at the standard of living you require at your initial retirement age. The rest you leave invested and as inflation bites into your income, you start to draw a second amount or 'segment' and so on until all your investments have been converted from accumulating ones into income producing ones.

If your investment return is high compared to the rate of inflation over a period of 15 years, in reality your retirement income may be much higher.

Your attitude towards risk

Different types of investments have different degrees of risk. There are three main types of risk:

● Risk of losing your money because the investment is one where the value is not fixed - like shares, stocks and investments in foreign currency; or investments like investment trusts, unit trusts and offshore funds which are linked to funds of stocks, shares, etc.

● Risk of losing your money because the organisation which you deposit or invest money with (eg a bank or life insurance company) goes bust because of mismanagement or fraud.

● Risk of losing money because the agent or financial adviser who is introducing you to an investment does not pass the money on and goes bust because of mismanagement or fraud.

There is no protection from the first risk. If you don't like the idea, avoid those types of investment where capital values fluctuate like shares, unit trusts and stocks although eventually they may turn out to be very profitable. In the case of the other two, you must take care to whom you entrust your money, although in many cases there are compensation schemes to protect you. In Part 2, each different type of investment has the position summarised under the heading *Risk*. The position of agents and financial advisers is considered in Chapter 2.

Your tax rate

Despite the considerable reduction in direct taxes and the simplification of rules between 1979 and 1988, investment decisions still depend on your tax position. This is described in *Chapter 3 Keeping Down Your Tax Bill* and *Chapter 5 Capital Gains Tax and Inheritance Tax.*

Different types of investment are dealt with in different ways for tax and this is explained in *Chapter 4 How Different Types of Investment are Taxed.* It's also summarised in Part 2 under the heading *Tax* for each individual type of investment. When describing the plus and minus points of an investment under the heading *How worthwhile* in Part 2, in most cases it states whether an investment is good for basic taxpayers, higher rate taxpayers, non-taxpayers or 20% taxpayers.

Money tied up in your home

One investment which you shouldn't forget is the value of your home. There are four ways with which you can utilise this value:
● If you live in an area which has high property values, you can move or retire to an area with lower values.
● If you live in a large house, when your children leave home or you retire, you can move to a cheaper or smaller one or to a flat.
● Provided the value of your home is significantly greater than your existing mortgage, you can borrow against the value of your home - as a further advance on your mortgage or as a second mortgage. The loan can often be paid off when you sell or die The schemes are usually called *equity release*. Most lenders require you to pay interest.
● You can take out a *Life Insurance Home Income Plan* when you are 65 or older to boost your income. Details are given in the entry in Part 2.

Remember that when you sell an owner occupied home, it's exempt from capital gains tax. If you have more than one home you can choose which one is your *main residence* which will be exempt. You can back-date the choice by up to two years by writing to your tax office. If one or more of the homes are jointly owned, both owners must sign the letter. However if you rent out the home or use it for a business for part of the time, there may be some tax to pay.

A record of your investments

It's always a good idea to keep methodical records of your investments. The cheapest way is to buy a few different coloured envelope files from a newsagent or stationers. Use one file for each different type of investment - eg red for shares and unit trusts, green for bank and building societies, yellow for pensions and life policies. Then whenever you want to check out your investments, everything should be clear and in order. Always keep copies of letters you send to the organisations which look after your investments, and make a note of any telephone conversations and the date.

Another good way to keep track of your investments is to assemble them on a computer spreadsheet program.

Crossing cheques A/C Payee

If you send large sums of money through the post, there is a chance that someone will steal the cheque and pay it into another account. To protect yourself you should use cheques which are crossed and have the words A/C Payee written within the crossing. This stops the cheque being signed over to someone else's account. New cheque books usually have these printed automatically, but if not, you can add two lines across the middle of the cheque and write in A/C Payee yourself. When you send a cheque through the post payable to a building society, an added precaution is to add the name of your account and your number after the name of the society. For instance: Pay Halifax Building Society A/C J R Williams No 4577762.

2

Best Advice and How To Get It

The Financial Services Act regulates investments and investment advisers. It was intended to improve the quality of financial advice you are given and to reduce the chance of you losing money through fraud or incompetence by an agent of an investment institution. The Act has been in force since April 1988.

One achievement of the Act is to compile lists of people who are allowed to be financial or investment advisers. Only firms or people on these lists, apart from the media which is in most cases exempt, are allowed to give investment advice to the public. Originally none of the list makers attempted to judge the competence or qualifications of advisers although most of the advisers will have been qualified by experience as having given investment advice in the past.

Since 27 August 1988 there has been *The Investors Compensation Scheme* if an adviser goes bust after that date owing you money. This applies to all authorised UK financial advisers who are members of the three main regulatory authorities PIA, IMRO or TSFA (for what these initials mean see later in this Chapter). In some cases if you invested money after 18 December 1986, you are covered. The scheme pays 100% compensation on the first £30,000 and 90% on the next £20,000. So the maximum compensation is £48,000 which can be scaled down if total claims for any one authority exceeds £100 million in a year.

If your adviser belongs instead, or in addition, to one of the other regulatory organisations like the Insurance Brokers Registration Council (IBRC) or the Law Society, you can be entitled to better compensation, see *The advisers* later in this Chapter. These other schemes may also cover incidents which occurred before 1986.

If you want to check whether an adviser is fully authorised, and by whom, phone the Securities & Investment Board Central Registry on 0171 929 3652 and they will tell you over the phone.

Which investment advice

The Financial Services Act does not cover deposits in banks, building societies, co-operative societies or National Savings. So anyone is allowed to give you advice on these types of investment. **Advisers registered under the Financial Services Act have strict rules about how they should give advice. These rules don't apply to advice on deposits in banks etc. So it's possible that you can get bad advice on one of these deposits and have no come-back on the adviser.**

Banks and building societies which offer deposit based pension schemes (ie additional voluntary contributions or a personal pension) based on their own deposits, as opposed to pension schemes issued by life insurance companies and unit trusts for which they act as agents, are not covered by the Act either.

Which type of adviser

According to the rules an adviser can be one of two types: an *appointed representative* or an *independent financial adviser*. Appointed representatives are only allowed to advise on the products of one single company or group of companies. Independent financial advisers are supposed to choose the companies they use from all the ones available and only to recommend the best products for each particular client's circumstances. This rule is called *polarisation*.

Banks and building societies although not covered by the Act for their own deposits are covered when they act as agents for life insurance policies and unit trusts for example. Most banks and building societies are now appointed representatives of one company.

Few banks and building societies are now independent financial advisers. But many will obtain independent advice on request. See the box overleaf for who does what.

Best advice

Financial advice is supposed to be best advice. That means the adviser is supposed to get detailed financial information from you before he or she gives you advice. If you are reasonably well informed, as you will be as a reader of this book, you may find this rather tedious. If you don't want to give the adviser confidential information about yourself, you will probably have to sign a form saying so in which case you may not have a come-back if the advice turns out to be poor.

Independent advisers	Appointed representatives (of company in brackets)
Bradford & Bingley	Abbey National (Abbey National Life) [1]
Clydesdale [2]	Alliance & Leicester (Scottish Amicable) [1,2]
Co-operative Bank	Bank of Scotland (Standard Life) [1]
Girobank	Barclays Bank (Barclays Life) [1]
Yorkshire Bank [2]	Birmingham Midshires (Sun Life) [1]
Yorkshire Building Soc.	Bristol & West (Eagle Star)
	Britannia (Britannia Life)
	Chelsea (Guardian)
	Coventry (Commercial Union)
	Derbyshire (GA Life)
	Halifax (Halifax Life) [1]
	Leeds & Holbeck (GA Life)
	Leeds Permanent (Leeds Life) [1]
	Lloyds Bank (Black Horse Life) [1]
	Midland Bank (Midland Life) [1]
	National & Provincial (National & Provincial Life)
	Nationwide (Guardian) [1,2]
	Nat. West. (Nat. West. Life) [1]
	Northern Rock (Legal & General) [1]
	Portman (Commercial Union)
[1] Has independent subsidiary	Royal Bank of Scotland (Royal Scottish)
[2] From 1996 will be appointed	Skipton (GA Life)
representative of own life company	TSB (TSB Life)
with independent subsidiary.	Woolwich (Woolwich Life) [1]

Commission

Some independent financial advisers work on a fee basis. They charge, say, £250. Commission on £10,000 invested in a unit trust or lump sum pension could be 2% to 5% which comes to £200 to £500. The difference is refunded to you, usually by enhancing the allocation of your investment. In the example with only 2% commission you don't benefit from paying a fee. But with larger investments, this method can amount to a very effective discount: eg 5% of £20,000 is £1,000 less £250 gives you £750. *Money Management* magazine maintains a register of independent financial advisers which operate on a fee basis. Phone the magazine's friendly computerised voice mail service in Bristol on 01 17 976 9444 for the names of up to six advisers in your area. The service is free. Bear in mind some may charge fees far in excess of £250 - so find out the basis at the outset. There are also some advisers who split the commission with you. Be careful with those which charge by the hour; their bill could give you a shock.

It may be that you decide you don't want independent financial advice. You may therefore be inclined to deal with the financial institution (eg unit trust group) direct. However if you employ a solicitor or accountant and pay them fees to do other work for you, you would be better off using them as a post box for your application forms. The financial institution will pay the solicitor or accountant commission usually at the same rate as to any other financial adviser. The solicitor or accountant will set this amount as a credit against fees you incur with him for other work he does.

You complete the application form and make the cheque payable to the unit trust group or whatever in the usual way. On the form you will find a space for the 'Stamp' of an independent financial adviser. You can usually just write in the name and address of your solicitor or accountant. Or if you prefer, you can send the cheque and form to your solicitor or accountant and ask them to forward it to the financial institution for you after stamping it with their stamp.

Either way write to the solicitor or accountant saying you are nominating them to receive the commission so that it can be used against fees incurred by yourself or members of your family. If you send the form direct, send the solicitor or accountant a photocopy of the form, so he or she is in the know.

This only really works well if you don't ask for advice; if you do, you can expect the solicitor or accountant to charge a fee for the advice which will use up part or all of the commission. State in your letter to the solicitor or accountant that 'I don't require and have not received any financial advice from you and this transaction is on an execution only basis'.

The advisers

The advisers you are likely to come across are as follows:
- *Stockbrokers* for individual stocks and shares. Most banks and many building societies will introduce you to a stockbroker if you ask. Stockbrokers are regulated by *The Securities & Futures Authority (TSFA)*. Some stockbrokers have subsidiaries which belong to PIA.
- *Independent financial advisers (IFAs)* for buying life insurance policies, pensions and unit trusts. With unit trusts you can always go direct to the unit trust company. These advisers are now usually regulated by the *Personal Investment Authority (PIA);* they were previously usually regulated by *FIMBRA*. Some are regulated by *IMRO (Investment Managers Regulatory Organisation)* or by *SIB (Securities & Investment Board)*.
- *Insurance brokers* for life insurance policies, pensions and unit trusts. Insurance brokers are regulated by *The Insurance Brokers*

Registration Council (IBRC). Insurance brokers which specialise in investment advice also belong to PIA. The compensation scheme if you lose money through an insurance broker is normally 100% of what you have lost. If the broker is also a member of PIA, you may have to claim first to PIA and go to the IBRC for the balance.

● *Chartered accountants* for tax avoidance, trust and estate planning, life insurance policies and pensions. They will normally charge you by the hour for advice and if they receive commission on products you invest in, this should be set against the fee. Some chartered accountants may also be members of PIA. The compensation scheme if you lose money through a chartered accountant is normally 100% up to a maximum of £50,000 and only applies to advice given or transactions made after 28 August 1988.

● *Solicitors* for trust and estate planning although some may give personal financial advice. Solicitors will usually charge you a fee for advice given and should set against it any commission they receive on products you invest in. Solicitors in England and Wales are regulated by the Law Society. *The Law Society Compensation Fund* pays 100% of what you lose with a maximum of normally £1 million for each case. There are separate schemes in Scotland and Northern Ireland.

● *Consulting actuaries* are mainly used for setting up company pension schemes but some may give personal financial advice.

Other regulatory organisations

The managers and promoters of the investments themselves are also regulated as follows. You may need to get in touch with these organisations if you have a complaint.

● *PIA (Personal Investment Authority)* also regulates sales and marketing by UK authorised unit trusts and UK authorised life insurance companies and appointed sales representatives of both.

● *IMRO (Investment Managers Regulatory Organisation)* mainly covers UK unit trusts and investment managers.

● *SIB (The Securities and Investment Board)* is the organisation which oversees all the other regulatory bodies. Some organisations are directly regulated by SIB instead of being regulated by PIA, IMRO or TSFA.

● *Lautro (Life Assurance and Unit Trust Regulatory Organisation)* has now had its functions taken over by PIA.

If you have to complain

If you have a dispute with any financial organisation which is not resolved to your satisfaction by the manager of the department you are dealing with, you should find out the name of the Chief Executive and write with your complaint. If your complaint is still not resolved, you can then try and use one or other of the various Ombudsman schemes listed below. They don't all cover every type of complaint but can award compensation of up to £50,000 to £100,000.

● *Banking Ombudsman.* This scheme excludes anything covered by the Financial Services Act but includes complaints about 'phantom' cash dispenser withdrawals, bank charges, cheque guarantee cards, foreign currency, credit and debit cards, delays and so on. If in doubt, it's worth a try. Most banks belong to it.

● *Building Societies Ombudsman.* The scope of the scheme is wider than the banking one but a building society can reject the findings within 28 days of you accepting it. This only happens occasionally. All building societies belong.

● *Personal Investment Authority Ombudsman Bureau* for complaints about marketing by PIA members and also for complaints about administration for those PIA members which have opted to be covered.

● *Investment Ombudsman* for members of IMRO.

● *Insurance Ombudsman Bureau.* Excludes some major complaints like surrender values on life and pensions policies. Can consider claims which have been rejected by insurance companies. Covers some Lautro members which have not yet transferred to the PIA. May cover administrative complaints for some companies.

● *Pensions Ombudsman.* Includes job and personal pensions but not the State scheme. No maximum on the amount of compensation. Some complaints may be referred to the PIA Ombudsman instead.

● *National Savings Ombudsman* for complaints about National Savings.

● *Inland Revenue Adjudicator* for complaints about your tax office.

Protecting yourself

One of the easiest ways to protect yourself against fraud is always to make your cheque payable to the final institution you want to invest with. This is not possible when buying shares on the stock exchange. Don't be persuaded by an investment adviser that it's 'easier' to make the cheque payable to his firm. An 'A/C Payee' cheque can only be paid into the account of the organisation it's payable to; if these words are not already printed on it, write them between the two lines crossing the centre of the cheque.

3

Keeping Down Your Tax Bill

To choose the right investments, you have to invest by the best way for your own personal tax position. This Chapter tells you how to work out whether you are a non-taxpayer, a 20% taxpayer, a basic rate taxpayer or a higher rate taxpayer (or the equivalent of one). **Before you take any investment decision you need to know which type of taxpayer you are.**

Income tax

Everyone has heard of income tax. Most people would prefer not to pay it. But lots of people pay more than they need, especially on their savings, through not knowing how the system works.

You don't pay tax on all your income. The taxman lets you off paying tax on the first so many pounds. How much depends on whether you are married, single, divorced or widowed and whether you are a one parent family. Elderly people on small incomes also pay less tax.

—————————————————————————————Income tax allowances

Allowance	This tax year 1995-96	Last tax year 1994-95
Personal	£3,525	£3,445
Married [6]	£1,720 [4]	£1,720 [5]
Additional [1]	£1,720 [4]	£1,720 [5]
Personal age (65-74) [2]	£4,630	£4,200
Personal age (over 75) [2]	£4,800	£4,370
Married age (65-74) [2,6]	£2,995 [4]	£2,665 [5]
Married age (over 75) [2,6]	£3,035 [4]	£2,705 [5]
Widow's bereavement [3]	£1,720 [4]	£1,720 [5]
Blind person's	£1,200	£1,200

[1] For one parent families. [2] Applies to modest incomes only - see Chapter 13. [3] See page 73.

This income, on which you don't have to pay tax, comes under the heading of *allowances*. **Everyone is entitled to a *personal allowance* or *personal age allowance*. Other allowances are given in addition. All are listed in the table below.** Personal allowances give tax relief at your highest rate; others marked with a footnote, give 15% relief.

The taxman also lets you off paying tax if you have certain expenses: mortgage interest or pension contributions for example. These are called *outgoings* but the tax relief on outgoings is often restricted too.

Some forms of income are *exempt* from tax: these are listed overleaf. Others which are taxed differently are explained in Chapter 4.

Having deducted your allowances and allowable outgoings (and ignoring income exempt from tax), the taxman taxes your income up to a certain level at the *reduced rate* of 20%. Then the next slice is taxed at the 25% *basic rate*. If your income is above the basic rate level, you have to pay tax on the extra amount at the 40% *higher rate*.

The amount of income tax allowances and the levels at which the higher rate of tax begin to apply used to be changed each year. In theory they are automatically linked to the rise in the official Retail Prices Index for the previous year to September. So if prices go up by 3% from September 1994 to September 1995, then allowances and tax bands should be raised by 3% for the tax year starting on 6 April 1996. But the Government can decline to act on this decision in its annual Budget. Or it can raise the allowances and tax bands by more. Another possibility is to raise some allowances by more, and others just by the rise in the cost of living or not at all. At the same time the Government also announces changes in the tax rates (up or down) and changes in tax rules designed to block up loopholes or to encourage certain types of investment or incentive.

and income tax rates

	This tax year 1995-96		Last tax year 1994-95	
Reduced rate	first £3,200	20%	first £3,000	20%
Basic rate	next £21,100	25%	next £20,700	25%
Higher rate	anything more	40%	anything more	40%

Maximum tax payable on reduced rate band

£640	£600

Maximum tax payable on basic rate band

£5,275	£5,175

[4] Tax relief at 15% only. [5] Tax relief at 20% only. [6] Only one for each married couple.

Exempt from income tax

Investments

Personal Equity Plan.

TESSA kept going for 5 years.

£70 interest a year on a National Savings Ordinary Account

National Savings Certificates (including Index-linked Issues) and Ulster Savings Certificates.

National Savings Children's Bonus Bond

National Savings Yearly Plan*

Interest on a tax rebate.

Interest awarded by a Court on damages for personal injury or death.

Premium bond prizes; betting winnings; National Lottery prizes.

Save As You Earn (SAYE) bonuses.

Some Friendly Society savings schemes or part of some schemes.

Pensions

Christmas bonus for pensioners.

Income support or supplementary pension.

Industrial disablement pensions and allowances paid to the injured person.

Part of the income from an immediate annuity purchased from a life insurance company.

Part of pensions paid to firemen or policeman injured on duty and possibly part of pension payable to others injured at work.

Pensions, pension additions or annuities, to holders of most gallantry medals from the armed forces.

Pensions paid by German or Austrian governments to the victims of Nazi persecution.

War disablement pensions.

War widows and orphans pension

Social security benefits and grants

Assisted places grant.

Attendance allowance.

Child and One-parent benefit.

Child's special allowance, Industrial death benefit for a child., Guardian's allowance.

Council tax benefit.

Disability living allowance, Disability working allowance, Severe disablement allowance, incapacity benefit, Industrial disablement pension.

Family credit.

Foreign social security benefits similar to those exempt in UK.

Home improvement and insulation grants.

Housing benefit

Income support (benefit paid instead of basic unemployment benefit or to dependants of strikers is taxable).

Increases for dependent children paid with widow's allowance, widowed mother's allowance, invalid care allowance, retirement pension.

Invalidity pension, Invalidity allowance (if paid with invalidity pension), Non-contributory invalidity pension.

Mobility allowance.

Sickness benefit and Maternity allowance paid directly by the Department of Social Security.

Social fund grant.

Student grants and scholarships.

Training allowance.

Widow's payment of £1,000.

*No longer available to new investors.

Knowing your tax rate

Most people with jobs are basic rate taxpayers. Retired people may not pay tax if their main source of income is the State Retirement Pension. If you have a large income, you pay higher rate tax.

What tax rate you pay depends on your income. But when you decide where to invest, also think whether the income from that money will put you into a higher tax band. The tax rates and bands mentioned in the following examples are for the 1995-96 tax year.

Take a married man earning £27,000 a year. The first £3,525 is not taxable because of his *personal allowance*. Suppose he makes pension contributions of £2,000 a year before tax. This is an outgoing which gains full tax relief. It cuts another slice off his taxable income. The first £3,200 is taxed at 20%. So £3,525 plus £2,000 plus £3,200 comes to £8,725 which is tax free or taxed at 20%. The rest (£27,000 minus £8,725 equals £18,275, is taxed at the 25% basic rate. Any extra income he receives from investments would also be taxed at the basic rate until the balance of his income exceeds £21,100. So he is called a basic rate taxpayer because extra income up to £3,937 (ie £21,100 minus £18,275) would be taxed at the basic rate.

A wife is treated in exactly the same way for her own income.

They can get up to another £258 off one of their tax bills in 1995-96 because of the *married allowance* (15% of £1,720*)*; in 1994-95 the amount was £344 (20% of £1,720). The same relief is given to single parent families and to widows in the year they are widowed. Unfortunately this allowance no longer acts as a tax band and does not raise the amount when 20% , basic or higher rate tax starts to bite.

There is also tax relief on a mortgage. But this relief is limited to the interest on up to £30,000 borrowed on one mortgage at a tax relief rate of 15% for 1995-96 (20% in 1994-95). Again this relief does not effect when you pay 20% , basic or higher rate tax.

Now consider a more wealthy set-up. Suppose a couple each has an income of £30,000 a year. Husband and wife each makes £1,500 pension contributions. So each has allowances and outgoings which total £5,025. That leaves £24,975 to be taxed. The first £3,200 is taxed at 20%; the next £21,100 is taxed at 25%; the rest, £24,975 minus £3,200 minus £21,100 which is £675 is taxed at 40%. So any extra income from investments is taxed at the higher rate of 40%. **Therefore both husband and wife are higher rate taxpayers even though most of their incomes is taxed at the basic rate**. However if the wife's income is only £25,000 a year, then she is a basic rate taxpayer - and her husband a higher rate taxpayer. So there would be a tax advantage in transferring high yield investments to her name; see Chapter 10. If your earnings or pension put you close to the limit where tax starts, or the higher tax band starts to bite, then you need to work out carefully whether you are liable for tax on your investments and at what rate. If you are 65 or over during the tax year, see also Chapter 13.

Minimising your tax

Often minimising your tax is the best way of maximising your investment return. In Part 2, each investment described tells you whether it's suitable for non-taxpayers, 20% taxpayers, basic rate taxpayers or higher rate taxpayers.

Sometimes the tax position does not make much difference. Take the example of three similar sorts of investments: building societies where basic rate tax is deducted from the interest; National Savings Investment Account where no tax is deducted but you pay it later; and National Savings Certificates where the interest is tax free.

Suppose the National Savings Investment Account pays, say, 7.8% interest and a building society account pays, say, 5.85% after tax. To a basic rate taxpayer after tax, the difference is of little consequence, as the Investment Account interest is taxable and you should pay basic rate tax on it later. This will reduce the National Savings Investment Account interest to 5.85% after tax, the same as the building society pays. National Savings Certificates are exempt from tax. The 42nd issue pays 5.85% so you get the same whatever your tax rate.

Therefore for basic rate taxpayers it's often as important to consider other factors in addition to the tax saving. These are:

● convenience: whether you want the money back easily or prefer to tie it up for a longer period to obtain a higher return.

● whether you expect interest rates to rise or fall over the period of your investment (if you expect them to fall, you should choose an investment where the interest rate is fixed).

● how secure or risky the investment is.

If you are a higher rate taxpayer, there is extra tax to pay on both building society and National Savings Investment Account interest reducing your return to 4.68% a year but none on National Savings Certificates where the return remains at 5.85%. How much the extra tax reduces your return can influence you, as a higher rate taxpayer, in favour of a tax free investment.

Non-taxpayers should consider investments where tax is not deducted because it saves them the trouble and delay of claiming a rebate. 20% taxpayers can claim a rebate or pay the tax later.

Free tax leaflets

From Inland Revenue (HM Inspector of Taxes) or Inland Revenue, Public Enquiry Room, West Wing, Somerset House, London WC2R 1LB.

IR1	Extra-Statutory Concessions
IR6	Double Taxation Relief
IR16, 17	Share Options
IR20	Residents and Non-Residents: Liability to Tax in the UK
IR24	Class 4 National Insurance Contributions
IR26	Business Profits, Changes of Accounting Date
IR28	Starting in Business
IR33	Income Tax: School Leavers
IR34	PAYE
IR37	Appeals
IR41	Income Tax and the unemployed
IR42	Lay-Offs and Short Time Work
IR43	Income Tax and Strikes
IR45	When Someone Dies
IR46	Clubs, Societies and Associations
IR53	Thinking of Taking Someone on
IR56	Employed or Self-Employed
IR57	Working for Yourself
IR58	Going To Work Abroad
IR60	Income Tax and Students
IR65	Giving To Charity (Individuals)
IR68	Accrued Income Scheme
IR72	Investigations: The Examination of Business Accounts
IR73	Investigations: How Settlements Are Negotiated
IR78	Personal Pensions
IR80	Income Tax: Married Couples
IR81	Have You Anything to Declare?
IR87	Rooms to Let (Plus Insert)
IR89	Personal Equity Plans
IR90	Tax Allowances and Reliefs
IR91	Widows and Widowers
IR92	One Parent Families

IR93	Separation, Divorce and Maintenance Payments
IR95, 96	Profit Sharing Schemes
IR97	SAYE Share Options
IR 98, 99, 100	Executive Share Options
IR103	Private Medical Insurance
IR104	Simple Tax Accounts
IR105	How Profits Are Taxed
IR106	Capital Allowances
IR110	Guide For People with Savings
IR113	Gift Aid: A Guide for Donors and Charities
IR114	TESSA
IR115	Tax And Childcare
IR119	Tax Relief on Vocational Training
IR120	You And The Inland Revenue
IR121	Tax And Pensioners
IR123	Mortgage Interest Relief
IR127	Are You Paying Too Much Tax On Savings?
IR131	Statements of Practice
IR133	Company Cars
IR134	Relocation Packages
IR136	Company Vans
IR137	The Enterprise Investment Scheme
IR141	Open Government
IR142	Self Assessment
CGT4	Capital Gains: Owner Occupied
CGT6	Retirement Relief on Disposal of a Business
CGT11	Capital Gains Tax And The Small Businessman
CGT13	Indexation Allowance for Quoted Shares
CGT14	Capital Gains Tax: An Introduction
CGT15	Capital Gains Tax: Married Couples
CGT16	Indexation Allowance: Disposal After 5 April 1988

4

How Different Types of Investments Are Taxed

Almost all forms of interest and dividends are taxable and should be disclosed to the Inland Revenue on your tax return when you are sent one, generally in April each year. Interest credited or accumulated in a bank or savings account or re-invested in a unit trust counts just as much as interest paid out to you.

If you don't receive a tax return for a few years, don't assume you will escape paying tax on interest where tax has not been deducted before you received it. When you have income liable for tax, it's up to you to ask for a tax return if you have not been sent one.

Tax free investments

Forms of income which are truly tax free which you can invest in and don't need to be disclosed to the taxman are interest on a Tessa kept going for 5 years, the proceeds of all types of Personal Equity Plans, National Savings Certificates (including the Index-Linked Issues), SAYE and Premium Bond winnings. The first £70 interest from a National Savings Bank Ordinary Account is also tax free. A husband and wife can each get up to £70 tax free.

You can also rent out a room - see *Rents* later in this chapter.

Interest with tax deducted

Many investments pay interest after deducting basic rate income tax. These include UK banks, building societies, local authority loans and National Savings First Option Bond. So if the interest rate used is 7% a year, and you have £10,000 invested, your before tax or gross interest is £700. With a 25% basic rate of income tax, then 25% is deducted by the building society or whatever, which comes to £175, and you are left with £525 after tax or *net*. The building society, bank or local authority should provide you with a *tax voucher* saying how much interest was paid and how much tax has been deducted although you may have to wait until the end of the tax year to receive it.

If you are not liable to UK tax on this interest, you can reclaim the tax from the Inland Revenue. The Inland Revenue will ask you to send it the tax voucher, so keep it in a safe place. If you are not sent a tax voucher, the bank or building society must give you one on request.

If your entire taxable income (excluding any income, pensions or social security payments which are tax exempt - see list on page 26) is less than your personal tax allowances (personal or personal age - see list on page 24), then you can fill in a form which allows the bank or building society to pay your interest without deduction of tax. You need a separate form for each individual account you have. The form is on the back of Inland Revenue leaflet *IR110 A Guide for People with Savings* and is available from banks and building societies and the Inland Revenue.

If you have a joint account and only one of you is eligible to have interest paid without deduction of tax, the one who is eligible can have half the interest paid without deduction of tax. Many banks and building societies allow this - check if yours does.

If your income is mainly from investments with tax deducted but your taxable income is more than your personal allowances, you are not eligible to have interest paid without deduction of tax. You will need to claim a rebate from the Inland Revenue. This can occur if you have retired early and don't receive a job or State pension.

If you are a higher rate taxpayer, you have to pay extra, based on your before tax or *gross* income. You will receive a tax bill from the Inland Revenue separately.

Before 6 April 1991

Interest paid to UK resident individuals on or before 5 April 1991 by UK banks and building societies and on local authority fixed term loans normally came *basic tax paid*. Individual investors who were basic rate taxpayers did not have to pay extra tax but non-taxpayers cannot claim the tax back.

Tax disclosure

Whether or not interest has tax deducted, UK banks, building societies, local authorities and National Savings provide details of all interest paid or credited to your account to the Inland Revenue.

Interest not taxed before you get it

Interest from the National Savings Bank Investment and Ordinary Accounts, National Savings Income, Capital and Pensioners Bonds, British Government Stocks bought through the National Savings Stock Register (and War Loan however bought), interest on deposits with co-operative societies and interest from abroad (eg offshore bank accounts including the Channel Islands and the Isle of Man) does not have tax deducted from it. Nor does interest paid to someone with a UK bank account for a fixed term which was opened on or before 5 July 1984, nor (until 5 April 1996) on deposits by trustees of a Discretionary or Accumulation Trust (see Chapter 11), nor by someone resident abroad or on certain fixed term deposits over £50,000 with a bank or building society.

They are therefore convenient investments for non-taxpayer because you don't have the trouble of claiming a tax rebate. Taxpayers, however, have to pay tax on the income from these investments and the income should therefore be included on your tax return.

For new accounts opened since 6 April 1994, interest is taxed on a *current year basis* - ie you pay tax on the interest paid or credited in the tax year it is paid or credited.

If your account was opened before 6 April 1994, your interest may have been taxed on a *preceding year basis*. This is now being phased out. If you are taxed on a *preceding year basis*:

● Tax for the 1995-96 tax year will be based on interest paid or credited during the 1994-95 tax year.
● Tax in the 1996-97 tax year will be based on your total interest in the 1995-96 tax year and the 1996-97 tax year divided by two.
● Tax in the 1997-98 and subsequent years will be on the interest in the same tax year as it is paid or credited ie the *current year basis*.

Tax assessed under these rules is payable in one lump sum on 1 January each year. Where the interest is relatively low compared with your salary or pension from your former job, instead of asking for a lump sum, the taxman will collect the interest from your earnings or job pension by reducing the allowances on your PAYE code number by the amount of the interest.

Rents

You pay tax on rents you receive on 1 January of the tax year in which you receive them. That means you may be paying tax on income you have not yet received (on rent payments due from January to March each year). However rent is normally paid quarterly in advance. A quarterly rent payment on 25 March is for the period April to June and would normally be regarded as being due for the next tax year.

The Inland Revenue makes an estimated assessment based on the previous year's rents - and then after you have made your tax return, adjusts the assessment and either gives you a rebate, or asks for more.

You can claim tax relief on various expenses you incur such as legal costs, estate agents charges, insurance, repairs, maintenance and decorations, electricity and other utilities etc. If the tenants reimburse you for all or part, you should add the amount to the rent you declare. You can also claim on interest of a loan to buy a commercial property up to the amount of rent you receive on all your properties. So if your rents don't exceed the interest you pay, you won't get full tax relief. Unused tax relief on interest can be claimed in future years provided you don't sell the property on which you incurred the interest.

Rent a room in your home Since 6 April 1992, you don't have to pay tax if the rent comes to £3,250 or less in the tax year and the room is furnished and in your only or main home. If the rent comes to more than £3,250 you can pay tax on the extra rent over £3,250 or you can pay tax on the whole amount in the normal way (and claim allowances for depreciation on furniture etc). For more details see the Inland Revenue leaflet *IR87 Rooms To Let (Plus Insert)*.

Life insurance policies

Life insurance companies pay tax. But the proceeds of a life insurance policy (endowment, unit-linked, whole life, etc.) are normally free of basic rate income tax and capital gains tax. The proceeds are the amount paid out when the policy matures or when you die

Although you are exempt from capital gains tax on your life policy, the insurance company is not. Capital gains tax may be deducted before you receive the proceeds of some unit-linked policies; with others the deduction is reflected in the price of the units. The rate of tax for life companies on these policies is 25% for both income and capital gains.

Higher rate taxpayers are usually liable to pay extra income tax when they receive the proceeds of a single premium life insurance policy (or on death); or when they cash a regular premium policy which has not been going for ten years (or three-quarters of the original term if less) or a regular premium policy which is not a qualifying one .

Single premium policies (investment bonds) often allow the policyholder to draw a tax free income each year. Such a payment does not count as income for tax purposes and up to 5% of the original investment can be drawn for 20 years, even by higher rate taxpayers, without any liability to pay extra tax. If you don't draw 5% in one year, the allowance can be carried forward and used in a subsequent year. If you make a withdrawal of more than 5% in a year which cannot be set off against unused allowances for withdrawals in previous years, the excess over 5% is taxed at the difference between the basic and the higher rate of tax if you arc liable to the higher rate of tax. The amount of extra tax is 15%, that is 40% minus 25%. The amount of tax may sometimes be reduced by using *top slicing relief.* Consult an accountant before you cash a large policy.

As mentioned before, a basic rate taxpayer has no liability to pay tax on the proceeds of such insurance policies although a higher rate taxpayer does. The point to watch out for is that a large policy showing a large profit paid out in one tax year could convert a basic rate taxpayer into a higher rate taxpayer whereas without the proceeds being paid he would not be. For this reason such policies are often sold in *segments* (eg five £5,000 policies instead of one £25,000 policy) to enable you to avoid receiving large amounts in any one tax year, by cashing in each one in a separate tax year.

A large policy cashed after you retire could also reduce Age Allowance and so raise your tax bill - see Chapter 13.

Regular premium life insurance policies (eg monthly or yearly) taken out on or before 13 March 1984 are eligible for tax relief on the premiums. Tax relief is not available for single premium policies nor on policies started after that date. The tax relief is already included in the premiums you pay. The relief is currently 12½% and is likely to be reduced to 10% eventually.

Dividends and unit trust distributions

Dividends from shares you hold in companies and income distributions from unit trusts come with a tax credit. Since 6 April 1993 this tax credit has been equivalent to the 20% rate of tax. Basic rate taxpayers don't pay extra tax. Non-taxpayers can claim a rebate; 20% taxpayers cannot. Higher rate taxpayers pay 20% extra. The 20% tax rate for tax credits does not affect the 20% tax band which is available in full to everyone in addition. Some unit trusts which invest in cash or stocks come with 25% tax deducted. For the 1992-93 tax year and earlier years, the tax credit for all dividends and distributions was 25%.

Personal pensions and retirement annuities

How pensions are taxed is described in Chapter 9.

Accrued income

If you have invested in *Building Society Permanent Interest Bearing Shares, Stock Convertible Loan, Stock Government Fixed Interest, Stock Government Index-Linked* or *Stock Loan and Debenture* and the total *nominal value* of all stocks of these types you own is more than £5,000, then the accrued income scheme applies when you acquire or dispose of any stock of this type.

When you buy or sell stock, the stockbroker (or Department for National Savings if you buy or sell through them) will work out how much accrued interest applies and will add it to, or deduct it from your contract note.

When you buy a stock, if accrued interest is added to the amount you pay, you can claim tax relief on this amount against your other income. If accrued interest is deducted, so you pay less, then you have to declare this amount on your tax return and pay tax on it.

When you sell a stock, if accrued interest is added to the amount you receive, you have to declare this amount on your tax return and pay tax on it. If accrued interest is deducted, so you receive less, then you can claim tax relief on this amount against your other income.

There is a free Inland Revenue explanatory leaflet *IR68 Accrued Income Scheme*.

Equalisation on unit trusts

When you buy any kind of unit trust and some offshore funds, your first distribution or dividend will be equal to the amount you would have received had you owned units for the whole period since the last dividend payment even though you have not owned them for the full time. The amount relating to the period before you bought your units is called *equalisation*. This equalisation payment is not liable to income tax - so only the taxable part should be declared on your tax return.

However you should keep a record of any equalisation payments as they count as a return of capital and should be deducted from your purchase cost when you calculate the amount for capital gains tax if this is applicable.

5

Capital Gains Tax and Inheritance Tax

Capital gains tax

When you sell or give away an asset for more than you paid (or it's worth more than when you were given it) you have made a capital gain. Most capital gains are liable to capital gains tax but because of the various exemptions and the index-linking provisions many gains can escape the tax altogether.

You *dispose* of an asset when you sell it or give it away. When you buy an asset or are given one, you *acquire* it.

For assets disposed of on or after 6 April 1988 the original cost is taken as the value of the asset on 31 March 1982 if you acquired it on or before that date, or the actual cost if you acquired it later.

If you incur any expenses while buying or selling an asset (eg stockbroker's or agent's commission, stamp duty, legal fees) you are allowed to add these to your original cost. If you make a loss when you sell or give away an asset, this loss can be set against any gains you have made on other assets before the tax is levied. If your losses come to more than your gains you can carry forward the losses indefinitely to be set against gains you make in the future.

The first £6,000 of capital gains you make in the 1995-96 tax years (£5,800 1994-95) is tax free. The balance is added to your income and taxed at 20%, 25% or 40% depending on your total income and gains for the year. **Husband and wife each have their own limit.** So if an asset is owned equally, husband and wife can each use their own exemption limit. Each child has a separate exemption limit. Most trusts have a separate limit for capital gains tax of £3,000 in 1995-96 (£2,900 1994-95). Trusts currently pay tax at 35%.

Exempt Certain assets are exempt from capital gains tax. These are your main home (if you own more than one, you can choose which one is your main home within two years of buying the second; you can also change your mind, and back date the new choice by up to two years); private cars; National Savings Certificates; SAYE; Personal Equity Plans; National Savings Yearly Plan; betting and lottery winnings and Premium Bonds; life insurance policies if you are the original owner. British Government Stock is exempt and so are other stocks bought after 13 March 1984. Also exempt are shares in Business Expansion Scheme Companies and Enterprise Investment Fund Schemes sold for the first time, having been held 5 years, and bought after 18 March 1986. Foreign currency *spent* (eg on holidays and holiday homes abroad) is exempt although currency bought and sold for gain is not. Things like boats and caravans which are not expected to last for more than 50 years are also exempt. Tangible moveable assets (ie personal belongings furniture, jewellery) worth less than £6,000 at the time of disposal (a set of objects, eg a pair of ear-rings, usually counts as one object) are also exempt. If the proceeds are more than £6,000 from each object, the taxable gain is $^5/_3$ rds of the excess over £6,000 if this is less than the actual gain.

There is no capital gains tax payable on your estate on death but see *Inheritance tax* below.

Indexation Capital gains tax takes account of inflation. Instead of deducting the original cost from the sale price, to work out the gain you take that original cost (plus any allowable expenses on purchase) and normally uplift it by an *indexation allowance* based on the change in the Retail Prices Index from the date of purchase to the date of disposal. This will reduce your gain and possibly eliminate it altogether. There are two Inland Revenue leaflets available on the indexation allowance *CGT13 Indexation Allowance on Quoted Shares* and *CCT16 Indexation Allowance: Disposals after 5 April 1988.*

For assets acquired before 31 March 1982, the indexation allowance is worked out as if the asset was acquired in March 1982. So the acquisition value is based on the value at 31 March 1982, not what you actually paid.

For assets acquired after 31 March 1982, the indexation allowance is worked out according to the month in which you acquired the asset and the month in which you disposed of it.

You can no longer create a tax loss or increase a tax loss by using the indexation allowance although from 30 November 1993 to 5 April 1995, you can do so up to a maximum of £10,000 in each tax year.

Unit Trust Savings Plan or Investment Trust Savings Plan Where you invest monthly, you don't have to use monthly indexation figures. You can use the indexation allowance for July each year instead.

Gifts and gains tax If you make a gift of an asset you may be liable to pay capital gains tax if the gain is large. So give away cash or assets which are exempt, see list on the next page. Gifts to a trust incur gains tax in the same way as gifts to an individual. Gifts between husband and wife and vice-versa are ignored. When it comes to working out the gain, the date the original owner acquired the asset counts, ignoring any transfers between husband and wife.

Business assets. There are exemptions when you retire from a business. And if you give away a business asset, you can agree with the person you gave it to defer any gains tax. See Inland Revenue booklets *CGT11 Capital Gains Tax and the Small Businessman* and *CGT6 Retirement Relief on Disposal of a Business.*

Time to pay Where you make a gift of land (eg a house) or controlling shareholding of a company or a minority holding in an unquoted company, capital gains tax can be paid over ten years, but interest must be paid unless it's agricultural property.

Inheritance tax

Inheritance tax is a tax on what you leave in your will (and on gifts you make in your lifetime to some trusts and companies). It only affects people who are likely to leave more than £154,000 in 1995-96 (1994-95 £150,000).

Where the estate, plus non-exempt gifts which were made within seven years before death, comes to more than £154,000, then the tax starts to bite at a rate of 40% of the excess. So if your estate is worth £300,000 (after deducting debts like mortgages, bank loans and outstanding bills) then deduct £154,000 which leaves £146,000 and the tax is 40% of £146,000 which is £58,400.

Non-exempt gifts made within 3 years of death are added to the estate. For gifts made between 3 and 7 years of death only part of the gift is added to the estate: 80% is added for gifts made more than 3 but less than 4 years before death; 60% is added for gifts made more than 4 but less than 5 years; 40% is added for gifts made more than 5 but less than 6 years; 20% is added for gifts made more than 6 but less than 7 years. Seven years after the gift is made, it is no longer taxable.

Exempt gifts which are not added to the estate even if the giver dies within seven years of making them are:
● Any amount to your husband or wife (even if you are not living with them or are separated but not divorced) which is also tax free on death.
● In addition £3,000 in any tax year. If you don't use all the allowance in one tax year, you can use the balance in the next one, after you have used up that year's allowance. Husband and wife each have a £3,000 a year allowance. So between the two they can give £6,000 a year - or £12,000 if neither has used the allowance from the previous tax year.
● In addition, wedding gifts: £5,000 by each parent (including step-parents). £2,500 by each grandparent or great-grandparent and also the bride and groom to each other; and £1,000 by anyone else.
● In addition, money spent on your own child's education or maintenance if he or she is under 18 or still in full time education; or reasonable provision for the care or maintenance of a *dependent relative.*
● In addition, *normal expenditure* gifts which you give out of your after tax income and which don't affect your standard of living, ie you don't have to draw on capital to make them.
● You can also give up to £250 each tax year to any number of different people provided they have not received any other gifts from you (say under the above exemptions) in the same tax year.

Other exemptions are available on 100% of the value of assets in unincorporated businesses, owner-occupied farms and farm tenancies, and holdings of over 25% in unquoted or USM companies.

There are 50% exemptions for controlling holdings in quoted companies and holdings of 25% or less in unquoted or USM companies and certain other assets including the interest of a landlord in let farmland.

You can also avoid tax on works of art thought to be part of the National Heritage provided these are listed on The Register of Conditionally Exempt Works of Art and are available for view by the public by appointment. The computerised register can be viewed at the Victoria & Albert Museum, National Library of Scotland, National Museum of Wales and Ulster Museum.

A free booklet *Inheritance Tax (IHT1)* is available from the Capital Taxes Offices of the Inland Revenue in London, Edinburgh and Belfast.

6

Spread Your Money Around

However much money you have, you want to make the most of it. But making the most of your money does not mean ploughing it all into one investment. You need different investments to suit different needs.

Emergency fund

This is the first purpose of having any investment: a sum of money which you can get at immediately without any penalty if something unexpected happens. For people who have little money, an emergency fund may be their only form of investment.

How much you should have in an emergency fund depends on how worried you are about an emergency. People do fall ill, have accidents, lose their jobs or have to carry out major repairs on their homes. It makes life much easier if you have ready cash to pay for some or all of these things should they occur.

A fund of £500 might do for a young single person. A married couple with children might aim for £2,000 to £3,000. If you are more cautious your emergency fund might be as high as £4,000 or £5,000. The higher your income and expenditure, the higher emergency fund you are likely to need as you will not only use it for emergencies but also to help pay for larger items of spending (say holidays or house repairs). People with jobs might think in terms of three months' pay.

An emergency fund of £3,000 (per couple) will not affect your right to state means tested Family Credit, Income Support, Council Tax Benefit (formerly called rate rebate) or Housing Benefit (formerly called rent rebate). One between £3,000 and £8,000 (£16,000 for Housing Benefit and Council Tax Benefit) will reduce the state benefits but not eliminate them. Each child has a £3,000 limit of its own.

However, there is no need to have the rest of your money readily available. If you are particularly worried about running out of funds, you should tie up as much as you can spare so that it becomes available at regular intervals, say, every year or every two years. Then every year or two, you should check whether your emergency fund is large enough and if necessary replenish it. If you have no savings, it's worth making a commitment to invest so much each month by a method which does not tie up your money for too long, in order to build up an emergency fund for the future.

Don't tie up your money for too long

Time may pass quickly. But when you find you are short of money or interest rates have changed, time can pass all too slowly for you. So unless you have a great deal of money, don't tie up your money for too long; you are quite likely to want it back early. Getting back a long term investment early usually makes it worse value than having left the money immediately available all the time.

Also be warned against tying up your money at a fixed rate of interest for more than two to four years at a time. If meanwhile other rates rise and offer a better return, you may then find yourself lured into changing your plans and suffer a penalty.

Compensation funds

Even if you invest in a way where your capital does not fluctuate in value, there is always a chance that the body you are investing in will go bust. It may be rare but it should not be forgotten. With some forms of investment there are compensation funds designed to refund some of your money if this happens. The funds are summarised below:

Banks which are licensed by the Bank of England are covered by a compensation scheme for 75% (90% from 1 July 1995) of the first £20,000 of each investor's total deposits with a bank (ie £40,000 for a joint account owned equally by two people). Maximum payment is £15,000 per investor (£18,000 from 1 July 1995). Deposits for an original term of over 5 years and in currencies other than sterling are excluded. (From 1 July 1995 all European Union member currencies and the ECU are included). See also *offshore banks* below.

Building societies are protected by a scheme which pays 90% of the first £20,000 of each investor's deposits (ie £40,000 for a two person joint account). Maximum payment is £18,000 per investor. This scheme includes all currencies although UK building societies don't currently offer foreign currency deposit facilities.

UK authorised insurance companies are covered by the Policyholders Protection Act which gives a 90% compensation less *excessive benefits*, a concept determined by a Policyholders Protection Board.

Overseas insurance companies (Isle of Man, Jersey, Guernsey and Gibraltar count as overseas) not authorised by the Department of Trade must say they are not authorised in any advertisement or circular; don't invest in them.

UK authorised unit trusts These are covered by *The Investors Compensation Scheme* which covers each investor for 100% of losses up to £30,000 and for 90% of the next £20,000 making a maximum payment of £48,000. This applies to investments made no earlier than 18 December 1986. There is no compensation for a fall in unit or share prices, only if there is a loss due to mismanagement or fraud by the managers.

Personal equity plans are covered by *The Investors Compensation Scheme*.

Friendly societies are covered by *The Investors Compensation Scheme*.

Co-operative societies are covered by a compensation scheme which has the same limits as for UK banks.

Local authorities don't have a formal compensation scheme but the Government would probably stand behind any authority liable to default on its loans.

Department for National Savings is a government department and therefore has a government guarantee.

Financial advisers Most are covered by *The Investors Compensation Scheme*. For more on advisers, and higher limits for solicitors and insurance brokers, see Chapter 2.

Offshore banks with branches abroad can advertise for deposits in the UK and have representative offices here even though they are not licensed by the Bank of England. They are not covered by the UK bank compensation scheme; nor are branches of UK banks in Guernsey, Jersey, Alderney or the Isle of Man.
● Isle of Man banks and UK bank branches in the Isle of Man are covered by a local compensation scheme for 75% of the first £20,000 of each investor's total deposits with a bank (ie £40,000 for a joint account owned equally by two people). The maximum payment is £15,000 per investor and includes deposits in any currency.
● If you open an account at a bank in the USA you are covered for 100% of up to US$100,000 per person (ie US$200,000 on a joint account or US$400,000 where an account is in four names) if the bank belongs to the Federal Deposit Insurance Corporation.

Offshore funds Where a fund is located abroad and the fund is *recognised* by the Securities & Investment Board, there are compensation funds with similar limits to *The Investors Compensation Scheme*.

● Isle of Man, Jersey for *recognised* funds: limits same as for *The Investors Compensation Scheme* in the UK but with a lower overall yearly total pay out for all claims.

● Guernsey for *recognised* funds: compensation for each investor of 90% on the first £50,000 and 30% on the next £50,000.

● Bermuda for *recognised* funds: 100% on the first US$50,000.

So for a £100,000 investment, in Guernsey the maximum payment would be £60,000 whereas in the UK it would be £48,000. But for £30,000, in the UK, Isle of Man and Jersey the compensation would be £30,000, whereas in Guernsey it would be £27,000. Not all funds in these territories are recognised.

● Ireland and Luxembourg have *recognised* funds but it is not clear what compensation arrangements, if any, exist at the time of writing. Such schemes are not yet compulsory within the EU.

All funds mentioned in this book were *recognised* at the time the book went to press. The Financial Times lists recognised funds in its prices page and these funds are allowed to be promoted in the same way as UK based unit trusts.

A longer term strategy

If you really want to tie up your money, don't put all your eggs in one basket. Suppose you have £14,000 and you are a basic rate taxpayer. For your emergency fund put £3,000 into a *Building Society Instant Access Account* or ❀*Building Society Postal Account*.

You now have £11,000 to invest. You may be tempted to tie this up for 5 years or even longer - don't. An emergency fund must be available to be spent. Once you have spent it, you will need another.

So wherever you invest the next £3,000 of your money, make sure you can get it back after two years. Another £4,000 might be tied up for, say, 4 to 5 years. And the remaining £5,000 can be put into long-term investments like ❀*Investment Trust Personal Equity Plan*, or ❀*Unit Trust Personal Equity Plan*. Other long term investments include different types of Unit Trusts, Investment Trusts and Shares. For the more cautious there is ❀*Stock Government Index-Linked* and ❀*Stock Personal Equity Plan*.

7

Turning Income into Capital

You may inherit money or win it in the National Lottery or the football pools. But you can't count on such a windfall and if you want to build up a capital sum, you will have to do it by turning your income into capital. This Chapter gives you a few hints on how best to go about it.

The investments you choose need to be those which give a good return but are also convenient for your purpose. Building capital requires investments where income and capital gains can accumulate.

In order to build up such a capital sum, you have to invest regularly. This is a commitment each month usually by direct debit or standing order or by direct deduction from your pay.

Don't over commit yourself. That is probably the biggest pitfall of regular investors. Only invest as much as you can afford when you start and choose a means of investing which allows you to raise your contribution when you are able to.

Borrowing and investing

Before you set about investing towards something, think about your borrowing. Investing and borrowing are the reverse of each other. You would do better to reduce the amount you are borrowing rather than saving up separately. So if you are paying high interest on a borrowing, like a credit card bill which you don't pay off in full at the end of each month, pay that off first before you start investing. By paying off your credit card bill you may save paying 17% to 25% interest a year whereas your investments may only generate 4% to 7% interest a year. These actual rates may change but rates for lenders and borrowers go up and down together - and it's always the borrowers who end up paying more.

There is another reason to pay off borrowing before you start to invest up capital. You generally have to pay income tax on the interest you receive from investments. But you rarely receive tax relief on interest you pay on borrowed money.

In general terms the cheapest form of borrowing is a mortgage to buy your own home. The most costly is a credit card from a store or chain of stores. If you are self-employed, you can benefit from tax relief on most borrowing for the business including overdraft interest. So borrow for the business and not for yourself.

Investing to buy a home

Mortgages continue to be easy to get although interest rates have risen since their low at the beginning of 1994. Since the peak in the housing market in 1988, house prices have fallen in many parts of the country. In some areas by as much as 30% or even more. But forced sales where borrowers can no longer afford to pay their mortgages are much reduced - and further falls in house prices seem unlikely. Some forecasters say they will start to rise again but that remains to be seen.

It usually takes about two months from seeing a home and deciding to buy it to the *exchange of contracts* where you need to pay over the deposit. You can therefore invest your money into a *Building Society 30 Day Notice Account* or a *Building Society 60 Day Notice Account* once you have reached the minimum investment and get higher interest.

Investing towards a mortgage is best done monthly. An amount to aim for are the payments you expect on your mortgage.

Save to buy a home with:
Building Society Regular Monthly Savings Account
Building Society Instant Access Account
❀ *Building Society Postal Account*
Building Society 30 Day Notice Account
Building Society 60 Day Notice Account

Investing towards a family

A young couple who are both working need to invest as much as possible if they want to start a family. It's very important that this money is not tied up: five years should be the maximum.

Invest towards a family with:
Building Society Regular Monthly Savings Account
Building Society Instant Access Account
❀ *Building Society Postal Account*
Building Society 30 Day Notice Account
Building Society 60 Day Notice Account
Building Society 90 Day Notice Account
For five years only:
❀ *Building Society Tessa Account*

Investing for holidays

Investing for holidays is usually very short term. Most people will want to go on holiday once a year- and if you go abroad it's likely to be quite costly: £1,500 plus for a family of four might be a typical figure. You will know from last year how much your next holiday is likely to cost you. Most years you can add on a bit for inflation and add or deduct from the cost depending on whether the pound is weak or strong. Unless you are investment for that special big holiday, there is not much point in committing yourself to a regular monthly saving.

Several building societies offer discounts or 'free' spending money on inclusive holidays or air fares booked by customers of certain accounts. This is equivalent to a discount of about 5%. Similar schemes are run for credit card holders like Access and Barclaycard.

Invest for a holiday with:
✻ *Building Society Cheque Account With Interest*
  Building Society Instant Access Account
✻ *Building Society Postal Account*
  Building Society 30 Day Notice Account

You might also consider for spending money:
  Offshore Bank Foreign Currency Account
✻ *Offshore Single Foreign Currency Fund*

Investing for a car

Cars wear out. So if you can afford to, it's as well to put aside a regular amount towards the deposit on a new one. If you can't pay cash, the cheapest way to borrow is from a building society; hire purchase or a loan from a bank will always be more costly. On a new car a bank or building society may require you to put up 10% to 20% in cash. Occasionally you are offered interest-free hire purchase instead of a discount for cash. If you don't have the cash, it's well worth taking. Invest for a car with:
  Building Society Instant Access Account
✻ *Building Society Postal Account*
  Building Society 30 Day Notice Account

8

How Best to Invest in Stocks and Shares

The aim of making a profit from shares is to buy when they are cheap and to sell when they are expensive. There are two strategies for share buying and selling:

● You can buy the market as a whole. That is you invest in a portfolio of, say, 20 shares and then forget about them using any dividends to boost your income.

● You can be an active investor, a speculator even, and buy and sell shares every week or month, seeking to make a profit from the ups and downs of the stock market.

Buying new issues

Many people start to build up a portfolio of shares by investing in the Government privatisation share issues. You could have built up quite a wide portfolio consisting of BAA, British Airways, British Aerospace, British Gas, BP, British Telecom, Cable & Wireless, Rolls Royce and the electricity and water companies, if you had gone in for these new offers. You might also have bought other recommended shares which were offered for the first time like Laura Ashley, TSB, Wellcome, Abbey Life and Abbey National.

With these offers it was easy to buy because all you had to do was fill in a form and send off your money. You also had the advantage of not having to pay stockbroker's commission which is now normally a minimum £15 to £20 per transaction (or 1% to 1.9%) and stamp duty of ½ %. But there remains little left to privatise as most State industries have already been sold off.

Building societies

Following the lead of Abbey National, other building societies may convert to public limited companies (Plc) and become banks. The Halifax and the Leeds Permanent have announced they will merge and then become a Plc. If you have an account which counts as a *share account* with either, don't close it as you will lose the right to receive a bonus or shares. The same applies to the Cheltenham & Gloucester Building Society which is being taken over by Lloyds Bank, giving a significant windfall to investors. Unfortunately these societies have taken steps to prevent new investors from benefiting from any eventual pay out. However if you want to participate in other conversions or takeovers, make sure you and your husband or wife each have £100 or more invested in separate *share* accounts in each of the societies you think will convert. You need to have been investors for at least two years to participate. The largest societies are listed in order of size under *Where from* on page 112. There will be a cut off date, so the earlier you invest the better.

Buying individual shares

You may want to buy individual shares other than on a new issue. Which ones to buy and when to sell is something even the experts don't agree on, so there is an opportunity for individuals to use their judgement and luck to choose shares themselves. There is no shortage of advice. Most newspapers and specialist magazines like *Investors Chronicle* (weekly) and *Money Observer* (monthly) regularly tip share purchases. There are special newsletters which give share tips and stockbrokers often give their clients recommendations.

If you just follow the published advice, you will often find that the share price has risen by the time you get round to buy the shares. That is because whenever a share tip is published, all stock market dealers automatically raise the price. If the tip is found to be correct, then the price will probably rise further. But if it's a dud, the price will fall back to the original level, and you can end up paying more for a share than you need have. You can follow the performance of all UK shares in tables published in *Money Observer* each month.

You should have a portfolio or spread of investments in different companies - at least seven but no more than 20 otherwise you can't keep track of them. The minimum of seven is so you don't suffer unduly if a single company you invest in goes bust or the shares fall very steeply.

Under £9,000 a year to invest

If you have £9,000 or less a year which you want to invest in the stock market, but still want to invest directly in shares, you might consider doing this through a ❀*Shares Self Select Personal Equity Plan* **with no tax on income or gains. The limit is per person - so a husband and wife can invest £18,000 a year between them.**

There are two types of personal equity plan investing directly in shares - one where the managers choose the shares for you, rather like a unit trust but generally with fewer shares; the other is the do-it-yourself type where you can choose the shares. The advantage of a personal equity plan is that you can usually avoid high minimum commission charges when you buy and sell individual shares and your entire investment is tax free (both income and capital gains). Personal equity plans are probably more suited to people who want to buy and hold shares than those who want to trade. Alternatively if you already hold a portfolio of shares, you could put one (or two) which have a high yield into your personal equity plan. Full details are given in the entry in Part 2 under the heading ❀*Shares Self Select Personal Equity Plan*.

Buying and holding

If you decide you want to buy shares and hold on to them for a long time, you may be better off investing in shares through a unit trust or an investment trust. You certainly will be if you have less than £5,000 to invest. The problem with these, especially unit trusts, is that there are almost as many unit trusts to choose from as there are actual shares to invest in.

More details are given in Part 2 under the headings:
Unit Trust Index Tracker
Unit Trust Invested in Shares
❀ *Unit Trust Personal Equity Plan*
Investment Trust Shares
❀ *Investment Trust Personal Equity Plan*

The share market was in a *bull* or upward stage for about two years until the beginning of 1994 when it fell sharply by about 20%. Part of this loss was recovered during 1994 but then it fell again. At the time of writing it is not clear whether the market will rise higher or turn into a *bear* or downward phase. It's likely that there will be wide differences in the performance of individual shares so you will need all the skill and luck you can get to invest successfully in shares over the lifetime of this edition of this book. Note that there has to be a UK General Election by May 1997 which is also likely to affect the UK Stockmarket.

Regular investment in shares

If you don't want to keep following the share market waiting for the right time to invest, your best bet is to invest on a regular basis month by month. Over the years you will accumulate money in shares through unit or investment trusts but you should wait until share prices are high before you sell. you can invest regularly through the following which have full details given in Part 2:

❀ *Investment Trust Personal Equity Plan*
❀ *Investment Trust Savings Plan*
❀ *Unit Trust Personal Equity Plan*
  Unit Trust Savings Plan

You can also link a regular investment to shares through *Life Insurance Unit-Linked Savings Plan* but such plans generally have high charges and are less flexible than the other alternatives unless you wish to use them for inheritance tax planning with the proceeds to go *in trust* to your children or grandchildren on your death.

Finding a good stockbroker

If you want to follow the market and buy and sell shares then you need a good stockbroker who you can deal with direct and who can give you trading buy and sell prices for your shares by phone.

The best way to find a good stockbroker is by recommendation. If you don't know anyone who is pleased with theirs, the Stock Exchange will send you a list of brokers willing to take on new private clients. You can also ask your bank to introduce you to their own stockbroker.

Find out how much they will charge - and if you are likely to buy or sell in amounts of less than £1,500 at a time, what their minimum commission is. The commission rate is likely to be 1% to 1.9%, for transactions of £5,000 or less. There is also a contract levy of £1 on each transaction of £10,000 or more.

Some brokers have two levels of service: the ordinary service where they give advice and the *execution only* service where they just do what you tell them - you make up your own mind about which shares to buy and sell, and when. Magazines and newspapers survey stockbrokers which offer low cost dealing services from time to time.

Fixing the price

When you buy or sell shares, the deal is often not actually made on the phone when you are speaking to your stockbroker. It's therefore very important that you place a *limit* on the transaction. A limit is the minimum price you will sell at or the maximum price you will buy at.

When you consider the selling price is too low, or the buying price too high, you can ask for the limit to be held for a week or longer. The stockbroker must then sell shares at the limit price or better if the shares reach the limit within the period stipulated. Some stockbrokers are reluctant to accept limits beyond the same day.

When you make transactions by phone, especially with limits, you should make a note of the conversation and date it. Stockbrokers usually make tape recordings of phone transactions and they may be able to play back the conversation in the event of disagreement over what was intended.

Be an active investor

There is a lot more you can learn about share strategy. A good start is *Shares A Beginners' Guide to Making Money* by Harold Baldwin (Wisebuy £2.95). Most large bookshops and branches of WH Smith now have an investment/financial section where you can find other more advanced and detailed books on share strategy. You also need to regularly read the financial pages of a newspaper.

Be a speculator

Consider gambling with traded options or warrants. Details are summarised in Part 2 under the heading *Shares Traded Options* and *Investment Trust Warrants*. If you are a pessimist you can still make money while share prices crash by using *put options*.

Shareholder perks

Some people buy shares for the fringe benefits. Surveys listing companies which offer perks are published from time to time by *Money Observer* and by stockbrokers Henry Cooke Lumsden. Check with the company before you buy the shares that they still offer the perks. Ask for the company secretary.

9

Saving Towards a Pension

Everyone who has earnings from a job or who is self-employed can contribute to a pension scheme with full tax relief on the contributions, subject to certain limits. Once contributions are invested the income and capital gains in the pension fund are tax exempt. And when you take the pension you can normally draw around a quarter of your pension fund as a tax free lump sum. The rest must be in the form of a pension for the rest of your life - and for the rest of your husband's or wife's life too if you want - although there will soon be more flexibility for ✿*Pension Personal Pension.*

Because these tax advantages are good, anyone investing towards retirement should do so through one type of pension scheme or another. Only people not eligible for a pension scheme should consider other types of investments; these are summarised at the end of this Chapter.

The State retirement pension

There are two parts to this. The first is the State flat rate or basic retirement pension which depends on the contributions made by employees and the self-employed. The current pension (for 1995-96) is £3,060 a year for a single person plus an additional £1,833 for an adult dependent or non-working wife who hasn't earned her own pension. The pension rises each year in April in line with increases in the Retail Prices Index to the previous September.

The second part, the State earnings related or additional pension (SERPS) is available to employees only. The Government has made a concerted effort to encourage people to opt out of SERPS through a personal or job pension. It has also significantly reduced the amount of pension earned under the scheme.

Generally speaking you should opt out if you are a man under age 41 now or woman under age 36. It could be worth opting out at slightly older ages but the decision is not so clear cut and depends on how well the investments in personal pensions do.

If you are currently in a job pension there are five possibilities:

● You wish to stay in SERPS because of your age (see above).

● Your job pension is already *contracted-out* of SERPS.

● You can contract-out of SERPS by taking out a special personal pension, called a *minimum contribution personal pension*. This minimum contribution personal pension has some restrictions (which don't apply to a ❀*Pension Personal Pension* which is described in Part 2). The minimum contribution personal pension has no lump sum on retirement, retirement age is a minimum of age 60 women, 65 men (compared with 50 for a personal pension) and you have to have a pension which increases each year and pays a pension to your widow or widower.

● You can contract-out of SERPS through *Pension Free Standing Top Up Plan* (see below) but this is not recommended as in this particular instance there is no tax relief on all of the contributions .

● You can leave your job pension and take a personal pension instead. This is only worth considering if you are under age 35 and unlikely to remain with your employer until retirement. If you do leave your job pension, you should also contract-out of SERPS. Part of the pension will be a *minimum contribution personal pension* with the restrictions described above and the rest will be an ordinary ❀*Pension Personal Pension* as described in Part 2.

If you are an employee but you are not in a job pension you can contract-out of SERPS by taking out a personal pension. This will also be part *minimum contributions personal pension* and part ❀*Pension Personal Pension*.

A job pension

Job, company or occupational pensions are optional. That doesn't mean you should always leave. The decision to leave depends on your age, whether you will stay with the company until retirement, and how good the job pension scheme is. You can get free advice on what to do and what your rights are from the Occupational Pensions Advisory Service (OPAS) which is an educational charity.

If you decide to stay with your job pension scheme, you can boost the pension you get on retirement by investing in additional voluntary contributions. There are two types and these are considered in Part 2 under the headings:

Pension In-House Top Up Plan
Pension Free Standing Top Up Plan

If you think you are entitled to a pension from a company you used to work for, but the company has moved or gone out of business, you will be able to use the Registry of Occupational Pensions which is run by the Occupational Pensions Board, a government department. In 1993-94 10,591 people asked the Registry for help and it succeeded in tracing 9,464 people's pension scheme.

A personal pension

If your job doesn't have a pension scheme, if you are self-employed or if you have two jobs and the second doesn't have a pension scheme, you are allowed to tax relief at your highest rate on contributions to a personal pension issued by a life insurance company, building society, bank or unit trust group.

When a pensions company invests your money in one of these schemes, it is exempt from income tax and capital gains tax on any income or gains it makes. So as well as obtaining tax relief, your money accumulates tax free. If you are an employee, you get basic tax relief when you pay the contribution; if you are self-employed you have to reclaim all the relief.

However, once you have committed yourself to a personal pension, you cannot get anything back until you are 50. If you are a professional sportsman, the pension can start to be paid at 35 or 40; other special cases will be considered. You can also start to draw your pension under 50 if you become permanently disabled. You cannot continue to pay contributions or start to receive benefits after the age of 75.

The proceeds of the policy come in the form of a pension for life (which counts as earned income) and 25% of the accumulated pension fund can be paid as a lump sum which is tax free.

If you are already age 50 you can get an instant pension provided you still have eligible earnings.

Contributions are restricted to 17½% of your *net relevant earnings* (ie earnings which are not counted for an occupational pension scheme) in the tax year if you are 35 or less. The limits are higher the older you are rising from 20% at age 36, to 40% at 61 (see table overleaf). Contributions paid in one tax year can be claimed (fully or partly) against your taxable income in the previous tax year instead of the current one provided there was sufficient relief in the previous year (or carried forward to the previous year from earlier years) to cover the contributions carried back. **You can make use of unused relief from previous tax years for up to 6 years (7 years if you elect to have the contributions count against your income in the previous tax year).**

Although you may not be able to afford the maximum contribution, you can use up past years' relief if you come into a windfall and want to invest it to provide you with a pension from age 50. The schemes accept single contributions as well as regular contributions - both count equally for tax relief. Personal pensions are covered in Part 2 under the heading ❀*Pension Personal Pension*.

Retirement annuity

Until 1 July 1988 a pension similar to a personal pension was available but only through life insurance companies called a *retirement annuity*. You cannot take out a new retirement annuity contract after that date. But if you already have one, you can make additional single or regular contributions provided they are under an existing policy number which you already have. Retirement annuities can give a larger lump sum, up to 37½% of the accumulated pension fund especially if you retire at the maximum age of 75. However if the starting pension is low, perhaps because the pension rises year by year, or you are a woman, or you want to retire at 60 or all three, the maximum lump sum could be slightly lower for a retirement annuity than for a personal pension. The lower lump sum need not worry you as you are allowed to transfer a retirement annuity into a personal pension at any time before you draw the pension.

Contribution limits

Contribution limits for personal pensions and retirement annuities are partially interchangeable. For instance if your net relevant earnings are £10,000 and your allowance is 17½%, then you can get tax relief on £1,750 worth of personal pension contributions. However at age 37, for example, you are entitled to an allowance of 20% for a personal pension but only 17½% for a retirement annuity. What you can do is contribute £1,750 to the retirement annuity and a further £250 to a personal pension. Instead of course, you can contribute the full £2,000 to a personal pension or any mixture provided the lower limit for a retirement annuity is not exceeded.

There is also a maximum overall level of net relevant earnings above which there is no further personal pension allowance. This usually rises each year in line with the Retail Prices Index:

- 1989-90 £60,000
- 1990-91 £64,800
- 1991-92 £71,400
- 1992-93 £75,000
- 1993-94 £75,000
- 1994-95 £76,800
- 1995-96 £78,600

This maximum does not apply to retirement annuities. This means that people with earnings over the limits listed at the bottom of the previous page, who are 35 and under, can make higher contributions to a *retirement annuity* (provided they already have one they can add to) than to a *personal pension*. However for those over age 35 the earnings level at which they can pay higher contributions to a retirement annuity rather than a personal pension is somewhat higher and depends on age. The company which you have your retirement annuity with or your independent financial adviser should be able to tell you the current level.

If you pay more in contributions than your allowances, you don't get tax relief on the contributions. In the case of a retirement annuity you are allowed to leave the money in the plan to accumulate tax free until you draw the pension. However that part of the pension you draw will then count as investment income (under current tax rules this would not result in more tax but it might do by the time you retire). If you pay more contributions than your allowances to a personal pension, the pensions company will be told to refund you the amount overpaid.

Contributions limits as % of salary

Personal Pensions for 1989-90 to 1995-96

Age at start of tax year	%
35 or under	17½
36 to 45	20
46 to 50	25
51 to 55	30
56 to 60	35
61 to 74[1]	40

Personal Pensions For 1987-88 and 1988-89		Retirement Annuities All years	
Age at start of tax year	%	Age at start of tax year	%
50 or under	17½	50 or under	17½
51 to 55	20	51 to 55	20
56 to 60	22½	56 to 60	22½
61 to 74[1]	27½	61 to 74[1]	27½

[1] You cannot pay contributions once you reach age 75.

Not eligible for a pension

The following investments (in alphabetical order) are worth considering if you are not eligible for a pension scheme because you are not working:

For regular investment:

❀ *Bank Tessa Account (5 years)*
❀ *Building Society Tessa Account (5 years)*
❀ *Investment Trust Personal Equity Plan*
❀ *Investment Trust Savings Plan*
   Life Insurance With-Profits Endowment Policy
❀ *Stock Personal Equity Plan*
❀ *Unit Trust Personal Equity Plan*
   Unit Trust Savings Plan

For lump sums not needed for up to 10 years or more consider:

❀ *Investment Trust Personal Equity Plan*
   Investment Trust Shares
   Life Insurance Mixed Bond
   Life Insurance Property Bond
   Offshore Managed Currency Fund
❀ *Offshore Single Foreign Currency Fund*
   Offshore Stock and Bond Fund
   Property Commercial Direct Investment
   Property Residential Direct Investment
   Shares Ordinary Quoted
❀ *Shares Self Select Personal Equity Plan*
❀ *Stock Government Index-Linked*
❀ *Stock Personal Equity Plan*
   Stock Private Index-Linked
   Unit Trust Index Tracker
   Unit Trust Invested in UK Shares
   Unit Trust Invested in Overseas Shares
❀ *Unit Trust Personal Equity Plan*
   Unit Trust Stock and Bond Fund

None of the above have tax relief on the contributions. However ❀*Bank Tessa Account,* ❀*Building Society Tessa Account,* ❀*Investment Trust Personal Equity Plan,* ❀*Shares Self Select Personal Equity Plan,* ❀*Stock Personal Equity Plan* and ❀*Unit Trust Personal Equity Plan* are completely exempt from tax on income or gains. With Tessas you lose the tax exemption if you cash early.

When you need to draw a pension

Personal pensions or retirement annuities are an ideal way of accumulating money towards a pension. You can start to draw your pension between age 50 and 75. You don't have to retire to do so.

When you finally want to draw your pension (or you reach age 75 when you have to), you should shop around, using the *open market option* to reinvest your pension money with the life insurance company offering the highest *pension annuity* rates available at that time. You have the option to take 25% of the accumulated pension fund as a tax free lump sum which you will probably want to invest separately elsewhere to obtain a better return. Even a *Life Insurance Annuity* gives a better return than a *pension annuity* because part of a *Life Insurance Annuity* is regarded as a return of capital and is tax exempt.

From mid-1995 you have the opportunity to draw an interim income from your *Pension Personal Pension* without committing yourself to a fixed pension annuity rate. There will be a range within which you draw, similar to the income you might get at that age if you started the pension proper. All the income withdrawn will be taxable as earnings. But you are then committed to drawing the income and cannot stop receiving payments or make extra contributions to the same personal pension. However, if later you want to take your cash lump sum, you can do so but you have to convert the remainder of your fund to a pension annuity, using the *open market option* if you wish.

If you have several *retirement annuities* or *personal pensions* with different companies, you can start to receive pensions from them at different times. Some companies offer *personal pensions* as *segments* where you can start to draw a pension from each segment at different times.

Another option to consider is an increasing pension annuity, either by a fixed amount, linked to the Retail Prices Index or on a *with-profits* basis. The different income you would get from these at different ages are shown in the table on the next page. The actual return of all these types of pension varies depending on the level of interest rates at the time you start to draw the pension.

How much yearly pension a £100,000 accumulated fund will buy

Age when you start pension £	Fixed £	Increasing at 4% a year[1] £	Index-linked £	With-profits[2] £
Man				
50	9,140	6,109	5,499	9,140
55	9,788	6,802	6,199	9,788
60	10,599	7,668	7,073	10,599
65	11,645	8,776	8,192	11,645
70	12,984	10,195	9,624	12,984
75	14,625	11,945	11,394	14,625
Woman				
50	8,545	5,468	4,853	8,545
55	8,965	5,955	5,352	8,965
60	9,554	6,609	6,016	9,554
65	10,375	7,492	6,910	10,375
70	11,507	8,691	8,118	11,507
75	13,028	10,294	9,736	13,028
Joint man and woman of same age				
50	8,121	5,072	4,466	8,121
55	8,375	5,433	4,847	8,375
60	8,739	5,911	5,345	8,739
65	9,260	6,549	6,005	9,260
70	9,982	7,399	6,877	9,982
75	10,955	8,514	8,018	10,955

Assumes pension is paid monthly in advance and guaranteed for five years [1]Figures for pension in first year. [2]If bonuses, both declared and final, are at 5.5%, the annuity will remain level. If bonuses are higher than that, the payments will rise; if lower, the payments will fall. *Source: Equitable Life.*

10

Wives' Income and Investments

A wife's income

Since 6 April 1990 a wife's income has been treated separately from her husband's. A wife has her own personal tax allowance which can be set against investment income as well as earnings. She also gets her own tax return if necessary although not everyone is sent a tax return every year.

Working wives There is no longer any distinction between earnings and investment income as far as tax is concerned. Both types belong to a wife and investment income is no longer added to a husband's income, for instance, for the purpose of working out higher rate tax.

Non-earning or part time earners Where a wife has no earnings, or her earnings are below her *personal tax allowance* for the year, she will be a non-taxpayer and should be able to avoid tax on income from investments worth up to about £44,000 each year - more if the investments are in shares with a low dividend yield.

Minimising tax on investment income

Both husband and wife each have their own 20% reduced rate and 25% basic rate tax band as well as their own personal tax allowance. Where a husband pays tax at a higher rate than his wife, it's worthwhile arranging for the wife to receive all or most of any investment income so that it's taxed at a lower rate, if at all.

If a wife doesn't have money of her own, a husband can give her money (or assets such as shares or commercial property with rental income) to enable her to have income which can be tax free up to the amount of her own personal tax allowance and then will be liable to the 20% and 25% tax rates.

There is no capital gains tax, inheritance tax or stamp duty to pay on a transfer of money or assets to a wife. Money can simply be taken from bank, building society or other accounts in the husband's or joint names and put it into an account or accounts in the wife's sole name. Income from accounts in a single name will be treated as the income of the person whose name it's in.

If this does not appeal to you, assets (eg shares, unit trusts) can be held jointly and husband and wife can make a declaration that the asset is owned in unequal shares or indeed entirely by one of you (in which case declare that the other is acting as a *nominee*). This should be done on Form 17 (from the Inland Revenue).

Signing a declaration which says a husband or wife owns, say 95%, of a jointly held asset, legally makes him or her the owner of it. In the event of a separation or divorce, that spouse would be entitled to the money.

The Inland Revenue will not accept a declaration that a bank or building society account is owned in unequal shares.

Despite this, it's probably possible for you to own such investments in unequal shares. This would only be of any practical significance in the event of subsequent separation, divorce or death. In order to do this husband and wife should type or write the following on a sheet of paper substituting their own names, appropriate percentages and details of the account:

"We Sara Jane Smith and Arthur Peter Smith of 24 Rose Crescent, London SW16 declare that our joint account at ABC Building Society No S9076655 (or all our bank and building society joint accounts) are beneficially owned as tenants in common in the following proportions: Sara Jane Smith 95%, Arthur Peter Smith 5%." The document should be signed, witnessed and dated and kept by the spouse with the larger ownership.

In this case, the Inland Revenue will tax you as if the account is owned in equal shares but Sarah Smith retains ownership of 95% of the money.

Payment without deduction of tax

Where one spouse's total income in the tax year is less than his or her personal tax allowances (single or age), interest from UK banks and building societies can be paid without deduction of tax. Details are in a leaflet *IR110 A Guide For People With Savings* which also has an application form at the back; you need one leaflet and form for each different account. Many banks and building societies allow you to have half the interest on a joint account paid without deduction of tax where only one of the holders is eligible.

However if a wife's income is, say, £4,000 a year (which is above her personal tax allowance) she is not eligible for interest to be paid without deduction of tax, even though most of her income may be not liable for tax. In that case she should invest in an investment where no tax is deducted as follows:

Co-operative Society Term Account
National Savings Capital Bond
National Savings Investment Account
National Savings Income Bond
❀ *Offshore Bank Instant Access Account*
Offshore Bank Notice Account
Offshore Sterling Currency Fund

Dividends

Where a wife has shares in UK companies which pay dividends, these come with a tax credit. Tax credits paid to a wife on or after 6 April 1990 can be reclaimed if the wife is otherwise not a taxpayer. This even applies to joint holdings, in which case the wife can only claim half the tax credit. Keep the tax vouchers, the counterfoils which come with the cheque; the Inland Revenue will want them as evidence that you have received the tax credit.

Interest with basic rate tax deducted

Most banks, building societies and local authorities deduct basic rate tax before you get your interest. This tax can be reclaimed if you are not a taxpayer on part or all of your income. The same applies to *Stock Loan and Debenture*; and to *Stock Government Fixed* and ❀*Stock Government Index-Linked* if you buy through a stockbroker. Keep these vouchers too.

Getting a tax rebate

If tax is deducted from income of any type and a wife has been unable to make use of her personal tax allowance, she can claim a tax rebate. Details on how to go about this are contained in a free leaflet *IR110 A Guide for People with Savings* from any Inland Revenue tax office. You can make a claim for income or interest received since 6 April 1990. But in the period 5 April 1990 to 6 April 1991 you can't get a refund of any tax deducted on a UK bank, building society or local authority fixed term loan.

Husbands with a low income

A husband has a married couple's tax allowance as well as his own personal allowance. If his income is not high enough to make full (or any) use of it, he can transfer it to his wife or they can split it between them. This might occur when a husband is disabled and receives tax exempt benefits or he is unemployed and has a very low income.

Capital gains tax

A wife is completely separately taxed for capital gains tax. Transfers between husband and wife and vice-versa, however, can be made without any penalty or tax in order to utilise the capital gains tax exemption limits. The starting point for working out the gain on an eventual disposal is the date and value of the original acquisition (not the transfer to a spouse).

Husband and wife can only own one main residence between them. If they have more than one they can choose which is to be the main one and it's therefore exempt from capital gains tax. This contrasts with an unmarried couple with two homes who can get two main residence exemptions if they own one home each and each choose the one they own as their main residence.

Wives over age 65

If you are age 65 or over, or your husband is or you both are, turn to Chapter 13. Separate taxation of husband and wife may cut your tax bill by even more.

Mortgage interest

Where a married couple has a mortgage in joint names, it's assumed that the interest is paid in equal shares. If it's in a single name, interest is assumed to be paid by the person whose name it's in. Either way, if you don't want these rules to apply, you can complete and send Form 15 to the Inland Revenue and make an allocation of interest election. There are two situations when you might want to do this:
- Where the mortgage is outside the MIRAS scheme and one partner is a non-taxpayer - or whose income after deducting the personal allowance is less than the mortgage interest.
- One of you is over 65 and might be eligible for Age Allowance or more Age Allowance.

11

Children's Investments

A child's income and tax allowance

Children are children until they reach age 18 as far as the law is concerned. Up to that age you can hold money in your own name (or in your husband's or wife's name or jointly) which legally belongs to your child. At age 18 the child can demand that the money is put in his or her own name unless the money is given under a formal trust which provides for the trustees (which can be you and your husband or wife) to hold on to it for longer.

The way in which a child's investment income is taxed does not depend on whose name the money is in. It can be in the child's own name, a parent's name or a grandparent's name for example. It depends on who gave the money in the first place, whether the income or interest from it is accumulated or spent, and the terms of any trust which the money is subject to.

A child has a personal tax allowance from the day he or she is born. This is the same as anyone else's and is £3,525 for the current 1995-96 tax year. In addition each child also has his or her own reduced rate band £3,200 in 1995-96, (£3,000 in 1994-95) and his or her own basic rate tax band (£21,100 in the current 1995-96 tax year). So each child with investment income of up to £3,525 a year can pay £1,410 less tax than an adult who pays higher rate tax.

Where a child's income is below his or her personal tax allowance, it's best to find an investment where income tax is not deducted, so as to avoid the trouble and delay of obtaining an income tax rebate. In the unlikely event that the best account happens to be a UK bank and building society account, the account can be made into one which does not deduct tax by getting a copy of Inland Revenue leaflet *IR110 A Guide for People with Savings* for each account you want to have this done on. There is a form at the back of the leaflet for you or the child (over age 16) to complete. However some of the better investments for children don't have tax deducted for anyone, see below.

Should a child invest in an account where tax is deducted but he or she is not be liable for it, this tax can be reclaimed using a special Tax *Repayment Claim Form R232*. This form is sent to a tax office specialising in repayment claims, with the relevant tax deduction certificates or tax vouchers once the child's income for the year is known. Up to 5 April 1991 no repayment is due on bank and building society interest, but rebates can be obtained on tax deducted on unit trust distributions, share dividends, stock interest and trust income belonging to children.

Investments for a child in his or her own name

For money held in a child's own name consider the following:
Bank Cash Card Account (over age 12 or 13)
Bank Children's Account (better gifts than building societies usually)
Building Society Cash Card Account (over age 14)
Building Society Children s Account
Building Society Instant Access Account
National Savings Capital Bond
National Savings Investment Account (1 month notice)
National Savings Ordinary Account

Income from money given by parents

The taxman prevents parents from making direct use of their own child's tax allowance through giving money to them, by counting as a parent's income, any income over £100 a year from money or investments given to their child (or to any type of trust for their child). So if you give your child £1,000 and he or she gets £70 interest on it, that £70 counts as the child's income and is effectively tax free. However if you give the child £1,500 and the interest is £105, this amount is added to your income and taxed at your rate (40% if you are a higher rate taxpayer). This counting of a child's income as his or her parent's carries on until the child reaches age 18 or gets married over age 16 if earlier.

There is an exception to this rule. Where you give money to a child *absolutely* **and it accumulates in an account (preferably one which doesn't deduct income tax) until the child is 18 or marries, all interest counts as the child's. So the child can have a tax free income which accumulates provided it, and the rest of the child's income, is less than his or her personal tax allowance each year and the child receives the income after age 18 (or after she marries over age 16).**

If any money is withdrawn from the account before the child is 18 or marries, that amount is added to the income of the parent who gave the money and is taxable in the tax year in which the withdrawal is made. This type of arrangement is not very satisfactory except for smallish amounts as the child is entitled to demand the money at age 18.

However at age 18 this changes. So if you want to help out a student or son or daughter who is unemployed, you could put money in their name which will not be taxable. However once the capital sum exceeds £3,000 it affects State means tested benefits. If you want to give more than, say, £5,000 to your child, you should consider setting up a formal trust so you can keep control of the money until age 25 or even longer - see *Trusts* at the end of this Chapter. If the money is in trust, then only the income paid by the trust will affect means tested benefits, not the capital.

Investments suitable for gifts from parents where it's intended that the income is accumulated to age 18 are:

Offshore Bank Notice Account
National Savings Capital Bond (provided child at least 13)
❀ *National Savings Children's Bonus Bond* (tax exempt so can be in addition to any others)
National Savings Investment Account

Investments suitable for gifts from parents who don't want to bother with a formal trust (or in addition or separate from one) but may want to spend some income on the child (eg school fees, holidays) are:

National Savings Capital Bond
❀ *National Savings Children's Bonus Bond* (tax exempt so can be in a addition to any others)
❀ *National Savings Fixed Issue Certificates* (tax exempt)
❀ *National Savings Index-Linked Certificates* (tax exempt)

The maximum limit for National Savings certificates can be doubled as investment can be made *once* up to the maximum in each child's own name, and *once again* in one or both of the parent's name as trustees for each child. Depending on how you fill in the form, the child may or may not have to sign when you cash these *in trust* holdings. Get advice from National Savings before you invest. These holdings are in addition to any the parents may have of their own (or in trust for each other). As these investments are tax exempt they are especially suitable for higher rate taxpayers - though some issues don't represent good value to basic taxpayers. Investments in a child's own name requires his or her signature for withdrawal from age 7.

Income from other money

Where money comes from any source other than a parent, and including money left to a child by a parent who has died, a child is taxed completely separately from his or her parents. So gifts from relatives and grandparents and money from Saturday jobs and newsrounds etc. can all be invested and interest received tax free up to the full personal tax allowance.

For money from this source, which can be held in a parent's name as *nominee or bare trustee*, consider accounts where tax is not deducted as the Inland Revenue form IR110 does not provide for this situation:

    Co-operative Society Term Account
    National Savings Investment Account
❀ *Offshore Bank Instant Access Account*
    Offshore Bank Notice Account
    Offshore Sterling Currency Fund
    Stock Government Fixed Interest (invested through the National Savings stock register).

If you want to invest longer term, consider the following:
❀ *Investment Trust Personal Equity Plan* (when child over age 18)
❀ *Investment Trust Savings Plan*
    Investment Trust Shares
    Unit Trust Savings Plan
    Unit Trust Index Tracker
    Unit Trust Invested in Shares
❀ *Unit Trust Personal Equity Plan* (when child over age 18)

Also consider investments listed below under the heading School fees.

School fees

Private education is extremely expensive and most people are unlikely to be able to pay for it out of their income. Specialists in this field recommend people to start investing when a child is born in order to spread the burden. But because the rise in school fee charges can exceed the return from most schemes, people have been disappointed .

One way of lightening the burden of fees is to ask grandparents to contribute. Another way if you have a child who can get into a private school and a low income, is to apply for a grant under the Assisted Places Scheme. Your income needs to be under around £25,000 a year for any contribution at an expensive day school but fees are currently paid in full at an income of less than £9,352 a year. If you have more than one child, the means test bites at a higher level. Details from Independent Schools Information Service, address in Appendix 1.

The investments listed below are suitable for basic and higher rate taxpayers. Non-taxpayers and reduced rate taxpayers are unlikely to be able to afford to pay for private education from their investments.

Invest regularly for school fees with:	Fees needed
Building Society 90 Day Notice Account	Up to 4 years
❀ *Building Society Tessa Account†*	5 years
❀ *Bank Tessa Account†*	5 years
❀ *Investment Trust Personal Equity Plan†*	5-17 years
❀ *Investment Trust Savings Plan*	5-17 years
Unit Trust Savings Plan	5-17 years
❀ *Unit Trust Personal Equity Plan†*	5-17 years
Life Insurance With Profits Endowment†	10-17 years

Lump sums for school fees:	Fees needed
❀ *Building Society Postal Account*	Up to 4 years
Building Society 90 Day Notice Account	*Up to 4 years*
Life Insurance Growth Bond	2-5 years
❀ *Building Society Tessa Account†*	5 years
❀ *Bank Tessa Account†*	5 years
Stock Government Fixed Interest	Up to 6 years
❀ *Stock Government Index-Linked†*	6, 8, 9, 11, 13, 16 years
Life Insurance School Fees Educational Trust†	3-15 years
Life Insurance Property Bond	8-17 years
Life Insurance Mixed Bond	8-17 years
❀ *Investment Trust Personal Equity Plan†*	8-17 years
❀ *Shares Self Select Personal Equity Plan†*	8-17 years
Offshore Managed Currency Fund†	8-17 years
Unit Trusts	8-17 years

†Especially higher rate taxpayers.

Lump sums of more than a year's fees which you want to earmark for school fees can usually be paid in advance to the school; check that there is no penalty if the child later changes schools. The lump sum earns interest and when the fees come due, both the lump sum and interest are available to pay them. The tax position is similar to *Life Insurance School Fees Educational Trust* which is explained in Part 2.

Large lump sums intended as payment for school fees and donated by a wealthy grandparent would be best invested through an *accumulation and maintenance trust* - consult a solicitor or qualified accountant for advice on how to set one up, see also below.

Income from money inherited by a child, or received as a gift from anyone other than its parents is not taxable to the extent of the personal tax allowance; choose instead investments listed under the heading *Income from other money* on page 67.

Different types of trust

There are three types of trust:
- *Accumulation and maintenance trust*
- *Discretionary trust*
- *Absolute trust.* This type of trust usually exists where someone holds assets as a *nominee* for someone else. Formally constituted absolute trusts are not recommended.

Confusingly an *accumulation and maintenance* trust is sometimes described as *discretionary*, because the trustees usually have discretion to decide whether the income from the trust is accumulated or spent for the benefit of the beneficiaries or actually paid to them if they are over age 18.

Accumulation and maintenance trust

With an accumulation and maintenance trust a *settlor*, eg a grand-parent, gives a sum of money, say £5,000, to a trust for at least one named beneficiary. The trust deed should be drafted by a solicitor or chartered accountant with experience in drafting such deeds and might cost you £50 to £500. Once the trust is set up, provided the trust says so, anyone else can add money to it (as well as the original settlor) but this should not be a parent - see *Trust income* overleaf.

The trust usually gives trustees discretion to pay the trust income for the education, maintenance or benefit of the beneficiary up to the age of 25 at which time the income must be paid to the beneficiary. These trusts usually specify that the capital of the trust can be distributed to the beneficiaries at any date after the youngest beneficiary is age 25. The trust can provide for it to continue for the whole life of a beneficiary and there are usually provisions for the wife and children of a beneficiary to receive the income if the beneficiary dies while the trust is still in existence. The trust can last for up to 80 years, say, or when the original beneficiary's youngest child reaches the age of 21.

The *primary beneficiaries* of such a trust are the people named in the trust deed. However they need not yet be born. The deed might specify 'my grandson Simon Jones and any other grandchildren'. While Simon is the only grandson he is entitled to 100% of the income of the trust; but if later four brothers and sisters and cousins arrive, he will only be entitled to a fifth of the trust.

With an *accumulation and maintenance* trust, the trustees have no discretion about who gets income and capital. The share of each beneficiary must be according to the original trust deed. The only discretion is whether to pay out income to a beneficiary. If it is paid out to one beneficiary and not to another, then records have to be kept, showing each beneficiary's share, so that a beneficiary whose share has been accumulated does not get less.

Discretionary trust

With a *discretionary trust* you don't need to specify who the beneficiaries are. They can be in rather general terms like 'any of the descendants of John and Jane Brown'. The trustees can choose to whom they pay income to, and when; they can decide whether and to whom to advance any capital; when the trust is finally closed down, they can decide to whom the money is given. The settlor can leave informal instructions to the trustees on how they should use their discretion (for instance they could be told not to pay any income to anyone who spends it on gambling or illegal drugs).

Discretionary trusts have a few snags, however. Whereas there is no inheritance tax on a gift to an accumulation and maintenance trust, there can be where money is given to a discretionary trust. It comes into effect once cumulative gifts exceed the inheritance tax threshold (currently £154,000) and is at half the rate paid on death (currently 20% instead of 40%). Discretionary trusts also have to pay inheritance tax once every ten years on the capital value of their assets if they are worth more than the inheritance tax threshold at the time. Currently that tax is not very large but could be raised by a new Government.

If a discretionary trust is set up below the inheritance tax threshold, there is no inheritance tax when it is set up. There is nothing to stop a husband setting one up for £154,000 and his wife setting up a separate trust with identical provisions for a further £154,000. Both would remain below their respective thresholds and no inheritance tax would be payable. However if after 10 years, the value of assets grew above the then inheritance tax threshold, there could be some inheritance tax in the future on the then capital value in excess over the then threshold.

Trust income

Income from a *discretionary trust* or an *accumulation and maintenance trust* is currently taxed at one rate of 35%. Income paid by a trustee to a beneficiary is paid with this tax deducted at 35% but the beneficiary (even a child) can reclaim all (or part) of the tax if he or she is not liable to pay the full amount deducted.

Income paid to unmarried children under 18 from a trust set up by a parent usually counts as the parent's income so no tax rebate is due. and it's not usually worth a parent setting up a such a trust. Such trusts are usually set up by grandparents.

The *settlor*, the person who gave the money to set up the trust, must not benefit from it; otherwise there are no tax advantages.

The tax repayment claim when the income counts as the child's is made by the parent on the child's behalf using *Tax Claim Form R232*. The trustees must fill in *Form R185E* giving details of the amount of trust income paid to the parents or spent as well as the tax deducted and give the form to the parent who sends it in with the claim.

If parents are trustees, trust income must be spent on education (eg school fees), maintenance (eg clothes) or benefit (eg holidays) to count as having been distributed by the trust and to enable the parent to claim a tax rebate. If the income of the trust is not spent, the 35% tax cannot he reclaimed. But if in a future year the income is spent (in addition to income in that year) the tax can be reclaimed then provided the child (or children) has enough tax allowances in that year.

The Inland Revenue sometime considers capital as well as income payments from *discretionary trusts* and from *accumulation and maintenance trusts* as the income of the beneficiary. Any payments are deemed to be *after* deduction of 35% tax. This doesn't apply when the trust is wound up, nor to payments of school fees out of capital which normally don't count as income.

12

Change in Plan

Redundancy

Redundancy payments don't usually amount to a lot - £2,000 is the average. But if you have worked with the same company for many years, you might get much more. If you have been in a company's pension scheme and are over age 50, you may get a pension plus a lump sum from the pension scheme at the same time as your redundancy money .

Lump sum redundancy payments or pay in lieu of notice are normally tax free if they currently amount to less than £30,000 and are paid after you have ended your employment; the balance is taxed in full. Lump sums paid as a *commutation* of pension rights are also tax free.

However when a company goes into liquidation, liquidators deduct what they call 'tax' from pay in lieu of notice money. This deduction is not tax and is not paid to the Inland Revenue but the House of Lords has ruled that your statutory pay in lieu of notice amounts to take home pay, and as personal tax allowances are usually used up by unemployment benefit, liquidators are correct to make a deduction.

Unemployment benefit is taxable. So while you receive unemployment benefit, part or all of your tax allowances are set against your benefit.

If you remain unemployed for more than a year (or after six months when the new rules start) after which unemployment benefit ceases, you are likely to be a non-taxpayer and will probably need to spend some of your capital in order to maintain your standard of living.

If you have retired early (ie before 65 for men, before 60 for women) and receive a pension from a former job, your personal tax allowances will be set against part or all of your job pension. Only if your job pension is less than your personal tax allowances and outgoings will you be a non-taxpayer as far as part or all of your investments are concerned. See also advice in Chapter 13.

Unless you regard your unemployment as early retirement, don't tie up your money: you may need it.

Taxpayers and non-taxpayers should invest in:
❀ *Building Society Cheque Account With Interest*
Building Society Instant Access Account
❀ *Building Society Postal Account*
Building Society 30 Day Notice Account

Non-taxpayers should also consider:
National Savings Investment Account
❀ *Offshore Bank Instant Access Account*
Offshore Bank Notice Account

Widows under retirement age

Widow's pensions and widowed mother's allowance are taxable. But if they are less than her personal tax allowance and if she has little other income, she may not be a taxpayer. The £1,000 payment made to widows under 60 without children is tax free. If she has children she may get *child addition* paid with her widow's benefit; this child addition is also tax free. As a single parent looking after children she is entitled to the *additional personal tax allowance for children* which now only gives 15% tax relief. If she has little additional income she may not be a taxpayer.

On the other hand, if a widow earns, she continues to receive her widow's benefit and will almost certainly be a taxpayer even if the job is only part time. Her personal tax allowances are first set against her widow's benefit and then against her earnings.

The proceeds of life insurance policies on death don't count as income - even the family income benefit policies which pay out monthly, quarterly or half-yearly instalments. But a pension paid to a widow by her former husband's firm and income from a personal pension or retirement annuity which continues count as income.

In the year of a husband's death there may be less tax to pay. Any investment income received by the husband in the part of the tax year up to the date of death counts as his income (together with his earnings or pension) against which the married man's tax allowances can be set. Investment income received during the remainder of the tax year (ie until the following 5 April) counts as the widow's; she can set her personal tax allowance plus her widow's bereavement tax allowance against this. The widow's bereavement allowance is given in the tax year of the husband's death and the following year only but now only gives 15% tax relief. There is a free Inland Revenue leaflet *IR91 A Guide for Widows and Widowers*.

Separated or divorced

Maintenance payments under a court order or an enforceable separation deed made before 15 March 1988 count as income in the hands of the recipient and may be taxable. Such payments paid to a child count as the child's income and are not liable for tax up to the value of the child's personal allowance assuming the child has no other income.

Voluntary payments and payments which started on or after 15 March 1988 don't count as income so there is no tax for the recipient to reclaim or pay but the payer cannot set them against his income. For more information see two free Inland Revenue leaflets *IR92 One Parent Families* and *IR93 Separation, Divorce and Maintenance Payments*.

Living abroad

If you are serving overseas with the armed forces or diplomatic service, your pay is taxable in the UK and your tax position is usually the same as anyone else. If you are serving for a fixed term you may have a good idea of how long you want to invest your money: you will want it back when you return to the UK.

If you are working overseas continuously for more than a full tax year, you will be non-resident for that tax year. In other cases you may have to wait three years before your non-resident status is agreed by the Inland Revenue. Particularly during those three years, and afterwards, you must be careful about the timing and length of visits to the UK. More information from an Inland Revenue leaflet *IR20 Residents and Non-Residents Liability to Tax in the UK*. While not liable for UK tax as a non-resident, UK banks and building societies can pay you without deduction of tax. But you may be liable for tax in the country in which you live or the country where you invest (which need not be the same). Taxmen in different countries swap information about interest paid on bank accounts.

13

Boosting Your Retirement Income

Age allowance

In the tax year in which you have your 65th birthday you can be eligible for higher personal tax allowances called *age allowance*. These are at a higher rate from the tax year when you reach the age of 75.

The way the rules for age allowance work can mean that to get the best after tax return, and thus the highest retirement income, your choice of investments must be divided between those suitable for a non-taxpayer where tax is not deducted, a basic rate taxpayer and a higher rate taxpayer.

If you receive the State retirement pension and no other pension or a very small pension or another pension which is fully or partly exempt from tax (see list on page 26) it's likely that some of your income from investments is not liable to income tax. If you are in this position you may have to claim a rebate of tax deducted from income on your investments.

Age allowance is given instead of the normal personal tax allowance if your income is below a certain level. The age allowance income limit for 1995-96 is £14,600 or less (1994-95 £14,200 or less). If your income comes to above this limit, your age allowance is reduced gradually as your income rises until it comes down to the normal personal tax allowance.

There are two scales of age allowance: if you are 65 to 74 the allowance for 1995-96 is £4,630. If you are 75 or over the allowance is £4,800.

There is also an extra married age allowance of £2,995 (£3,035 if one of you is 75 and over). But the extra married age allowance only gets tax relief at 15% in the 1995-96 tax year. Only one partner of the married couple gets the married age allowance, the other gets the age allowance only - or you can have half each.

Married couples

Separate taxation of a husband and wife's income applies to pensioners just like any other married couple. **Provided couples can split their income more or less equally between them, that can give rise to a considerable tax saving**.

If both husband and wife are over age 65, they are each entitled to age allowance on their own income. A husband and wife can each have an income of up to £14,600 and get full age allowance. So a couple both over age 65 can have a combined income of £29,200 in the 1995-96 tax year and each get full age allowance.

If a couple has an income of £29,200 which comes mainly from investments and they can arrange matters so that they each have half the income, that is £14,600 each, and they can split the married age allowance between them (half each). Their total tax bill will be £743 a year less than compared with the situation before they were 65.

Married couples with large pensions Pensions count as the income of the person who receives them. So you each have your personal tax allowance of up to £3,525 set against it if you are under 65 or the personal age allowance of £4,630 (age 65-74) or £4,800 (age 75 or over). The married age allowance can be set against either spouse's pension - or you can have half each.

There is no scope for switching pensions from husband to wife or vice-versa once they have started to be paid. But people planning to retire should aim to try and equalise their pensions in retirement to enable them to pay the least tax under these rules.

Juggling investments

It's quite permissible to transfer money and assets from husband to wife and vice-versa in order to try and equalise your incomes as far as possible. Joint holdings will be taken by the Inland Revenue to be owned half each unless you tell them otherwise by signing a form. Your tactics should be the same as for a wife under retirement age - see Chapter 10.

Tax effective investments

Here is how to work out your most tax effective investment strategy which as mentioned above may mean choosing some investments suitable for non-taxpayers, some suitable for basic taxpayers and even some suitable for higher rate taxpayers.

Taxable pensions less than total tax allowances

If that is the case you should invest in the following investments (in alphabetical order) where tax is not deducted until the interest on your investments plus your taxable pensions reaches your tax allowances. This will save you the trouble of having to claim a tax rebate. However if you don't mind claiming a rebate, use the other investments mentioned later in the Chapter as well.

Bank Cheque Account with Interest (at an offshore branch)
Co-operative Society Term Account
National Savings Investment Account
National Savings Income Bond
National Savings Pensioners Income Bond
❀ *Offshore Bank Instant Access Account*
Offshore Bank Notice Account
Offshore Managed Currency Fund
Offshore Stock and Bond Fund
Property Commercial Direct Investment
Property Residential Direct Investment

Marginal age allowance

If your income is over £14,600 you lose £1 of age allowance for every £2 by which your income exceeds this figure until the age allowance is reduced to the level of the ordinary personal tax allowance. This marginal age allowance income limit for 65 to 74 year olds in 1995-96 comes to an end when a single person's income reaches £16,804; or when one of the married couple's income reaches £19,360 and the other's £16,804. The limits are a shade higher for the over 75's: £17,150 for a single person and £19,780 for one of a married couple.

These income limits refer to before tax or gross income. If part of your income is from dividends or unit trust distributions you must add the tax credit to determine whether they fall within the limits.

By losing your age basic age allowance within these income bands, although you are only a basic rate taxpayer, you are in effect being taxed at a higher rate - in fact at a rate of 37½%. If your income falls within these bands you might consider investments suitable for higher rate taxpayers to reduce your taxable income to £14,600. These are:

❀ *Bank Tessa Account*
❀ *Building Society Tessa Account*
❀ *Investment Trust Personal Equity Plan*
  Life Insurance Mixed Bond
  Life Insurance Property Bond
  (with the two above income must be 5% or less of original cost to leave age allowance unaffected).
  Life Income Bond
❀ *National Savings Fixed Certificates* (only issues paying reasonable interest)
❀ *National Savings Index-Linked Certificates*
❀ *Stock Government Index-Linked*
❀ *Stock Personal Equity Plan*
❀ *Unit Trust Personal Equity Plan*

More on all these investments in Part 2 under the individual entry.

Alternatively if you think you will be a basic taxpayer after next 6 April but are a marginal age allowance taxpayer this tax year, transfer your building society investments to a society which pays interest once a year instead of monthly or half yearly. Some societies pay yearly in April which makes tax planning easier.

Summary

To summarise: if you, or your husband or wife, are over 65 and your or your spouse's total income (from investments and taxable pensions) is below the actual age allowance levels applicable to each of you (ie £4,630 or £4,800 single, £7,625 or £7,835 married) you are a non-taxpayer. Only one married partner gets the married allowance as well, the other gets the single allowance.

If your income is above the age allowance levels but under the £14,600 age allowance income limit, you are a basic rate taxpayer on the excess over the age allowance but still a non-taxpayer on any amount below the allowance which is not set against taxable pensions.

If your income is above £14,600 but below the marginal age allowance income limits (£16,804 or £17,150 single) then extra income between these limits reduces your age allowance and is taxed at the basic rate of tax which together is equivalent to a tax rate of 37½%. As the extra married age allowance now gives relief at only 15%, you need not be so concerned at losing that. So your investment strategy for income between these bands is the same as a higher rate taxpayer.

The best income

In retirement you usually want to get the highest income you possibly can from your investments. The income can be fixed or variable - and the money you invest can also be fixed or variable. The most convenient income is monthly but it may be easier to have the income paid half-yearly when you have less than, say, £5,000 to invest.

Fixed income and fixed capital. With these investments you know the return you are going to get at the outset, usually for a fixed period of time called the term or with an annuity for the rest of your life.

Building Society Escalator Bond
Building Society Term Account
Co-operative Society Term Account †
Life Insurance Annuity (fixed)
Life Insurance Income Bond
National Savings FIRST Option Bond
National Savings Pensioners Income Bond †
National Savings Capital Bond * †
✱ *National Savings Fixed Issue Certificates* *
Local Authority Fixed Term Loan

Variable income and fixed capital. Here your capital does not vary but the income can go up and down. These include:

Bank deposits (most)
✱ *Bank Tessa Account* ‡
✱ *Building Society Postal Account*
Building Society accounts (most)
✱ *Building Society Tessa Account* ‡
Life Insurance Annuity (increasing, with profits or index-linked)
National Savings Income Bond †
National Savings Investment Account †
✱ *Offshore Bank Instant Access Account* †
Offshore Bank Notice Account †

Fixed income and variable capital. Investments where the income is fixed but where your capital can go up and down in value. These include:

Building Society Permanent Interest Bearing Shares
Stock Government Fixed Interest († through National Savings)
Stock Loan and Debenture
Shares Preference

---

*This investment doesn't pay out interest but accumulates, You should spend capital from another account if necessary, which you can replenish at the end of the term. †Tax not deducted from the income.
‡ Especially higher rate taxpayers.

Variable income and variable capital. Where neither the income nor the capital is fixed. These include:
Life Insurance Mixed Bond
Life Insurance Property Bond
(both the above using income withdrawal scheme)
❀ *National Savings Index-Linked Certificates* *
❀ *Offshore Single Foreign Currency Fund* †
Offshore Stock & Bond
Shares Preference (when you invest through a unit trust)
❀ *Stock Government Index-Linked* (†through National Savings)
❀ *Stock Personal Equity Plan*
Stock Private Index-Linked
Stock Unit Trust Invested in Gilts
Unit Trust Stock & Bond Fund

Riskier investments with variable income and capital. This is really the same as the last category except that they generally have a lower income and less certainty of what you will get. These include:
Investment Trust Shares
❀ *Investment Trust Personal Equity Plan* ‡
Investment Trust Split Level Shares (income shares)
Life Insurance Equity Bond
Life Insurance International Bond
Offshore Managed Currency Fund
Property Commercial Direct Investment
Property Enterprise Zone Trust ‡
Property Residential Direct Investment
Property Ground Rents
Shares Ordinary Quoted
❀ *Shares Self Select Personal Equity Plan* ‡
Stock Convertible Loan
Unit Trust Invested in Overseas Shares
Unit Trust Invested in UK Shares
❀ *Unit Trust Personal Equity Plan* ‡

---

*This investment doesn't pay out interest but accumulates. You should spend capital from another account if necessary, which you can replenish at the end of the term. †Tax not deducted from the income. ‡Especially higher rate taxpayers.

14

Summary of Investments

Here is a summary of the different types of investments. There are nine different categories:
- Investments you can get out immediately or within a few days.
- Investments for which you have to wait a week to a month.
- Investments for which you have to wait from a month to a year.
- Investments with money back from 1-7 years.
- Longer term investments suitable for 8 years or more.
- Getting a monthly income.
- Investing in shares.
- Investing in property.
- Index-linked investments (linked to the Retail Prices Index).

Sometimes a long-term investment can make short-term profits - but it can also mean short-term losses. All are listed alphabetically. The best are marked with a rosette ❀. Some are poor value.

Money back at once or in a few days
No penalty
  Bank Cash Card Account
  Bank Cheque Account With Interest
❀ *Bank Children's Account*
  Bank Higher Interest Deposit Account
  Building Society Cash Card Account
❀ *Building Society Cheque Account With Interest*
  Building Society Children's Account
  Building Society Instant Access Account
❀ *Building Society Postal Account*
  Building Society Regular Monthly Savings
  Building Society Share and Deposit Accounts
  Offshore Bank Foreign Currency Account
❀ *Offshore Bank Instant Access Account*
❀ *Offshore Single Foreign Currency Fund*
  Offshore Sterling Currency Fund
  Unit Trust Cash Trust

Small penalty
Bank 7 Day Account
Building Society 30 Day Notice Account
Building Society 60 Day Notice Account
Building Society 90 Day Notice Account
National Savings Ordinary Account

Money back in a week to a month
No penalty
Bank 7 Day Account
Bank Notice Account
Building Society Monthly Income Account
Building Society 30 Day Notice Account
National Savings Investment Account
National Savings Premium Bond
Offshore Bank Notice Account

Money back in more than a month but less than a year
Bank Notice Account
Bank Term Account
Building Society 60 Day Notice Account
Building Society 90 Day Notice Account
National Savings Income Bond
Offshore Bank Notice Account
Stock Government Fixed-Interest
❀ *Stock Government Index-Linked*
Stock Private Index-Linked

Investments probably suitable for 1 to 7 years See table opposite.

Investments probably suitable for 8 years or longer
Friendly Society Building Society Linked
Gold Coins
❀ *Investment Trust Personal Equity Plan*
Investment Trust Shares
❀ *Investment Trust Savings Plan*
Investment Trust Split Level Trust
Life Insurance Equity Bond
Life Insurance International Bond
Life Insurance Mixed Bond
Continued overleaf

Money back from 1 to 7 years

Investment	1yr	2yrs	3yrs	4yrs	5yrs	6yrs	7rs
✹Bank Tessa Account	□	□	□	□	■		
Building Society Escalator Bond	□	□	□	□	□		
Building Society Term Share	□	□	□	□	□		
✹Building Society Tessa Account	□	□	□	□	■		
Building Society Permanent Interest Bearing Share	□	□	□	□	□	□	□
Building Society Stock Market Bond			□		□		
Co-operative Society Term Account	■	■	■	□	□		
✹Investment Trust Personal Equity					■	■	■
Investment Trust Zero Dividend	□	□	□	□	□	□	□
Life Insurance Growth/Income Bond	□	■	■	□	□	□	□
Local Authority Fixed Term Loan	□	■	■	□	□	□	□
✹National Savings Fixed Certificate	□	□	□	□	■		
✹National Savings Index-Linked Cert.	□	□	□	□	■		
National Savings Capital Bond	□	□	□	□	■		
National Savings FIRST Option Bond	□						
National Savings Income Bond	□						
✹National Pensioners Bond	□	□	□	□	■		
Offshore Stock & Bond Fund	□	□	■	■	■	■	■
✹Offshore Single Foreign Currency	■	■	■	■	■	■	■
Property Ground Rents							■
Shares Enterprise Investment Fund					□	□	□
Shares SAYE Share Option					■		■
Stock Government Fixed Interest	□	□	□	□	□	□	□
Stock Loan or Debenture	□	□	□	□	□	□	□
✹Stock Personal Equity Plan	□	□	□	□	□	□	□
Stock Unit Trust Invested in Gilts	□	□	□	□	□	□	□
✹Unit Trust Personal Equity Plan	□	□	□	□	■	■	■
Unit Trust Stock & Bond Fund	□	□	□	□	□	□	□

■ Recommended investment period   □ Under terms of investment

Continued from page 82

Life Insurance Property Bond
Life Insurance With-Profits Bond
Life Insurance With-Profits Endowment Policy
Life Insurance With-Profits Flexible Policy
Offshore Investment Fund
Offshore Managed Currency Fund
Offshore Stock & Bond Fund
Pension Buy Out Bond
✱ *Pension Director's Pension*
Pension Free Standing Top Up Plan
Pension In-House Top Up Plan
✱ *Pension Personal Pension*
Property Commercial Direct Investment
Property Enterprise Zone Trust
Property Residential Direct Investment
Shares Enterprise Investment Fund
Shares Ordinary Quoted
✱ *Shares Self Select Personal Equity Plan*
Stock Convertible Loan
✱ *Stock Government Index-Linked*
Stock Private Index-Linked
Unit Trust Index Tracker
Unit Trust Invested in Overseas Shares
Unit Trust Invested in UK Shares
✱ *Unit Trust Personal Equity Plan*
Unit Trust Savings Plan
Unit Trust Stock & Bond Fund

Getting a monthly income
Not all the companies under each heading pay income monthly.
Bank Higher Interest Deposit Account
Building Society Monthly Income Account
Life Insurance Annuity
Life Insurance Equity or International Bond
Life Insurance Fixed-Interest, Gilt, Money or Convertible Bond
Life Insurance Mixed Bond
Life Insurance Property Bond
Life Insurance With-Profits Bond
National Savings Income Bond
National Savings Pensioners Income Bond
Offshore Bank Notice Account

Unit Trust Cash Trust
Unit Trust Invested in Shares

Investing in shares

Building Society Stock Market Guaranteed Bond
✱ Investment Trust Personal Equity Plan
✱ Investment Trust Savings Plan
Investment Trust Shares
Investment Trust Split Level Trust
Investment Trust Warrants
Life Insurance Equity Bond
Life Insurance Stock Market Guaranteed Bond
Life Insurance International Bond
Life Insurance Unit-Linked Savings Plan
Offshore Investment Fund
Pension Buy Out Bond
✱ Pension Director's Pension
Pension Free Standing Top Up Plan
Pension In-House Top Up Plan
✱ Pension Personal Pension
Shares Enterprise Investment Fund
Shares Ordinary Quoted
Shares SAYE Share Option
✱ Shares Self Select Personal Equity Plan
Shares Traded Options
Shares Unquoted
Shares Venture Capital Trust
Stock Convertible Loan
Unit Trust Index Tracker
Unit Trust Invested in Shares
✱ Unit Trust Personal Equity Plan
Unit Trust Savings Plan

Investing in property

Life Insurance Property Bond
Property Commercial Direct Investment
Property Ground Rents
Property Residential Direct Investment

Index-linked investments

✱ National Savings Index-Linked Certificates
✱ Stock Government Index-Linked
Stock Private Index-Linked

Lump sum investment table

Type of investment	Paid gross [5] ✓ or ✗	Quoted rate [1] %	After tax if you pay:[1]				Fixed/ varies F or V	See page
			Nil %	20% %	25% %	40% %		
Bank								
Cash Card Deposit £500	✗	3.80	3.8	3.0	2.9	2.3	V	92
Cheque Account With Int.	✗	6.25	6.4	5.1	4.8	3.9	V	93
Higher Interest Deposit £1 [2]	✗	5.50	5.6	4.5	4.2	3.3	V	95
Notice: 60 Day £10,000+	✗	6.00	6.0	4.8	4.5	3.6	V	96
90 Day £500+	✗	4.60	4.7	3.7	3.5	2.8	V	96
Term Account 3 years	✗	9.25	**9.3**	**7.4**	**6.9**	5.6	F	98
Tessa Account	✓	7.50	7.5	**7.5**	**7.5**	**7.5**	F	99
Building Society								
Cash Card Account £500	✗	4.25	4.3	3.4	3.2	2.6	V	100
Cheque Account £2,500+	✗	6.00	6.0	4.8	4.5	3.6	V	101
£10,000+	✗	6.25	6.3	5.0	4.7	3.8	V	101
£25,000+	✗	6.50	6.5	5.2	4.9	3.9	V	101
Instant Access £10+	✗	5.25	5.3	4.2	3.9	3.2	V	104
£2,000	✗	5.90	5.9	4.7	4.4	3.5	V	104
£20,000+	✗	6.90	6.9	5.5	5.2	4.1	V	104
Postal Account £1,000+	✗	5.85	5.9	4.7	4.4	3.5	V	110
£10,000+	✗	6.35	6.4	5.1	4.8	3.8	V	110
£50,000+	✗	6.70	6.7	5.4	5.0	4.0	V	110
30 Day Notice £25,000+	✗	6.60	6.6	5.3	5.0	4.0	V	105
£50,000+	✗	6.90	6.9	5.5	5.2	4.1	V	105
60-90 Day Notice £500+	✗	6.30	6.3	5.0	4.7	3.8	V	106-7
£2,000+	✗	6.55	6.6	5.2	4.9	3.9	V	106-7
£10,000+	✗	7.05	7.1	5.6	5.3	4.2	V	106-7
£25,000+	✗	7.30	7.3	5.8	5.5	4.4	V	106-7
£40,000+	✗	7.40	7.4	5.9	5.6	4.4	V	106-7
Permanent Int Brng Share	✗	10.70	**11.0**	**8.8**	**8.2**	6.6	V	109
Term Share : 3 years	✗	8.75	**8.8**	**7.0**	**6.6**	5.3	F	114
5 years	✗	8.70	**8.7**	**7.0**	**6.5**	5.2	F	114
Tessa Account: variable	✓	7.40	7.4	**7.4**	**7.4**	**7.4**	V	115
Tessa Account: fixed	✓	9.25	**9.3**	**9.3**	**9.3**	**9.3**	F	115
Co-operative Society								
1 Year Term £100	✓	8.00	**8.2**	**6.5**	**6.1**	4.9	V	116
3 Year Term £500	✓	8.50	**8.7**	**6.9**	**6.5**	5.2	V	116

Best rates in heavy black. These rates are liable to rise. Check the current rate before you invest. Correct at 14 February 1995. [1] The after tax return includes reinvestment of monthly, quarterly or half-yearly interest; see overleaf for conversion; the quoted rate does not. [2] Some pay more for higher amounts. [3] For a woman aged 70, paid monthly, guaranteed 5 years. [4] Assumes 3% a year rise in the Retail Prices Index. [5] Banks and building societies can pay with no tax deducted to non-taxpayers.

Lump sums (continued)

Type of investment		Paid gross ✓ or ✗	Quoted rate [1] %	After tax if you pay:[1] Nil %	20% %	25% %	40% %	Fixed/ varies F or V	See page
Life insurance									
Annuity [3]		✓ ✗	11.40	**12.0**	10.8	10.4	9.5	F	125
Income Bond: 3 years		✗	6.40	6.4	**6.4**	6.4	5.4	F	126
	5 years	✗	6.60	6.6	**6.6**	6.6	5.6	F	126
Local authority									
3 year term		✗	8.25	**8.4**	6.7	6.3	5.1	F	139
5 year term		✗	8.65	**8.8**	7.1	6.6	5.3	F	139
National savings									
Capital Bond 'I'		✓	7.75	7.8	6.2	5.8	4.7	F	140
FIRST Option	£1,000+	✗	6.40	6.4	5.1	4.8	3.8	F	142
1 yr term	£20,000+	✗	6.80	6.8	5.4	5.1	4.1	F	142
Fixed 42nd Certs: 1 year		✓	4.00	4.0	4.0	4.0	4.0	F	143
	5 year	✓	5.85	5.9	5.9	5.9	**5.9**	F	143
Index-linked Certs 5 year [4]		✓	6.00	6.0	6.0	**6.0**	**6.0**	V	144
Income Bond	£2,000+	✓	6.50	6.7	5.4	5.0	4.0	V	145
	£25,000+	✓	6.75	7.0	5.6	5.2	4.2	V	145
Investment: 1 month		✓	5.25	5.3	4.2	3.9	3.2	V	146
	£500+	✓	5.75	5.8	4.6	4.3	3.5	V	146
	£25,000+	✓	6.00	6.0	4.8	4.5	3.6	V	146
Pensioners Bond		✓	7.50	7.8	6.2	5.8	4.7	F	147
General extension rate		✓	3.51	3.5	3.5	3.5	3.5	V	207
Offshore Bank									
Instant Access £1,000+		✓	5.75	5.8	4.6	4.3	3.5	V	150
	£25,000+	✓	6.65	6.7	5.3	5.0	4.0	V	150
	£50,000+	✓	6.85	6.9	5.5	5.1	4.1	V	150
Notice 90 day	£5,000 +	✓	6.00	6.0	4.8	4.5	3.6	V	151
	£50,000+	✓	7.20	7.2	5.8	5.4	4.3	V	151
Offshore Fund									
Single Foreign	US$	✓	4.75	4.8	3.8	3.6	2.9	V	154
Currency	Yen	✓	0.88	0.9	0.7	0.7	0.5	V	154
	DM	✓	3.73	3.8	3.0	2.8	2.3	V	154
Sterling Currency Fund		✓	4.99	5.1	4.0	3.8	3.0	V	155
Stock & Bond Fund		✓	7.09	7.2	5.8	5.4	4.3	V	156
Stock									
Government Fixed 4 yrs		✓ ✗	-	**8.5**	7.2	6.9	**5.9**	F	176
	9 yrs	✓ ✗	-	**8.8**	7.1	6.6	5.3	F	176
Government Index linked[4]		✓ ✗	-	7.0	**6.4**	6.2	**5.8**	V	178
Personal Equity Plan		✓	8.76	**8.8**	**8.8**	**8.8**	**8.8**	V	181
Unit trust Invested in Gilt		✗	8.37	**8.5**	6.8	6.4	5.1	V	183
Unit Trust									
Cash Trust		✗	5.70	5.8	4.6	4.3	3.5	V	184
Stock & Bond Fund		✗	6.62	6.7	5.4	5.0	4.0	V	191

How much interest

The amount of interest you receive depends not only on the interest rate but also on how often you receive it. That is because with interest paid half way through the year you get the chance to earn interest on the interest as well as on the amount already in the account. For example, some banks and building societies pay interest half-yearly. The National Savings Bank Investment Account pays yearly.

Before you invest, as well as checking the interest rate, also check how often it's paid. The table on the right shows you how much you would get at the end of a year at various interest rates with interest paid and reinvested in the same account for the rest of the year. You can see it becomes less important when interest rates are low. This rate of interest is called the compound annual rate which is sometimes abbreviated as CAR.

Warning: many banks and building societies pay a lower rate for monthly interest compared with annual. But some don't pay the equivalent of the compound annual rate - they pay less. So the society with the best rate for yearly interest may not be the best for monthly.

| Quoted | Interest at year end on £100 if paid: | | | |
	Yearly	Half-yearly	Quarterly	Monthly
%	£	£	£	£
3	3.00	3.02	3.03	3.04
3.25	3.25	3.28	3.29	3.30
3.5	3.5	3.53	3.55	3.56
3.75	3.75	3.79	3.80	3.82
4	4.00	4.04	4.06	4.07
4.25	4.25	4.30	4.32	4.33
4.5	4.50	4.55	4.58	4.59
4.75	4.75	4.81	4.84	4.85
5	5.00	5.06	5.09	5.12
5.25	5.25	5.32	5.35	5.38
5.5	5.50	5.58	5.61	5.64
5.75	5.75	5.83	5.88	5.90
6	6.00	6.09	6.14	6.17
6.25	6.25	6.35	6.40	6.43
6.5	6.50	6.61	6.66	6.70
6.75	6.75	6.86	6.92	6.96
7	7.00	7.12	7.19	7.23
7.25	7.25	7.38	7.45	7.50
7.5	7.50	7.64	7.71	7.76
7.75	7.75	7.90	7.98	8.03
8	8.00	8.16	8.24	8.30
8.25	8.25	8.42	8.51	8.57
8.5	8.50	8.68	8.77	8.84
8.75	8.75	8.94	904	9.11
9	9.00	9.20	9.31	9.38
9.25	9.25	9.46	9.58	9.65
9.5	9.50	9.73	9.84	9.92
9.75	9.75	9.99	10.11	10.20
10	10.00	10.25	10.38	10.47
10.25	10.25	10.51	10.65	10.75
10.5	10.50	10.78	10.92	11.02
10.75	10.75	11.04	11.19	11.30
11	11.00	11.30	11.46	11.57
12	12.00	12.36	12.55	12.68
13	13.00	13.42	13.65	13.80

PART 2

Ninety Eight Ways
to Invest

What the headings mean

❀ The rosette award denotes a best value investment of its type. But read the "How worthwhile' section because an investment with a rosette award is not necessarily best value for everyone.

Name This describes the type of investment as it is generally known and is preceded by the type of institution which offers it. (eg Bank, Building Society, Life Insurance Company, National Savings) or the general nature of the investment (eg Offshore, Shares, Stock, Unit Trust).

What it is A summary of the main distinguishing points.

Who can invest Whether there are any age or other restrictions on the investor.

How worthwhile Which sort of taxpayer (non, 20%, basic or higher) should seek this type of investment. Cross-references to competing investments.

Minimum Minimum range of investment allowed by those schemes listed on the page. Higher minimum schemes may be available but have not been included unless they offer better value.

Maximum Maximum investment which is allowed by a single institution or scheme.

Suitable Whether suitable for lump sums, regular savings or both.

Money back How soon you can get your money back. Any penalties like loss of interest or capital.

Interest Whether the return from the investment is fixed or variable.

Interest paid How often the interest is paid, eg. half-yearly, yearly, quarterly or monthly. Whether interest is accumulated or paid-out, and if so, the method.

BUILDING SOCIETY

❀ Postal Account

(Also known as Balmoral, Capital Trust)

An account which pays a good interest rate and where you can withdraw immediately, generally without notice or penalty but only by post. Deposits generally also have to be made by post. You lose interest while your cheque is in the post, possibly for up to a week if you receive it before a weekend and can't pay into another account until Monday.

Who can invest Anyone.

How worthwhile Good value for readily available money. Better value if you make few transactions. Compare with *Building Society Cheque Account With Interest* (more convenient). Non-taxpayers and higher rate taxpayers compare with *Offshore Instant Access Account*. For small amounts also consider *Unit Trust Cash Trust.*

Minimum *£1,000:* Bradford & Bingley, Birmingham Midshires. *£2,000:* Britannia, Yorkshire. *£2,500:* Most others.

Maximum £100,000 to £3 million. Some are open for deposits from new customers for limited periods only.

Suitable Lump sums.

Money back A few days. You fill in a form and post it back to the Society which posts you a cheque by return. Minimum cheque sometimes £50 or £100.

Interest Variable. More interest usually paid for larger amounts eg when over £10,000, £25,000, £30,000, £50,000, £100,000.

Interest paid Usually yearly (half-yearly at Birmingham Midshires); direct to a bank account, or left to accumulate. Some also pay monthly but at a lower nominal interest rate and require 30 days notice, see *Building Society Monthly Income Account.*

Tax Basic rate tax is deducted from the interest. Non-taxpayers can reclaim the tax from the Inland Revenue (or have it paid with no deduction). 20% taxpayers can reclaim tax. Higher rate taxpayers pay extra.

Fees to pay None.

Passbook Statement usually sent with each transaction or yearly.

Children Unsuitable.

Risk 90% compensation scheme on the first £20,000 for each investor.

How to invest Subscribe to *Building Society Choice* (monthly) or phone one of the societies listed below at their special 'By Post' phone number.

Where from Birmingham Midshires (First Class), Bradford & Bingley (Direct Premium), Bristol & West (Asset) Britannia (Capital Trust), Nationwide (InvestDirect), Yorkshire (1st Class).

The rates on these accounts may be excellent when you invest but they don't always stay that way.

Tax How the investment is treated for tax in the UK. Whether tax is deducted at source; whether non-taxpayers can reclaim it; whether higher rate taxpayers pay extra and whether the investment is tax exempt.

Fees to pay Charges levied at the outset or regularly by the institution or financial adviser. These charges reduce the return on your investment.

Passbook Whether there is a passbook, certificate, statements or other document issued.

Children Whether the investment is suitable for a child's investment and any special conditions which apply. Child means someone under age 18.

Risk All savings and investments are equally affected by inflation which erodes their real value. This assesses the risk of losing your capital either because the investment fluctuates in value or the institution with which you invest gets into difficulties.

How to invest How to go about finding an institution which offers the scheme and what to do next. Where the best choice is constantly changing, how to find the best buy in other surveys.

Where from A list of the institutions which, at the times this book went to press, offered the best rates for the type of scheme described at the level of investment quoted. For example: '*Min £25,000:* Halifax' means Halifax is good value for sums over £25,000; the actual minimum for the account may be lower eg £500. Addresses and telephone numbers are given in *Appendix 1*.

BANK

Cash Card Account

(Also called Instant Savings Account, Saver Plus, Flexible Savings)

An account with a low minimum where you can easily pay in at a bank branch or by post and withdrawals can be made with a plastic card from a cash machine.

Who can invest Anyone. You do not need a bank current (cheque book) account. But to get large amounts out (other than in cash) you need to transfer the money to a cheque book account except at Abbey National and TSB.

How worthwhile Poor value for large amounts. Convenient if you make many cash transactions. Compare with *Building Society Cash Card Account* or *Building Society Cheque Account with Interest* pays better interest for larger amount and has the same cash card.

Minimum Nil.

Maximum None.

Suitable Lump sums. Regular savings

Money back At once from a cash machine £500 a day Midland, First Direct; £350 a day Clydesdale; £300 a day Royal Bank of Scotland; £250 a day Abbey National, Bank of Scotand; £200 a day Lloyds, TSB; from £50 a week to £250 a day Nat. West. Also over the counter at your own bank.

Interest Variable. Sometimes higher for larger amounts. Some banks (not listed here) pay very poor rates.

Interest paid Added to account monthly, quarterly, half yearly or yearly.

Tax Basic rate tax is deducted from the interest. Non-taxpayers can reclaim the tax from the Inland Revenue (or have interest paid with no deduction). 20% taxpayers can reclaim tax. Higher rate tax payers have to pay extra.

Fees to pay Abbey National 60p if withdrawal from a non-Abbey machine. Other banks may charge for withdrawal if you use another bank's cash machine unless there is a special arrangement, see note at the foot of this column. None from own bank.

Passbook Statements sent.

Children Over age 12 at Lloyds; 13 at Abbey National, Nat. West.; 14 at Royal Bank of Scotland; 16 at Midland. See also *Bank Children's Account.*

Risk 75% compensation scheme (90% from 1 July 1995) on the first £20,000 for each investor.

How to invest Check the rate offered. Some advertise out of date rates. Rates published in *Money£acts* monthly.

Where from Abbey National (Instant Saver), Clydesdale (Instant Solution), First Direct (High Interest Savings), Lloyds (Instant Savings), Midland (Saver Plus), Nat. West. (First Reserve), Royal Bank of Scotland (Gold Deposit), TSB (Flexible Savings).

Your card can be used in cash machines at other banks and building societies. Abbey National [2], AIB [1,2], Girobank [1,2], HFC Bank, Western Trust [2], Yorkshire Bank can use each other's Link machines (for other members and use abroad [1 or 2] see Building Society Cash Card Account). Barclays, Lloyds, Royal Bank of Scotland, Bank of Scotland (plus Link), can normally use each other's cash machines without charge. First Direct, Midland, Nat. West, Royal Bank of Scotland, Northern, TSB, Clydesdale, Bank of Ireland can use each other's with no charge. Visa cards can use each others' machines but if not listed above there may be a charge eg 1½%. Visa cards can be used abroad.

BANK

Cheque Account With Interest

(Also called High Interest Cheque Account, Prime Account, Premier Account)

An account with or without an initial minimum investment where money can be paid in and withdrawn with the cheque book provided, sometimes subject to a minimum withdrawal. Some allow you to overdraw, use direct debits and standing orders, have a cheque guarantee card. Some have a cash machine card.

Who can invest Anyone age 18 or over. Account can be in joint names.

How worthwhile A temporary home for money on its way somewhere else. High Street banks don't usually pay good interest but they pay more than ordinary cheque accounts. Compare with *Building Society Cheque Account With Interest, Offshore Bank Multi-currency Account.* If you have large sums of money credited to your account by Electronic Transfer, it may be more convenient to use an account at a bank which is itself a member of the bank clearing system.

Minimum *£1,000:* Barclays, Robert Fleming/S&P (Classic), UDT. *£2,000:* Citibank, Western Trust. *£2,500:* Bank of Scotland, Robert Fleming/S&P (Deposit).

Maximum Usually none.

Suitable Lump sums.

Money back Cheques or cash cards can be used for withdrawals (minimum cheque £100 at Midland and Nat. West.). Visa credit card paid off directly from the account at Robert Feming/S & P.

Interest Variable. Calculated daily. The High Street Banks tend to pay less.

Interest paid Added to account monthly, quarterly, half-yearly depending on the bank. Less or no interest while account balance below £1,000 - £2,500 .

Tax Basic rate tax is deducted from the interest. Non-taxpayers can reclaim the tax from the Inland Revenue (or have interest paid with no deduction). 20% taxpayers can reclaim tax. Higher rate taxpayers have to pay extra. Barclays Bank, Bank of Scotland, Robert Fleming offer these accounts in the Isle of Man where no tax is deducted; taxpayers should pay later.

Fees to pay Usually none. 75p Western Trust (2 free a month). Several charge £5 a month if balance below £2,500.

Passbook None. Statement issued monthly or quarterly.

Children Account Must be held in an adult's name.

Risk 75% compensation scheme (90% from 1 July 1995) on the first £20,000 for each investor.

How to invest Phone or call at one of the banks listed below Rates published monthly in *Money£acts.*

Where from *High Street Banks:* Bank of Scotland (Money Market), Barclays (Prime). *Other Banks:* Citibank (Money market Plus), Robert Fleming/S&P (Classic, Deposit), Western Trust (High Interest Cheque), UDT (Capital Plus).

Other cheque accounts which pay interest at High Street banks now pay at an almost non-existent rate of less than 1% a year.

BANK

Children's Account

A bank account with free gifts, money boxes, competitions and magazines. Most banks have different gifts for different ages eg under 9, 9-13, 14-17. BarclayPlus has £5 WH Smith discount voucher. Lloyds Headway has discount vouchers, £31 off driving lessons and at 16, a cheque book. Midland LiveCash £30 shop and mail order vouchers and 1 free driving lesson plus 5 discounted. TSB has discount vouchers at 300 cinemas for 11-15 year olds and reduced magazine subs plus high street discounts.

Who can invest Children. Abbey National: Up to age 15. Bank of Scotland: Up to 15. Barclays: Under age 19. Midland: 11-18. Lloyds: Under 18. Royal Bank of Scotland: 9-17. TSB: Up to 15.

How worthwhile A way to encourage children to save. Some of the banks have the best gifts but usually *Building Society Children's Account* pays better interest. Unsuitable for large amounts. Older children also consider *Bank Cash Card Account* and *Building Society Cash Card Account.*

Minimum £1.

Maximum None.

Suitable Lump sums. Regular savings.

Money back At Barclays 7 days' notice or immediately when you lose 7 days' interest At Abbey National, Midland, Lloyds, Royal Bank of Scotland, TSB immediately with no loss of interest. *Cash card for machine withdrawal* If age 11 or over at Lloyds (with parent's consent); 13 at Midland, TSB; 14 at Barclays; Royal Bank of Scotland. Under 7: parent must

sign, over 7 child can withdraw on own signature.

Interest Variable. Some pay more than others. Often better than an adult's account with a small balance.

Interest paid Added to account yearly, half-yearly, quarterly, monthly depending on the bank.

Tax Basic rate tax is deducted from the interest. Non-taxpayers can reclaim the tax from the Inland Revenue (or have interest paid without deduction). 20% taxpayers can reclaim tax. Higher rate taxpayers (eg where interest counts as a parent's income) pay extra. For how a child's income is taxed see Chapter 11.

Fees to pay None.

Passbook At Abbey National, TSB. Otherwise paying-in books provided. Statements usually twice yearly; quarterly at Royal Bank; monthly at Lloyds.

Risk 75% compensation scheme (90% from 1 July 1995) on the first £20,000 for each investor.

How to invest Call at some of the banks listed below and compare what they offer.

Where from TSB (FirstSave). *For good gifts but poor interest:* Barclays (BarclayPlus Junior 0-10, BarclayPlus 11+), Lloyds Bank (Young Savers, Headway), Midland (LiveCash). *For slightly better interest but poor gifts:* Abbey National (Action Savers Club), Bank of Scotland (Super Saver 5 0-16; Express 12-17), Royal Bank of Scotland (Cash Club 9-13; Route 17 1-17).

BANK

Higher Interest Deposit Account

(Also called Gold Deposit, Premium Reserve, Monthly Income)

An account with a minimum investment where you can easily pay in and withdraw by transfer to a cheque account.

Who can invest Anyone. Account can be held in joint names. At a High Street Bank you need a bank cheque book account with the same bank to operate such accounts conveniently.

How worthwhile Poor value at large banks. Possible risk of default at small less known ones. Consider instead *Building Society Postal Account.*

Minimum Usually £1 or £5.

Maximum None.

Suitable Lump sums. Regular savings.

Money back Usually immediately.

Interest Variable.

Interest paid Added to account monthly, quarterly, half-yearly depending on the bank. Can be paid into a current account or accumulated.

Tax Basic rate tax is deducted from the interest. Non-taxpayers can reclaim the tax from the Inland Revenue (or have interest paid with no deduction). 20% taxpayers can reclaim tax. Higher rate taxpayers have to pay extra.

Fees to pay None.

Passbook Statements usually sent yearly, half-yearly or quarterly depending on the bank. Passbook may be available with some banks.

Children Unsuitable.

Risk 75% compensation scheme (90% from 1 July 1995) on the first £20,000 for each investor.

How to invest At a bank branch or by post if you already have an account.

Where from *High Street Banks:* See under *Bank Cash Card Account. Other Banks:* See *Good Savings Guide* or *Money£acts* for up to date rates.

Interest rates on these accounts change frequently. High Street Bank accounts are less competitive when interest rates in general are low.

BANK

Notice Account

(Also called Investment, Gold Ninety ,Crown Reserve)

An account usually with a minimum investment which can be added to but notice of 60 or 90 days (2 or 3 months) must usually be given to withdraw.

Who can invest Anyone.

How worthwhile Compare with *Building Society 60 Day Notice Account* and *Building Society 90 Day Notice Account* which usually give better Interest. Non-taxpayers not eligible for interest to be paid with no tax deducted, consider instead *Offshore Bank Notice Account* or *National Savings Investment Account.* 6 or 12 months notice not recommended.

Minimum £500 to £10,000. Minimum deposit £500 at Abbey National.

Maximum None or £25,000-£50,000.

Suitable Lump sums.

Money back All or part after required notice given. Most allow early withdrawal for a charge. TSB withdrawal on demand if £5,000 remains. Royal Bank of Scotland (Gold 90) if £10,000 remains. Royal Bank of Scotland (Royal Reward) no early access. Abbey National 2 penalty free withdrawals of up to £15,000 each by cheque or £250 each in cash a year (6 if over £10,000 remains). Other withdrawals without notice incur loss of interest on notice period.

Interest Variable. Rates usually higher over £10,000, £25,000, £50,000. Royal Bank of Scotland (Royal Reward) gives a 2% bonus for each full year you remain invested.

Interest paid At Abbey National, TSB: yearly on 1 April. Royal Bank of Scotland: yearly on 30 April. By cheque, direct to a bank account, or left to accumulate. Often monthly income option to another account at higher minimum.

Tax Basic rate tax is deducted from the interest. Non-taxpayers can reclaim the tax from the Inland Revenue (or have interest paid with no deduction). 20% taxpayers can reclaim tax. Higher rate taxpayers have to pay extra.

Fees to pay None.

Passbook Statements usually sent yearly. Passbook at Abbey National; choice at TSB.

Children Unsuitable.

Risk 75% compensation scheme (90% from 1 July 1995) on the first £20,000 for each investor.

How to invest Call at or phone the companies listed below, ask for details and compare them.

Where from *60 day:* TSB (60 day). *90 day:* Abbey National (Investment), Royal Bank of Scotland (Gold Ninety), Royal Bank of Scotland (Royal Reward).

BANK

7 Day Account

(Also called Deposit Account)

An account where you can easily pay in. You withdraw at 7 days' notice or immediately with a loss of 7 days' interest.

Who can invest Anyone. Account can be held in joint names. You don't usually need a bank current (cheque book) account.

How worthwhile Poor value. Consider instead *Building Society Postal Account* and *Building Society Cheque Account With Interest.* For small amounts consider instead *Building Society Cash Card Account* or *Bank Cash Card Account.*

Minimum £1.

Maximum None.

Suitable Lump sums. Regular savings money can be transferred regularly from a current account.

Money back 7 days notice or immediately with loss of 7 days' interest.

Interest Variable. Current rates are usually displayed at bank branches and are virtually non-existent. Changes announced in newspapers.

Interest paid Added to account usually half-yearly in June and December. Lloyds Bank interest is added monthly or yearly

Tax Basic rate tax is deducted from the interest. Non-taxpayers can reclaim the tax from the Inland Revenue (or have interest paid with no deduction). 20% taxpayers can reclaim tax. Higher rate taxpayers have to pay extra.

Fees to pay None.

Passbook Usually none. Paying-in slips provided. Statement sent half-yearly.

Children Consider instead *Bank Children's Account.*

Risk 75% compensation scheme (90% from 1 July 1995) on the first £20,000 for each investor.

How to invest If you have one of these accounts, close it and move the money to one which pays better interest.

Where from Most banks.

Bank 7 Day Accounts are just one of a large number of superseded Bank and Building Society accounts which pay extremely poor interest, often ½% a year or less. A few banks automatically transfer you to the new version. Most don't. So an investor in what was once a good value account, may now be in one which is very poor value indeed. Always regularly check the current interest rate.

BANK

Term Account

(Also called Term Deposit Account, Fixed Term Deposits, Fixed Rate Bond)

Lump sum invested usually at a fixed rate of interest for a fixed term of 1 to 5 years. Usually no additions or withdrawals allowed. Higher rates of interest and different lengths of term can be negotiated for larger sums but usually only for terms under a year.

Who can invest Anyone

How worthwhile Compare with *Stock Government Fixed Interest.* Taxpayers compare with *Life Insurance Income Bond, Local Authority Fixed Term Loan.* Higher rate taxpayers compare with *National Savings Fixed Certificates.* Non-taxpayers compare with *National Savings Capital Bond, Co-operative Society Term Account.* Terms over 5 years not recommended.

Minimum £1,000-£5,000.

Maximum Usually none.

Suitable Lump sums.

Money back At end of fixed term when company usually notifies you. Some companies will return your money early if you have a good reason but may reduce the interest rate.

Interest Usually fixed. With all companies, interest paid monthly is less than the half-yearly or yearly rate.

Interest paid Half-yearly or monthly (a few companies pay yearly or quarterly): by cheque, direct to a bank account, or left to accumulate. Not all companies pay all these ways.

Tax Basic rate tax is deducted from the interest. Non-taxpayers can reclaim the tax from the Inland Revenue (or have interest paid with no deduction). 20% taxpayers can reclaim tax. Higher rate taxpayers have to pay extra.

Fees to pay None.

Passbook None. Statement usually sent half yearly.

Children Unsuitable.

Risk 75% compensation scheme (90% from 1 July 1995) on the first £20,000 for each investor.

How to invest Look for companies offering good interest rates in the newspapers. A list is published in *Money£acts* each month.

Where from Best rates usually from smaller, less well known banks. Best buys change frequently and are often issued as a limited offer.

Always leave some of your money invested where you can get at it at once or within a few days without penalty. Only tie up money for as long as you are sure you will not need it.

BANK

✹ Tessa Account

(Also called Tax Exempt Special Savings Account)

An account with a yearly maximum investment and no withdrawals for 5 years to receive interest tax free. You can either let the interest accumulate for 5 years or receive part of it each year. After 5 years you can continue to earn tax free interest on up to £9,000 in a Tessa.

Who can invest Anyone 18 or over. Joint accounts not allowed.

How worthwhile Good value for taxpayers, especially higher rate taxpayers but building societies usually pay better interest. Compare with *Building Society Tessa Account*. Non-taxpayers compare with *Building Society 30, 60 or 90 Day Notice Accounts, Offshore Bank Notice Account*.

Minimum £1 to £1,800. You can usually invest what you like, when you like, subject to the maximums.

Maximum £9,000 overall. £3,000 in year 1, £1,800 in years 2-4, £600 in year 5 (or up to £1,800 if less than maximum invested in previous years). You can only have one Tessa. When your Tessa matures after 5 years, you can reinvest up to £9,000 from it within 6 months in a new Tessa as one lump sum for another 5 years.

Suitable Lump sums, regular savings.

Money back After 5 years without penalty. Immediately (TSB or Lloyds Bank) or 28 days notice (Abbey National). If you withdraw more than an amount equal to what the accumulated interest less basic rate tax would be, the Tessa must be closed, transferred to a taxable account, and any interest earned so far becomes taxable. You can transfer your Tessa to another bank or building society and you won't lose the tax benefits. You may lose bonuses on early closure or transfer.

Interest Usually variable. Some offer fixed rates for all or part of the term.

Interest paid Usually added to account yearly. Part of the interest can usually be paid to another bank account. But the amount of interest equivalent to the basic rate of tax which would be deducted on a normal account must be accumulated for the full 5 years.

Tax Interest is tax free. It does not have to be included on a tax return.

Fees to pay Most banks have charges eg £20, £25, £50 if you want to move the account to another bank or to a building society, should their interest rate become poor value. Abbey National £20 charge if you don't give 28 days notice. Lloyds Bank 3 months loss of interest on switch to another Tessa. TSB no charge.

Passbook Statements usually sent.

Children Not eligible.

Risk 75% compensation scheme (90% from 1 July 1995) on the first £20,000 for each investor.

How to invest Call at, phone or write to one of the banks listed below. Look at surveys in the press or subscribe to *Money£acts* for up to date rates. You need your National Insurance or State Pension number, if you have one, for the application form.

Where from Abbey National, Barclays Bank, Lloyds Bank, TSB.

Check up from time to time that the interest rate remains competitive. If it isn't, transfer to a better Tessa Account at another bank or at a building society.

BUILDING SOCIETY

Cash Card Account

(Also called Cardcash, Cashbase, Cashcentre, Moneylink)

An account where you can easily pay in and withdrawals can be made from a cash dispenser usually 24 hours a day. Some cards can be used abroad.

Who can invest Anyone 12-16 or over.

How worthwhile Convenient if you make many cash transactions. Compare with *Bank Cash Card Account*. For larger amounts consider *Building Society Cheque Account With Interest.*

Minimum £1-£500.

Maximum Usually none.

Suitable Lump sums, regular savings. Deposits can be made at many machines. Salary can be paid direct into many accounts.

Money back Immediately from cash machine usually maximum £200-£300 a day. Some machines have maximum single transaction below daily limit. Over the counter at own society.

Interest Variable. Sometimes higher for larger amounts.

Interest paid Usually added to account yearly.

Tax Basic rate tax is deducted from the interest. Non-taxpayers can reclaim the tax from the Inland Revenue (or have interest paid with no deduction). 20% taxpayers can reclaim tax. Higher rate taxpayers have to pay extra .

Fees to pay Halifax charges 60p each time you use the card at a non-Halifax machine.

Passbook Yes or statements sent. Some machines can print statements and print your account balance.

Children Available at age 12 from Britannia, Halifax, Nationwide (see *Building Society Children's Account)*; 14 from Alliance & Leicester, Dunfermline, National & Provincial; 16 at most other societies.

Risk 90% compensation scheme on the first £20,000 for each investor.

How to invest Contact one of the societies listed below.

Where from Alliance & Leicester (Instant Access), Birmingham Midshires (Quantum Instant), National & Provincial (Instant Reserve), Nationwide (CashBuilder). See also Nationwide (InvestDirect) under *Building Society Postal Account.*

The following building societies belong to the Link network and their cards can be used at each other's machines, Post Offices and at banks' machines which belong to Link (see Bank Cash Card Account). Alliance & Leicester, Birmingham Midshires, Bradford & Bingley, Bristol & West, Britannia [1,2], Chelsea [1,2], Coventry [2], Derbyshire [1,2], Dunfermline [1,2], Halifax, Leeds Permanent, National & Provincial, Nationwide, Northern Rock, Norwich & Peterborough [2], Portman [2], Woolwich, Yorkshire Building Society [1,2]. Those marked [1] can use 4B Network machines in Spain, Multibanco in Portugal and Bancontact Mister in Belgium. Those marked [2] can use Plus machines in Canada, USA, Puerto Rico, US Virgin Islands, Mexico, Western Australia (Perth), Hong Kong, Singapore, Japan and Guam. To find the nearest machine in the USA phone 1 800 THE PLUS.

BUILDING SOCIETY

Cheque Account With Interest

(Also called Asset Reserve, Classic, Current)

An account with or without an initial minimum investment which can be added to (your salary or pension can be paid in direct) and withdrawals made or bills paid with the cheque book supplied or in the ordinary way at a building society branch. Some allow you to overdraw, use direct debits and standing orders, and have a cash machine and cheque guarantee card.

Who can invest Anyone 18 or over.

How worthwhile An alternative with better interest to a bank current (cheque book) account. With lower interest but possibly more convenient also consider *Bank Cheque Account With Interest.*

Minimum Initially *None:* Woolwich. *£500:* Northern Rock. *£2,500:* Chelsea (by post only). *£5,000:* Halifax.

Maximum None or £500,000.

Suitable Lump sums; regular payments (eg salary or pensions).

Money back Cheques can be used to pay bills or make withdrawals into other accounts. *Link* cash machine card available at Chelsea, Northern Rock, Woolwich.

Interest Variable. Usually more for larger amounts and poor while account below £2,500.

Interest paid Monthly at Northern Rock. Quarterly at Halifax. Yearly on 1 January at Portman. Yearly on 1 February at Chelsea. Yearly on 30 September at Woolwich. Interest accumulates in the account.

Tax Basic rate tax is deducted from the interest. Non-taxpayers can reclaim the tax from the Inland Revenue (or have interest paid with no deduction). 20% taxpayers can reclaim tax. Higher rate taxpayers have to pay extra.

Fees to pay None.

Passbook None. Statements sent.

Children Unsuitable.

Risk There is a 90% compensation scheme on the first £20,000 for each investor.

How to invest Phone or call at one of the societies listed below and ask for an application form.

Where from Chelsea (Classic), Halifax (Asset Reserve), Northern Rock (Current), Woolwich (Current).

These Building Society Cheque Account With Interest Accounts give the best rates of interest for an account with a cheque book. However they do not usually match the best rates overall.

BUILDING SOCIETY

Children's Account

(Also called Junior Savers , Young Saver, Little Xtra Club)

Building Society Share Account backed by popular children's characters, money boxes, free comics or magazines, letters, birthday cards and special promotions. A few offer discount vouchers or £1 or £5 cash added to account.

Who can invest Children. Maximum age depends on society, usualy 16. Some have 'teenage' accounts. Money can sometimes be tied up to age 18.

How worthwhile Good way to encourage younger children to save. Better interest for small amounts than in other building society accounts. Compare with *Bank Children's Account* and *Building Society Instant Access Account.* Age 12-14 and over compare with *Bank Cash Card Account* or *Building Society Cash Card Account.*

Minimum Usually £1.

Maximum Varies.

Suitable Lump sums. Regular savings.

Money back On demand: cash £250; cheque up to £5,000. Under 7 (10 Chelsea; 11 Halifax; 12 Bristol & West; 14 Leeds Permanent) parent must countersign. Over 7 (or when society thinks child responsible) child can withdraw on own signature. Cash card from age 12 at Britannia, Halifax, Nationwide. At 14 at Alliance & Leicester.

Interest Variable. Usually higher than the equivalent *Buildiing Society Instant Access Account* for the same amount

Interest paid Usually half-yearly or yearly to accumulate. Several send birthday cards.

Tax Basic rate tax is deducted from the interest. Non-taxpayers can reclaim the tax from the Inland Revenue (or have interest paid with no deduction). 20% taxpayers can reclaim tax. Higher rate taxpayers (eg where interest counts as a parent's income) have to pay extra. For how a child's income is taxed see also Chapter 11.

Fees to pay None

Passbook Often with a special cover.

Risk 90% compensation scheme on the first £20,000 for each investor.

How to invest Call at or phone one of the societies listed below

Where from *For better interest choose between:* Skipton (Young Sovereign), Market Harborough (Junior Bond), Tipton & Coseley (Top Class Saver), Vernon (Junior Saver) and Norwich & Peterborugh (Head Start, min. £250. *Otherwise:* Britannia (Brighter Saver, piggy bank 0-16; LTD 11-17), Dunfermline (HeadStart), Earl Shilton (£5 bonus for £5), Furness (£2.50 bonus on opening), Halifax (Little Xtra Club 0-11, Quest Club added to any account 12-16), Ipswich (TycoonRacoon, gifts 0-11), Leek United (Humphrey 0-13, height chart, money box; Pyramid Max 14-19 half price ticket to Alton Towers), Loughborough (Penguin money box, gift vouchers), Monmouthshire (Toy Squirrel or sports bag), Nationwide (Smart-2-Save 0-11, The Smart Account 12-17), Woolwich (For Kids).

Older children may be keener on higher interest or a cash dispenser card than low interest and special incentives.

BUILDING SOCIETY

Escalator Bond

(Aso called Escalating Term Share, Step Up Bond)

Lump sum invested for a term of 3, 4 or 5 years with the interest rate rising at yearly or 6 monthly intervals. No additions allowed. Withdrawals can sometimes be made, usually at 3 months' notice and losing 3 months' interest; some accounts are less restrictive. The interest rate is fixed at the outset.

Who can invest Anyone.

How worthwhile At the current fixed rates offered, good value provided you get as good, or nearly as good interest, as with a *Building Society Notice Account* in year 1 and you don't expect interest rates to rise to more than those offered by the Escalator Bond during the investment term. Poor value if interest rates rise unless withdrawal penalty is not severe. Non-taxpayers compare with *National Savings Capital Bond, Co-operative Society Term Account* (some offer Escalator Bonds). Higher rate taxpayers consider instead *National Savings Fixed Issue Certificates.*

Minimum Usually £500, £1,000, £2,000.

Maximum Usually none.

Suitable Lump sums.

Money back At end of term or earlier usually at 3 months' notice *and* 3 months' loss of interest. If you die, investment plus full interest up to date is paid out.

Interest Usually fixed for the term.

Interest paid Usually yearly. By cheque, direct to you, to a bank account, into another account. The money can't usually be left to accumuate. Monthly: into bank or other account see *Building Society Monthly Income Account.*

Tax Basic rate tax is deducted from the interest. Non-taxpayers can reclaim the tax from the Inland Revenue (or have interest paid with no deduction). 20% taxpayers can reclaim tax. Higher rate taxpayers have to pay extra.

Fees to pay None.

Passbook Or certificate issued.

Children Unsuitable.

Risk Full value of original investment returned on withdrawal. 90% compensation scheme on the first £20,000 for each investor.

How to invest Look for advertised special offers in the press. Get details from the companies listed below and compare them. Consult the list published in *Money£acts* each month.

Where from Coventry, Halifax, Lambeth, Newcastle, Portman, West Bromwich.

Some banks, offshore banks and co-operative societies also offer Escalator Bonds.

BUILDING SOCIETY

Instant Access Account

(Also called Gold Sovereign, Premium Access)

An account where you can with-draw immediately from a building society branch. Most pay more for larger account balances. Some societies with better value accounts ask you to open them by post but you can then use their branches for transactions.

Who can invest Anyone.

How worthwhile Can be good value for readily available money but *Building Society Postal Account* usually pays more. *Building Society Cheque Account With Interest* pays *less* but gives quicker access. Non-taxpayers and higher rate taxpayers also consider *Offshore Bank Instant Access Account.*

Minimum £500 to £2,500 to get a reasonable interest rate.

Maximum £100,000 to £1 million.

Suitable Lump sums. Regular savings.

Money back On demand: Usually at any branch. Cash £250 (£500 Halifax, Britannia, Northern Rock, Yorkshire; £300 Leeds & Holbeck). Cheques vary by society, check before you invest; usually £20,000 (up to £100,000 at large societies). Many allow withdrawals from any branch. Remainder usually in a few days but many societies say at a few month's notice in rules.

Interest Variable. More interest usually paid for large amounts eg over £5,000, £10,000, £25,000, £50,000, £100,000. No interest if balance less than £100 C&G; £50 Halifax.

Interest paid Usually yearly. By cheque, direct to a bank account or left to accumulate. Some also pay monthly: *see Building Society Monthly Income Account.*

Tax Basic rate tax is deducted from the interest. Non-taxpayers can reclaim the tax from the Inland Revenue (or have interest paid with no deduction). 20% taxpayers can reclaim tax. Higher rate taxpayers pay extra.

Fees to pay None.

Passbook Or receipt. Statement usually sent yearly.

Children Under 7: parents must sign. Over 7 (or when society thinks child responsible, say 10 or 12): child can withdraw on own signature. Compare with *Bank Children's Account* and *Building Society Chidren's Account.*

Risk 90% compensation scheme on the first £20,000 for each investor.

How to invest Subscribe to *Building Society Choice* or *Money£acts* (both monthly). See surveys in the press. Phone or call at the societies listed.

Where from *Your minimum £10:* City & Metropolitan. *£500:* Marsden, Portman. *£2,000+:* Northern Rock (Go Direct). *£2,000-£10,000:* Skipton (3 High Street).

The best interest on instant access accounts are now available mainly by post. See Building Society Postal Account.

BUILDING SOCIETY

30 Day Notice Account

(Also called One Month Notice, Special Option)

An account usually with a minimum investment which can be added to. Withdrawals can be made by giving 28 or 30 days notice. Some accounts have an option to withdraw immediately when you lose the equivalent amount of interest; a few have no loss of interest if £5,000 or £10,000 remains in account. Make sure you get the best interest for the amount you invest as most pay more for larger amounts. Generally only available from smaller societies.

Who can invest Anyone

How worthwhile You can get as good value with just a few days notice from larger societies. Consider instead *Building Society Postal Account* or *Building Society Instant Access Account*, If you don't mind a longer wait, compare with *Building Society 60 Day Notice Account*. Non-taxpayers not eligible for interest to be paid with no tax deducted consider instead *Offshore Bank Instant Access Account* or *Offshore Bank Notice Account*.

Minimum Usually £500 or £1,000.

Maximum £30,000 to £1 million.

Suitable Lump sums. Regular savings.

Money back All or part after the notice period, or, often, immediately with loss of interest on amount withdrawn.

Interest Variable. More interest paid for large amounts eg over £10,000, £25,000, £50,000.

Interest paid Yearly (half-yearly Hanley). By cheque, direct to a bank account or left to accumulate. Some also pay monthly: see *Building Society Monthly Income Account*.

Tax Basic rate tax is deducted from the interest. Non-taxpayers can reclaim the tax from the Inland Revenue (or have interest paid with no deduction). 20% taxpayers can reclaim tax. Higher rate taxpayers have to pay extra.

Fees to pay None.

Passbook Or receipt. Statements usually yearly.

Children Suitable for money earmarked for school fees as you know exactly when you need it and therefore when to give notice.

Risk 90% compensation scheme on the first £20,000 for each investor.

How to invest See surveys in the press and check adverts for latest offers. Subscribe to *Building Society Choice* or *Money£acts* (both monthly).

Where from Greenwich (Capital Shares), Harpenden (Hertfordshire), Manchester (Bonus 30), Nottingham (Autumn Bonus).

Even 30 days can seem a long time if you need money in a hurry, so always keep some immediately available.

BUILDING SOCIETY

60 Day Notice Account

An account usually with a minimum investment which can be added to. Withdrawals can be made by giving 60 days notice. There is usually an option to withdraw immediately when you lose the equivalent amount of interest. Make sure you get the best interest for the amount you invest.

Who can invest Anyone

How worthwhile Good value if you don't mind waiting to get (some of) your money back. Compare with *Building Society 90 Day Notice Account* and *Building Society Term Share*. Non-taxpayers not eligible for interest to be paid with no tax deducted, consider instead *Offshore Bank Notice Account*.

Minimum Usually £500 or £5,000.

Maximum £100,000 to £500,000

Suitable Lump sums. Regular savings.

Money back All or part after the notice period, or usually immediately with loss of interest on amount withdrawn.

Interest Variable. More interest paid for large amounts eg over £5,000, £10,000 £25,000, £50,000.

Interest paid Usually yearly. By cheque, direct to a bank account or left to accumulate. Some also pay monthly: see *Building Society Monthly Income Account*

Tax Basic rate tax is deducted from the interest. Non-taxpayers can reclaim the tax from the Inland Revenue (or have interest paid with no deduction). 20% taxpayers can reclaim tax. Higher rate taxpayers have to pay extra.

Fees to pay None.

Passbook Or receipt. Statements usually yearly.

Children Suitable for money earmarked for school fees as you know exactly when you need it and therefore when to give notice.

Risk 90% compensation scheme on the first £20,000 for each investor.

How to invest See surveys in the Press. Check adverts for latest best buys. Subscribe to *Building Society Choice* or *Money£acts* (both monthly). Phone or call at the societies listed below.

Where from *Your minimum: £500:* Consider *Building Society Instant Access Account* or *Building Society Postal Account* instead. *Your min: £2,500+:* Northern Rock (Postal 60). *Your minimum £10,000+:* Northern Rock (Postal 60).

Always leave some of your money invested where you can get at it at once or within a few days without penalty. Only tie up money for as long as you are sure you will not need it.

BUILDING SOCIETY

90 Day Notice Account

(Also called Extra Interest, Special, 90 Day Extra)

An account usually with a minimum investment which can be added to. Withdrawals can be made by giving 3 months or 90 days notice. There is usually an option to withdraw immediately when you lose the equivalent amount of interest. Usually no loss of interest if £10,000 remains. Make sure you get the best interest for the amount you invest.

Who can invest Anyone.

How worthwhile Good value if you don't mind waiting to get your money back. Compare with *Building Society 30 Day Notice Account, 60 Day Notice Account* and *Building Society Term Share.* Non-taxpayers not eligible for interest to be paid with no tax deducted, consider instead *Offshore Bank Notice Account.*

Minimum Usually £500 or £1,000.

Maximum £30,000 to £1 million.

Suitable Lump sums. Regular savings.

Money back All or part after the notice period, or, often, immediately with loss of interest on amount withdrawn. Bristol & West does not allow early withdrawals. Usually no loss of interest if £10,000 remains in the account; £5,000 at Halifax, Darlington, Mansfield, Progressive.

Interest Variable. More interest paid for large amounts eg over £5,000, £10,000, £25,000, £50,000, £100,000.

Interest paid Usually yearly. Most also pay monthly, see *Building Society Monthly Income Account.*

Tax Basic rate tax is deducted from the interest. Non-taxpayers can reclaim the tax from the Inland Revenue (or have interest paid with no deduction). 20% taxpayers can reclaim tax. Higher rate taxpayers have to pay extra.

Fees to pay None.

Passbook Or receipt. Statements usually yearly.

Children Suitable for money earmarked for school fees as you know exactly when you need it and therefore when to give notice.

Risk 90% compensation scheme on the first £20,000 for each investor.

How to invest See surveys in the press. Check adverts for latest best buys. Subscribe to *Building Society Choice or Money£acts* (both published monthly). Phone or call at the societies listed below.

Where from *Your minimum £1,000:* Teachers (Minster 90). *Your minimum £10,000+:* Chesham (Shire Bond), Bristol & West (Asset 90). Also consider Halifax (Premium Extra) which gives a ½ % bonus if you don't withdraw for a year.

Always leave some of your money invested where you can get at it at once or within a few days without penalty. Only tie up money for as long as you are sure you will not need it.

BUILDING SOCIETY

Monthly Income Account

An account which pays out interest monthly. The rate of interest depends on which type of account the money is invested in. Many societies allow monthly income based on any type of account. But it is best to use the ones which pay the highest interest which are generally *Building Society 90 Day Notice Account, Building Society Term Share* or *Building Society Escalator Bond*. See relevant page for details of each type of account.

Who can invest Anyone.

How worthwhile Convenient if you want a monthly income. Choose the society which gives the highest return. Compare the rates for monthly income which are not always equivalent to the yearly rates.

Minimum Usually £5,000 but £1,000 or £2,500 also available. Often higher than the minimum for the particular type of account where interest is paid yearly or half-yearly.

Maximum None.

Suitable Lump sums.

Money back Same conditions as for yearly or half-yearly interest payments. With *Building Society Instant Access Account* or *Building Society Postal Account* usually 1 month's notice required to close account (ie give notice during January receive the money 1 March).

Interest Variable unless your monthly income is based on a *Building Society Term Share* or *Building Society Escalator Bond* with a fixed rate. Rate slightly less than for half-yearly or yearly interest. It should be worth the same because it is paid monthly but some societies pay less than an equivalent rate; see page 88 for table of equivalent rates.

Interest paid Monthly by cheque, direct to a bank account or into another account at the society. Interest cannot be accumulated. Check the society you choose pays the interest where you want. Interest until the end of the first month is sent out with the following month's interest.

Tax Basic rate tax is deducted from the interest. Non-taxpayers can reclaim the tax from the Inland Revenue (or have interest paid without deduction). 20% taxpayers can reclaim tax. Higher rate taxpayers have to pay extra .

Fees to pay None.

Passbook Or certificate issued. Some societies send statements half-yearly or yearly.

Children Unsuitable.

Risk 90% compensation scheme on the first £20,000 for each investor.

How to invest See surveys in the press. Subscribe to *Building Society Choice* or *Money£acts* which include a table of rates updated each month. Check adverts for latest offers.

Where from Many building societies.

If you need to spend your interest, a monthly income account is a convenient way to have it paid to you. Some banks offer monthly interest accounts too.

BUILDING SOCIETY

Permanent Interest Bearing Share

(Also known as PIBS)

Lump sum invested in special shares issued by about 11 large and medium sized building societies at a fixed interest rate. There is no fixed life for the shares, which may be bought and sold at any time at the market price through a stockbroker. If the building society gets into financial difficulties, it may miss interest payments. You can also lose money if the market price has fallen by the time you sell (it would do this if interest rates rose). You could also lose money if the building society got into trouble as no compensation scheme applies. They are more like a Stock than a Share or Building Society Account.

Who can invest Anyone.

How worthwhile Good value for non-taxpayers and basic rate taxpayers provided interest rates don't rise after you buy in which case they may become poor value. Compare with *Shares Preference, Stock Debenture and Loan* or *Stock Government Fixed Interest.* Higher rate taxpayers compare with *Stock Government Fixed Interest.*

Minimum £1,000 to £50,000 depending on the society.

Maximum None. But some shares may be in short supply and a £20,000 maximum in any one share would be sensible.

Suitable Lump sums.

Money back About 10 days. You get the market price at the time you sell plus or minus *accrued interest,* see Chapter 3.

Interest Fixed. The rate at which the society pays is called the *coupon.* But the return you get is determined by the price you pay, which sets the *yield.* When the market price is above 100, the *yield* is less than the *coupon.*

Interest paid Usually half-yearly by cheque or direct to a bank or building society account.

Tax Basic rate tax is deducted from the interest. Non-taxpayers can reclaim the tax from the Inland Revenue. 20% taxpayers can reclaim tax. Higher rate taxpayers pay extra.

Fees to pay Stockbrokers commission when you buy and sell: On first £20,000 ¾% to 1%; less on larger amounts, minimum £17-£25. Some may charge more eg 1½% on first £7,000. Same when you sell.

Passbook Share certificate issued.

Children Under age 18 shares should be held in an adult's name but can be designated with the child's name.

Risk There is no compensation scheme. The society can stop or miss interest payments. Possible capital loss if interest rates rise and the market price of your shares fall.

How to invest Ask a stockbroker which Building Society's Permanent Interest Bearing Shares offer the best *yield.* If you want to invest a large amount, spread your investment between different societies.

Where from Stockbrokers.

Although these shares pay good interest they could lose you money if interest rates rise.

BUILDING SOCIETY

✻ Postal Account

(Also known as Asset, First Class, Capital Trust, InvestDirect)

An account which pays a good interest rate and where you can withdraw immediately, generally without notice or penalty but only by post. Deposits generally also have to be made by post. You lose interest while your cheque is in the post, possibly for up to a week if you receive a cheque before the weekend and can't pay it into another account until Monday.

Who can invest Anyone.

How worthwhile Good value for readily available money. Better value if you make few transactions. Compare with *Building Society Cheque Account With Interest* (more convenient). Non-taxpayers and higher rate taxpayers compare with *Offshore Instant Access Account*. For small amounts also consider *Unit Trust Cash Trust*.

Minimum *£1,000:* Bradford & Bingley, Birmingham Midshires, Yorkshire. *£2,000:* Britannia. *£2,500:* Most others. *£10,000:* Bristol & West.

Maximum £100,000 to £3 million. Some are open for deposits from new customers for limited periods only.

Suitable Lump sums.

Money back A few days. You fill in a form and post it back to the Society which posts you a cheque by return. Minimum cheque sometimes £50 or £100. Nationwide offers a cash machine card.

Interest Variable. More interest usually paid for larger amounts eg when over £10,000, £25,000, £30,000, £50,000, £100,000.

Interest paid Usually yearly. Direct to a bank account, or left to accumulate. Some also pay monthly but at a lower nominal interest rate and require 30 days notice, see *Building Society Monthly Income Account.*

Tax Basic rate tax is deducted from the interest. Non-taxpayers can reclaim the tax from the Inland Revenue (or have it paid with no deduction). 20% taxpayers can reclaim tax. Higher rate taxpayers pay extra.

Fees to pay None.

Passbook Statement usually sent with each transaction or yearly. Birmingham Midshires has passbook.

Children Unsuitable.

Risk 90% compensation scheme on the first £20,000 for each investor.

How to invest Subscribe to *Building Society Choice* (monthly) or *Money£acts* (monthly) or phone one of the societies listed below at their special 'By Post' phone number.

Where from Birmingham Midshires (First Class), Bradford & Bingley (Direct Premium), Bristol & West (Asset) Britannia (Capital Trust), Nationwide (InvestDirect), Yorkshire (1st Class).

The rates on these accounts may be excellent when you invest but they don't always stay that way. Make sure your account continues to pay a top rate or switch to another account which does.

BUILDING SOCIETY

Regular Monthly Savings Account

A commitment to save a certain amount each month in return for higher interest. Some societies allow you to raise or lower monthly payment and to miss a number of payments each year. Partial withdrawals may be allowed.

Who can invest Anyone.

How worthwhile Good value for short term savings starting with small amounts. But if you want to save for 5 years, taxpayers consider instead a monthly payment to a *Building Society Tessa Account* or a *Bank Tessa Account*. Higher rate taxpayers consider *Tessas*.

Minimum £1 a month at Darlington; £5 a month at Mansfield; £10 a month at City & Metropolitan, Dudley; £15 a month at Scarborough.

Maximum Usually £100 to £500 a month.

Suitable Regular savings. Sometimes a society allows up to 3 months payments to be made in advance. Sometimes payments can be missed.

Money back If account is closed: immediately or within a few days (sometimes 1 month). Partial withdrawals vary according to the society from none to 2 to 4 a year to as many as you like.

Interest Variable.

Interest paid Yearly.

Tax Basic rate tax is deducted from the interest. Non-taxpayers can reclaim the tax from the Inland Revenue (or have interest paid with no deduction). 20% taxpayers can reclaim tax. Higher rate taxpayers have to pay extra.

Fees to pay None.

Passbook Sometimes. Statement sent usually once a year.

Children Unsuitable.

Risk 90% compensation scheme on the first £20,000 for each investor.

How to invest To open an account, call at or phone a building society branch. Regular payment can then be made by visiting the branch, by post, bank standing order, direct debit or by credit transfer. A list of rates is published monthly in *Money£acts*

Where from Smaller building societies.

BUILDING SOCIETY

Share and Deposit Accounts

Ordinary share accounts were the original building society accounts. Money is easily paid in and withdrawn. Deposit accounts are the same but pay less interest although theoretically they have more security.

Who can invest Anyone.

How worthwhile Poor value. Consider instead *Building Society Cash Card Account* which usually pays the same interest or higher and is more convenient. If you have more than £1,000, consider instead *Building Society Postal Account.*

Minimum Usually £1.

Maximum Usually none.

Suitable Lump sums. Regular savings.

Money back On demand: cash £250 to £1,000; cheques usually £20,000 or more. Many societies allow withdrawals from any branch. Remainder usually in a few days but many societies say 1 month's notice in rules.

Interest Variable. Most societies pay poor interest on what are now almost entirely defunct accounts. Some small societies pay more but may require a few days' withdrawal notice. There may be no interest on balances under £50 or £100.

Interest paid Usually half yearly or yearly. By cheque, direct to a bank account or left to accumulate.

Tax Basic rate tax is deducted from the interest. Non-taxpayers can reclaim the tax from the Inland Revenue (or have interest paid with no deduction). 20% taxpayers can reclaim tax. Higher rate taxpayers have to pay extra.

Fees to pay Some societies levy charges on balances under £100.

Passbook Yes. Some societies don't send a yearly statement when the balance is small eg less than £100. Halifax sends statements on request or if passbook not updated during year.

Children Consider instead *Building Society Children's Account.*

Risk 90% compensation scheme on the first £20,000 for each investor.

How to invest If you have one of these accounts, close it and move the money to one which pays better interest.

Where from Most societies no longer have 'ordinary shares'. The largest 25 in order of size are: Halifax, Nationwide, Woolwich, Alliance & Leicester, Leeds Permanent, C&G, Bradford & Bingley, Britannia, National & Provincial, Northern Rock, Bristol & West, Yorkshire, Birmingham Midshires, Portman, Coventry, Skipton, Leeds & Holbeck, Chelsea, Derbyshire, Norwich & Peterborough, Cheshire, West Bromwich Principality, Newcastle, Staffordshire.

Note C&G is in the process of being taken over by Lloyds Bank when C&G will become a bank if shareholders agree. Halifax and Leeds Permanent want to merge and then convert the merged society into a bank.

Building Society Share Accounts are just one of a large number of superseded Bank and Building Society accounts which pay extremely poor interest, often ½% a year or less. A few societies automatically transfer you to the new version. Many don't. So an investor in what was once a good value account, may now be in one which is very poor value indeed. Always regularly check the current interest rate.

BUILDING SOCIETY

Stock Market Guaranteed Bond

(Also known as Share Index+)

An account which accumulates interest in line with the growth in value of the FT-SE 100 Share Index for 3 or 5 years. You are guaranteed to get your money back over five years and the schemes usually guarantee a minimum interest rate eg 4.5% a year too. If you want your money back early you get less interest but still get all your capital back. The bonds are issued for a limited time and different issues from the same society will have different guarantees.

Who can invest Anyone.

How worthwhile Potentially good value if you want to tie your money up for 3 or 5 years. But if the stock market is in the doldrums by the time the bond matures, you get a poor return although no loss of capital; if you stop early you also get a poor return. Higher rate taxpayers consider instead *Unit Trust Index Tracker.* The return counts as taxable interest in the year you cash the bond (your tax rate may also be higher in 5 years time). This type of investment is also available from Life Insurance companies and Banks but usually with higher charges.

Minimum £1,000 to £5,000.

Maximum Varies.

Suitable Lump sums.

Money back After 3 or 5 years depending on the society. Or at 30 days notice, usually on 4 or fewer fixed dates during the year.

Interest Variable. Linked to the rise in the FT-SE 100 Share Index with a guaranteed minimum.

Interest paid After 3 or 5 years depending on the society. Or when you cash, if you cash early.

Tax Basic rate tax is deducted from the gain which counts as interest in the year when you cash. Non-taxpayers and 20% taxpayers can reclaim tax from the Inland Revenue. Higher rate taxpayers pay extra tax, currently 15%, at the rate for the year in which they cash on the *grossed-up value* of the gain. The scheme is inefficient taxwise, because you get no indexation allowance nor the capital gains tax free limit.

Fees to pay Usually none but avoid those with a 5% initial charge.

Passbook Statement sent.

Children Unsuitable.

Risk 90% compensation scheme on the first £20,000 for each investor.

How to invest See surveys and adverts in the press. Ask for details and compare the guarantees, charges and terms of different societies.

Where from Building societies.

One problem with these bonds is the possibility of stockmarket manipulation by traders on the day your bond matures resulting in a fall in your maturity value. This has nothing to do with the building society but could effect the value of your investments.

BUILDING SOCIETY

Term Share

(Also called Fixed Rate Bond)

Lump sum invested for a term of 6 months to 5 years. The interest rate is usually fixed. Usually no additions allowed. Withdrawals can sometimes be made, usually by losing interest on the amount withdrawn for the whole term or 3 or 4 months interest.

Who can invest Anyone.

How worthwhile Where interest is fixed for the full term, good value provided you get as good, or nearly as good interest, as with a *Building Society Notice Account* and you expect interest rates to fall or remain the same during the investment term; poor value if they rise above the level you are paid. Non-taxpayers compare with *Co-operative Society Term Account, National Savings Capital Bond, National Savings Pensioners Bond, Stock Government Fixed Interest.* Taxpayers compare with *Life Insurance Income Bond, Local Authority Fixed Term Loan.* Higher rate taxpayers compare with *National Savings Fixed Certificates.*

Minimum Usually £1,000, £2,000, £5,000, £10,000.

Maximum None or £10,000 to £200,000.

Suitable Lump sums.

Money back At end of term or earlier usually at 3 months notice *and* 3 months loss of interest. If you die, investment plus full interest up to date is paid out. Also compare with *Building Society Escalator Bond* if you expect interest rates to rise.

Interest Usually fixed for the term.

Interest paid Usually yearly. By cheque, direct to a bank account, into another account, or left to accumulate. Monthly: into bank or other account see *Building Society Monthly Income Account.*

Tax Basic rate tax is deducted from the interest. Non-taxpayers can reclaim the tax from the Inland Revenue (or have interest paid with no deduction). 20% taxpayers can reclaim tax. Higher rate taxpayers have to pay extra.

Fees to pay None.

Passbook Or certificate issued.

Children Unsuitable.

Risk 90% compensation scheme on the first £20,000 for each investor.

How to invest Look for advertised special offers in the press. A list is published in *Money£acts* and *Building Society Choice* each month.

Where from A number of building societies. Best buys change frequently and are often issued as a limited offer.

Some building societies operate Term Shares where the interest rate is not fixed, but is guaranteed as a rate above the Share Rate, known as the 'differential'. Apart from this guaranteed differential, that type of account operates like a Building Society 90 Day Notice Account.

BUILDING SOCIETY

✳ Tessa Account

(Also called Tax Exempt Special Savinqs Account)

An account with a yearly maximum investment and no withdrawals for 5 years to receive interest tax free. You can either let the interest accumulate for 5 years or receive part of it each year. After 5 years you can continue to earn tax free interest on up to £9,000 in a Tessa.

Who can invest Anyone 18 or over. Joint accounts not allowed.

How worthwhile Good value for tax-payers, especially higher rate taxpayers. Compare with *Bank Tessa Account*. Non-taxpayers compare with *Building Society 30, 60 or 90 Day Notice Accounts, Offshore Bank Notice Account.*

Minimum Usually £1 to £500. £3,000 at Bristol & West, Dumfermlinɡ National Counties.

Maximum £3,000 in year 1. £1,800 in years 2-4. £600 in year 5 (or up to £1,800 if less than the maximum was invested in previous years). You can only have one Tessa. When your Tessa matures after 5 years, you can reinvest up to £9,000 from it within 6 months in a new Tessa as one lump sum for another 5 years.

Suitable Lump sums. Regular savings.

Money back After 5 years without penalty. Immediately or at up to 90 days notice depending on the society. If you withdraw more than an amount equal to what the accumulated interest less basic rate tax would be, the Tessa Account must be closed, transferred to a taxable account, and any interest earned so far becomes taxable. You can transfer your Tessa to another building society or bank and you won't lose the tax benefits. You may lose bonuses on early closure or a transfer.

Interest Usually variable.

Interest paid Usually added to account yearly or half yearly. Part of the interest can be paid by cheque or to a bank account. But the amount of interest equivalent to the basic rate of tax which would be deducted on a normal account must be accumulated for the full 5 years.

Tax Interest is tax free. It does not have to be included on a tax return.

Fees to pay Many societies have penalties if you want to move the account to another society or to a bank. With others you can avoid the charge by giving 7, 28 or 90 days notice.

Passbook Yes or statements sent.

Children Not eligible.

Risk 90% compensation scheme on the first £20,000 for each investor.

How to invest Call at, phone or write to one of the societies listed below. Look at surveys in the press or subscribe to *Money£acts* for up to date rates. It's best to invest as much as you can yearly and let your interest accumulate to benefit from the tax exemption. You have to put your National Insurance number or State Pension number on the application.

Where from Bristol & West, Lambeth, Market Harborough, Nationwide, Stroud & Swindon, Vernon, Yorkshire Building Society. Also consider Dumfermline, Market Harborough (maximum scheme), National Counties, Progressive, Tipton & Cosely, West Bromwich which pay a good return but have a transfer penalty.

Check from time to time that the interest rate remains competitive. If it isn't, transfer to a better account but beware of transfer penalties.

CO-OPERATIVE SOCIETY

Term Account

(Called Development Bond, Fixed Term Loan, Investment Bond, Unit Loan)

Lump sum invested at a fixed rate of interest for a term of 1 to 5 years. Interest is usually paid half-yearly or at the end of the term.

Who can invest Anyone age 18 or over.

How worthwhile Good value, especially for non-taxpayers, if you consider interest rates will fall or remain the same during the term; less good value if they rise. Compare with *Building Society Term Share, Local Authority Fixed Term Loan, Stock Government Fixed Interest, National Savings Capital Bond, National Savings Pensioners Bond.* Taxpayers also compare with *Life Insurance Growth or Income Bond, National Savings Fixed Certificates.*

Minimum Usually £100. £1,000 at CRS on some accounts. Sometimes a higher rate paid for £10,000+.

Maximum £50,000 for each account.

Suitable Lump sums.

Money back At end of term.

Interest Fixed. Rates vary at different times and between societies.

Interest paid Half-yearly by cheque or accumulated to end of term (you don't always have a choice).

Tax Not deducted. Taxpayers are liable to pay income tax on the interest which should be declared on a tax return .

Fees to pay None.

Passbook Certificate issued.

Children Investment must be made by a parent or grandparent on behalf of a child.

Risk 75% compensation scheme on the first £20,000 for each investor. Many small societies which have got into financial difficulties in the past have been taken over by CRS.

How to invest Phone the Investment Department of a co-operative society for the current rate and an application form.

Where from Subscribe to *Money£acts* which publishes a list of societies and current interest rates each month under the heading Retail Co-operatives. The largest society is CRS.

A few societies offer Esclalator Bonds which are Term Shares where the interest rate is fixed at a different and escalating rate each year eg Year 1: 6%. Year 2: 9%. Year 3: 12%. Compare these with Building Society Escalator Bonds.

FRIENDLY SOCIETY

Building Society Linked

A commitment to save a fixed amount, monthly or yearly for 10 years into a life insurance policy which after the deduction of a charge is linked to a tax free investment in a bank. After 10 years you stop saving and can continue to earn tax free interest.

Who can invest Anyone up to age 70.

How worthwhile Fair value for taxpayers, and higher rate taxpayers, who are sure they can save for 10 years. Unsuitable for non-taxpayers. Consider *Building Society Tessa Account* instead which has the same tax exemption and interest but lower charges.

Minimum £9 a month; £100 a year

Maximum Being raised in 1995 to £25 a month, £270 a year for each eligible person. A married couple can take £50 a month or £540 a year between them. Limits apply to premiums on all such policies with all Friendly Societies. *Beware of policies with higher premiums; you will not get full tax exemption.*

Suitable Regular savings. You can set up a transfer scheme: a lump sum is invested in a special account and each year the premium is automatically transferred to the friendly society policy. The interest on the decreasing balance in the account is not tax free but over 10 years allows the lump sum to fund the regular savings plan in full (eg 10 yearly premiums of £270).

Money back After 10 years. If you stop saving earlier, your return is reduced. Can be left longer to accumulate tax free.

Interest Variable Interest is accumulated within the policy.

Interest paid When you cash the policy after 10 years or more. If you die while the policy is in force, the greater of the value of your policy or the guaranteed life cover (usually £1,500 for an £18 a month payment) is paid.

Tax There is no tax on the proceeds nor on the interest accumulated of savings of up to £200 a year (to be raised to £270 a year) or or £18 a month (to be raised to £25 a month).

Fees to pay Deducted from your investment. 7½% initial on monthly premiums, 5% initial on yearly. Yearly ¾%. Check the exact charges before you invest.

Passbook None. Insurance policy issued. Yearly statement.

Children Each child can have its own policy.

Risk Friendly societies are covered by The Investors Compensation Scheme.

How to invest Phone or write for an application form.

Where from Homeowners Friendly Society. Bradford & Bingley (Prosperity Plan).

Some versions invest half your money in a unit trust. Avoid them as they sacrifice the flexibility of a Unit Trust Personal Equity Plan which has the same tax exemption. If you are offered a scheme with a premium over £270 a year or £25 a month, the excess does not benefit from the tax exemptions described above.

GOLD

Coins

A convenient means of investing in gold. You hope to make a capital gain by selling for more than you paid but you may end up with a loss by selling for less. The price of gold coins is closely linked to the price of gold but different coins may sell for a different *premium* over the price of gold. New rules on VAT from 1 January 1995 mean that you should be able to buy a second-hand gold coin or bar without paying VAT, with the dealer paying VAT on the dealer's overall sales margin. Previously a similar system applied to coins which were more than 100 years old, includiing sovereigns (which contain .2354 of a Troy ounce of pure gold). Other gold coins are the Britannia, Krugerrand, Maple Leaf, Double Eagle, Nugget. You normally have to pay 17½% VAT on the whole cost of a new coin or new bar. Half sovereigns and certain dates of sovereigns sell for a higher *premium* because of rarity.

Who can invest Anyone.

How worthwhile Gold is generally not a good investment when inflation is low as it is at present. Make sure you don't pay VAT on the whole price as the *dealer margin* scheme for second-hand coins is optional. Another way to invest in gold is to buy *Shares* of gold mining companies or a *Unit Trust* specialising in these companies.

Minimum The price of 1 coin. With gold at £239 a Troy ounce, a second-hand sovereign might cost £61 including VAT on the dealer's margin. Similar coins not sold under the scheme would cost £61 plus VAT which is £71.68. To sell you would get £55 each.

Maximum None.

Suitable Lump sums. Regular savings.

Money back At once at the market price.

Interest None.

Tax Gains you make on the sale of coins are liable to capital gains tax, see Chapter 5. If you deal frequently in coins you may have to pay income tax instead.

Fees to pay None: commission is usually included in the buying and selling price. If coins are delivered to you, postage and insurance. VAT at 17½% on the purchase price if you buy what is deemed to be a 'new' coin from a VAT registered supplier (most dealers are registered). You can buy second-hand coins or second-hand bars without VAT providing the dealer uses the scheme.

Passbook None. You get the coins.

Children Suitable as gifts especially from parents. Children's capital gains are not aggregated with their parents.

Risk High. The value of gold can go down as well as up. Keep the coins in a safe place like a deed box in a bank, and/or have them insured.

How to invest Check the current price in a daily newspaper. Check with a few dealers how much their coins will cost to buy. When you sell, do the same. When you ask for the price, don't say whether you are buying or selling. Check whether the price quoted includes any VAT and that you are not paying VAT on the whole price, only the dealer's margin at most.

Where from Spink & Son. A list of other coin dealers can be obtained free from Royal Mint Coin Club.

INVESTMENT TRUST

❀ Personal Equity Plan

(Also called Investment Trust PEP)

A means of investing up to £6,000 a year taxfree in investment trusts with at least 50% of their assets in UK or EU shares. Up to £1,500 can be in *non-qualifying* trusts with 50% of assets in shares but not necessarily UK or EU. It's easiest to invest monthly. You usually have a choice of trust and should choose one with a higher income *yield* to benefit from the tax exemption.

Who can invest Anyone 18 or over. Joint plans are not allowed but husband and wife can have one each. In any one tax year you can only invest in a Personal Equity Plan from one manager.

How worthwhile Good value for taxpayers, especially higher rate tax-payers. Compare with *Unit Trust Personal Equity Plan*. Higher rate tax-payers, see also *Shares Self Select Personal Equity Plan*. Unsuitable for non-taxpayers.

Minimum £30 *monthly:* Dunedin. *£50 monthly:* Alliance. *£100 monthly:* Fleming, Ivory & Sime, Moorgate.

Maximum £6,000 a year, £500 a month plus manager's charges. You have a choice of using your £6,000 limit instead on a fixed interest investment, see *Stock Personal Equity Plan*.

Suitable Regular savings. Lump sums sometimes have higher charges.

Money back 10 days after you sell; from June 1995 5 days. Managers don't usually deal every day. You get the market price when you sell. If you die the plan ends and your money is returned.

Interest Variable. Called *dividend*. The before tax interest is called the *yield* and trusts which show the highest yield are most attractive as they make the most use of the tax exemption.

Interest paid Dividends can be accumulated by being invested in more shares; or they can be paid by cheque to you or to a bank account half-yearly, quarterly or yearly.

Tax Income and capital gains are tax free and need not be entered on a tax return. Tax deducted from the dividend is reclaimed by the manager on your behalf and credited to your account.

Fees to pay When you buy stockbrokers commission from nil to 1.65%, stamp duty ½%. Initial set-up charge nil to 3% (nil to 1½% for companies listed here) or fixed charge £5 to £50; £30 Dunedin, £45 Murray Johnstone. Yearly management charge nil-1½%; nil Alliance, Ivory & Sime; ½% Dunedin; 1.25% (max. £45) Murray Johnstone. When you sell stockbrokers commission only.

Passbook None. Statements sent, monthly, half-yearly or yearly.

Children Not allowed

Risk High but not as risky as buying individual shares. The value of the share can go down as well as up.

How to invest Choose a trust or manager which operates a scheme. Choose a high yielding ordinary trust with a *discount* and *gearing*. Monthly investment is normally by direct debit or standing order from a bank account. Get a list of personal equity plans and trusts from the *Association of Investment Trust Companies* or contact the companies below.

Where from Alliance Trust Savings, Dunedin, Ivory & Sime, Moorgate, Murray Johnstone

An Investment Trust Personal Equity Plan is an excellent investment for a higher rate taxpayer.

INVESTMENT TRUST

❋ Savings Plan

A commitment to save a minimum amount regularly, usually monthly which is invested in shares in an investment trust (a company investing mainly in ordinary shares managed by professionals). *Investment Trust Shares* **broadly reflect the value of the ordinary shares held by the trust but can be less or more. You can top up with extra lump sums, raise or lower the monthly amount, or stop saving at any time. If you stop, you either sell the shares at the market price or continue holding them.**

Who can invest Anyone.

How worthwhile Flexible and potentially good value for taxpayers who want to invest regularly in a fund of ordinary shares. If you have less than £500 a month (£6,000 a year) to invest consider instead *Investment Trust Personal Equity Plan.* Also compare with *Unit Trust Savings Plan.*

Minimum £20 to £500 a month (usually £25 or £50) or £200 to £2,500 lump sum. You can buy more when you feel like it.

Suitable Regular savings.

Maximum None.

Money back 10 days after you sell; from June 1995 5 days. Managers, unlike stockbrokers, don't usually deal every day. You get the market price when you sell. Some allow partial withdrawals.

Interest Variable. Called *dividend.*

Interest paid The dividends can be paid to you by cheque, direct to a bank account or used to buy more investment trust shares.

Tax 20% tax is deducted from the dividend (called a *tax credit*). Non-

taxpayers can reclaim the tax credit from the Inland Revenue. Higher rate taxpayers have to pay extra; basic taxpayers don't. Gains on shares may be liable to capital gains tax (see Chapter 5) though the managers pay no capital gains tax when they make gains on ordinary shares held within the trust.

Fees to pay When you buy and sell: stockbrokers' commission usually nil to ¼%. Fees vary between managers. A few have high charges, like 4%, where co-mmission is paid; you may be able to avoid them by dealing direct. Stamp duty ½% when you buy only.

Passbook None. Statements of shares and dividends sent half-yearly or monthly.

Children Under 18 shares must be held in an adult's name and can be *designated* with a child's name or initials.

Risk By buying regularly you even out fluctuations in the market price eg. you buy when prices are high as well as low. You still need to choose the right time to sell. Otherwise the same as *Investment Trust Shares.*

How to invest Choose a trust which operates a scheme. Phone the managers and ask for their literature and an application form.

Where from A list of companies and 44 savings plans is available from the *Association of Investment Trust Companies* in its Monthly Information Service booklet.

An Investment Trust Savings Plan is a good way of regularly investing in shares. It's more flexible than an Investment Trust Personal Equity Plan. It usually has lower charges than a Unit Trust Savings Plan and income can be paid to you or accumulated.

INVESTMENT TRUST

Shares

Lump sum invested in the shares of a company which employs professional managers to invest its assets, mainly in *ordinary shares*. The price of investment trusts moves broadly with the value of its portfolio of shares. Sometimes the portfolio is worth more than the market value of the trust and the trust shares are said to be at a *discount*; the reverse is known as a *premium*. You usually receive an income and hope to make a capital gain by selling for more than you paid but you may end up with a loss by selling for less. There are around 260 investment trusts. Most specialise by type (eg Smaller Companies, Venture and Development Capital) or area (eg. Far East, Europe, Emerging Markets or a mixture). Most trusts are *geared* which means they go up and down more sharply than a unit trust with the same portfolio of shares.

Who can invest Anyone.

How worthwhile Good value as a long term investment for taxpayers if you buy and sell at the right time; poor value if you don't. See also *Investment Trust Personal Equity Plan*. Unsuitable for non-taxpayers.

Minimum £200 to £500 if you invest direct with managers; £1,000 with a stockbroker because min. commission.

Maximum None.

Suitable Lump sums. See *Investment Trust Savings Plan* for regular savings.

Money back 10 days after you sell; from June 1995 5 days. Stockbrokers deal every day; managers usually don't. You get the market price when you sell.

Interest Variable. Called *dividend*. The before tax interest is called the *yield*. Some aim for a high or rising income.

Interest paid Usually half-yearly. By cheque to you or direct to a bank account. About 5 weeks before the dividend is paid, the shares go *ex-dividend*; this means the seller gets the next dividend, not the buyer.

Tax 20% tax is deducted from the dividend (called a *tax credit*). Non-taxpayers can reclaim the tax credit from the Inland Revenue. Higher rate taxpayers have to pay extra; basic taxpayers don't. Gains on trust shares are liable to capital gains tax (but see Chapter 5) although no tax on gains on ordinary shares held by the trust.

Fees to pay When you buy and sell: stockbrokers' commission: On first £7,000 1% to 1.9%; then usually 0.5%; min. £15 to £30. Managers usually buy and sell free or for 0.15% to 1%; min. £10 to £20. Stamp duty ½% when you buy only.

Passbook Share certificate issued

Children Under age 18 shares must be held in an adult's name but can be *designated* with a child's initials or name.

Risk High. The value of shares goes down as well as up but little risk of the trust going bust as there may be with the shares of an individual company.

How to invest Get a copy of the latest Monthly Information Service booklet from the *Association of Investment Trust Companies*. It lists managers, savings schemes, PEPS, trust portfolios, speciality, discounts and gearing. Choose from the larger trusts of the type you want with the highest discount and gearing. Or ask a specialist stockbroker for advice.

Where from The trust managers or a stockbroker (list from *Association of Investment Trust Companies*).

INVESTMENT TRUST

Split Level Trust

(Also called Split Capital Trust, Dual Purpose Trust)

Lump sum invested in a company which employs professionals to invest its assets in shares. Unlike ordinary *Investment Trust Shares* the shares of a *Split Level Investment Trust* are (usually) split into two main types: *income shares* and *capital shares*. Income shares receive all the income from the trust all of which is paid out as dividends; capital shares receive no income. Split level trusts have a fixed life, like a Stock, at the end of which after 1 to 9 yrs, depending on the trust, the income shares are repaid at the price at which the shares were first issued and capital shareholders get the value of the investments in the company.

Who can invest Anyone.

How worthwhile *Income shares:* Potentially good value for non-taxpayers, 20% taxpayers and basic rate taxpayers but the high and rising income ceases when the trust comes to an end and you may incur a loss of around half your original investment if you don't sell some time before the end of the term. Higher rate taxpayers might consider investing through *Investment Trust Personal Equity Plan* (but there will be no tax relief for a loss). *Capital shares:* Potentially good value for higher rate taxpayers but the shares fluctuate a great deal in value.

Minimum Around £1,000 because of minimum commission.

Maximum None but some may be in short supply.

Suitable Lump sums. You can save regularly with some by using *Investment Trust Savings Plan.*

Money back At the end of the term. 10 days after you sell, if you sell early; from June 1995 5 days. Stockbrokers deal every day; managers usually don't. You get the market price when you sell early or a value calculated by the managers if you hold to redemption.

Interest *Income shares:* Variable. Called *dividend* The before tax interest is called the *yield.* You can expect this to rise year by year. *Capital* shares: None

Interest paid Usually half-yearly. By cheque to you or direct to a bank account. About 5 weeks before the dividend is paid, the shares go *ex-dividend;* this means the seller gets the next dividend not the buyer.

Tax 20% rate tax is deducted from the dividend (called *tax credit*). Non-taxpayers can reclaim the tax credit from the Inland Revenue. Higher rate taxpayers pay extra, basic taxpayers don't. Gains on trust shares are liable to capital gains tax (but see Chapter 5) although no tax on gains on ordinary shares held by the trust.

Fees to pay When you buy or sell: Stockbrokers' commission: 1% to 1.9% on first £7,000, then usually ½%; minimum £15 to £30. If you buy from the managers, commission can be nil to ¼%. Stamp duty ½% when you buy only.

Passbook Share certificate issued.

Children Unsuitable.

Risk Significantly higher than *Investment Trust Shares.*

How to invest Get advice from a specialist stockbroker.

Where from The *Association of Investment Trust Companies* has a booklet on Split Level Trusts. The *Association of Private Client Investment Managers* has a booklet with the names of specialist stockbrokers.

INVESTMENT TRUST

Warrants

You invest in a security which gives you the right to buy a certain number of investement trust shares at a fixed price on a fixed date or series of dates or during a specified period in the future before the warrant *expires* at the end of a fixed period determined when it is first issued. You can buy and sell warrants like *Shares* on the Stock Exchange. You rarely *exercise* the warrant (ie. buy the shares); to make money you aim to sell the warrant at a higher price than you bought it for. If you hold a warrant beyond its expiry, and it is not *excercised,* it is has no value. The value of warrants goes up and down much more quickly than the investment trust shares in which you have the right to buy.

Who can invest Anyone 18 or over.

How worthwhile Potentially good value if you like to speculate. Compare with the Capital Shares of *Investment Trust Split Level Trust.* You can lose most of your investment quickly if you predict investment trust share prices wrongly. If you are right you can make a lot of money in a short time. Dealing in warrants needs regular attention.

Minimum Around £1,000 to avoid minimum commission.

Maximum None.

Suitable Lump sums.

Money back When you sell the warrant before its expiry. You get the current market price which may be more or less than you paid.

Interest None usually.

Interest paid Not applicable.

Tax Any profits you make count as capital gains and are taxable - see Chapter 5. Any losses can be set against other capital gains.

Fees to pay Stockbrokers' commission 1% to 1.9% of what you pay; minimum £20 to £30; same when you sell.

Passbook Warrant certificate issued.

Children Unsuitable.

Risk High .

How to invest For a free leaflet on investment trust warrants, phone or write to *Association of Investment Trust Companies.* Its Monthly Information Service gives details of all warrants together with prices, premiums/discounts and gearing.

Where from A stockbroker who knows about warrants.

You can also buy warrants in some Shares Ordinary Quoted. These may be even more risky as the performance of an individual company can fluctuate more than that of an Investment Trust.

INVESTMENT TRUST

Zero Dividend Preference Shares

(Also called Zero Coupon Shares)

A certain type of share issued by an *Investment Trust Split Level Trust* which receive no income but are repaid at a fixed price at a fixed date in 1 to 13 yrs time (depending on the trust). Your return is equivalent to a fixed accumulating rate of interest. The return depends on the price you pay (plus commission etc) in relation to the price when the shares are repaid at the redemption date (or when you sell, if you sell before then); it also depends on how much tax you have to pay on your gain. They are more like a stock than a share.

Who can invest Anyone.

How worthwhile Potentially good value for basic rate and higher rate tax payers if the gain continues to be taxed as a capital gain rather than income, see *Tax.* Taxpayers compare with *National Savings Fixed Issue Certificates, Life Insurance Growth Bond.* Non-taxpayers and 20% taxpayers compare with *National Savings Capital Bond.*

Minimum Around £1,000 because of minimum commission.

Maximum None but some may be in short supply.

Suitable Lump sums.

Money back At the end of the term. 10 days after you sell, if you sell early; from June 1995 5 days. Stockbrokers deal every day; managers usually don't. You get the market price if you sell early or a fixed redemption value (although if the trust performs very badly, this may not be paid in full).

Interest None.

Interest paid When the shares are repaid.

Tax Gains on trust shares are liable to capital gains tax (but see Chapter 5). It is possible that gains on the shares will be liable to income tax instead of capital gains tax by the time many shares are repaid. Either way no tax is payable until after the shares are repaid (or you sell).

Fees to pay Stamp duty ½% when you buy. When you buy or sell: Stockbrokers' commission: 1% to 1.9% on first £7,000; then usually ½%. If you buy through the managers, commission nil to 0.2%.

Passbook Share certificate issued

Children Shares must be registered in an adult's name but can be *designated* with a child's name or initials. Possibly a suitable investment for an Accumulation Trust.

Risk Moderate. The investment trust might not have enough money to repay the shares in full - or if you have to sell early, and interest rates have risen since you bought, the price may have fallen.

How to invest Get advice and details of the available trusts and their *redemption yields* from a specialist stockbroker.

Where from The *Association of Investment Trust Companies* has a booklet on Split Level Trusts. The *Association of Private Client Investmen Managers* has a booklet with the names of specialist stockbrokers.

Future tax law changes may make this investment less attractive. There are also Stepped Preference Shares which offer dividends which rise at a predetermined rate plus a fixed redemption value.

LIFE INSURANCE

Annuity

Lump sum invested with a life insurance company which usually cannot be returned. You receive a fixed income until you die. Better returns the older you are. Options, but with lower income, include a joint life annuity where payments continue until the second death or one guaranteed to pay for at least 5-10 years even if you die.

Who can invest Anyone but only suitable for over age 65 men, 70 women.

How worthwhile Designed to deal with the problem of outliving your capital. Because of inflation they are only worth considering if you are over age 70 men, 75 women. Using an annuity and a life insurance policy can reduce inheritance tax. Compare with *Property Ground Rents* and the Income Shares *of Investment Trust Split Level Trust.*

Minimum Around £10,000, otherwise charges reduce the return.

Maximum None.

Suitable Lump sums.

Money back Usually not possible. Surrender value, if available, is likely to be much less than the investment.

Interest Fixed or increasing at a fixed rate. Rates vary according to type of annuity. For Instance a fixed annuity for a man of 70 might pay £1,300 a year, whereas one rising by 4% a year might initially pay £1,000 a year. Current rates surveyed in magazines eg Money Management.

Interest paid Yearly, half-yearly, quarterly or monthly. By cheque to you or direct to bank account usually in arrears. Less income is paid for more frequent payment.

Tax The annuity payment is regarded as part taxable, part return of capital. The capital part is not taxable but this amount depends on your age when you buy it. For each £10,000 of purchase price, the capital part of the payment is:
At age 65: £570 (men), £485 (women).
At age 70: £705 (men), £601 (women).
At age 75: £884 (men), £763 (women).
At age 80: £1,114 (men), £985 (women).
These limits apply to new annuities; pre-1992 ones have a larger capital part. Basic rate tax is deducted from the taxable portion; non-taxpayers can have it paid without deduction of tax or can reclaim it; 20% taxpayers can reclaim part. Higher rate taxpayers have to pay extra tax on the taxable portion only.

Fees to pay None.

Passbook None. Annuity contract.

Children Unsuitable.

Risk UK authorised life companies are covered by a 90% compensation scheme less 'excessive' benefits. For complete safety use an old established company.

How to invest Get an independent financial adviser to obtain quotations for you; also get your own from Equitable Life and London Life which do not pay commission to advisers. If you want to avoid inheritance tax, ask a chartered accountant, solicitor or other adviser for advice.

Where from Most life companies.

Equitable Life offers unit-linked and 'with-profits' annuities where the income depends on the performance of the underlying investments, the income may go up or down. Annuities linked to the Retail Prices Index are also available. The initial income is often lower than with a fixed annuity.

LIFE INSURANCE

❀ Growth or Income Bond

Lump sum invested with a life insurance company at a fixed interest rate for terms of 1-10 years. Versions which pay out interest are called *Income Bonds*; those which accumulate income are called *Growth Bonds*.

Who can invest Anyone. Usually minimum age 18, 17 or 12; maximum none or 79-85.

How worthwhile Good value for basic rate taxpayers provided you don't expect interest rates to rise during the term of the bond. Some bonds pay better rates the older you are. Terms over 5 years not recommended. Higher rate taxpayers compare Growth Bonds with *National Savings Fixed Issue Certificates,* and *Income Bonds* with *Stock Government Fixed-Interest* Non-taxpayers and 20% taxpayers consider instead of Growth Bonds *Co-operative Society Term Account* or *National Savings Capital Bond,* and instead of Income Bonds, *Stock Government Fixed-Interest* or *Stock Debenture and Loan.*

Minimum £1,000 to £10,000.

Maximum None.

Suitable Lump sums.

Money back At end of term or when you die. Some bonds can be cashed early but you lose some of your money.

Interest Fixed. Many companies pay higher rates for larger amounts eg over £5,000, £10,000, £20,000, £50,000.

Interest paid With Income Bonds usually yearly (a few pay half-yearly; or monthly with £5,000 minimum investment); by cheque to you or direct to a bank account.

With Growth Bonds the interest is accumulated.

Tax The interest whether paid out or accumulated usually comes tax paid for basic rate taxpayers. Non-taxpayers and 20% taxpayers cannot reclaim the tax. Higher rate taxpayers have to pay extra, either each year, or when the bond matures. The income or proceeds of a Bond may reduce someone's entitlement to Age Allowance.

Fees to pay None.

Passbook Insurance policy issued.

Children Unsuitable.

Risk None provided you don't cash the bond early. UK authorised life companies are covered by a 90% compensation scheme less 'excessive' benefits. Don't invest in an Income or Growth Bond offered by an overseas life company which is not authorised in the UK as your protection is less and your income or growth could be liable to UK basic as well as higher rate tax.

How to invest Subscribe to *Money£acts* which publishes a list of bonds and rates monthly or look in the lists published in *Money Management* magazine or the Saturday and Sunday financial pages of the newspapers.

Where from See the National press for advertisements of limited offers; from an independent financial adviser or direct from a life company.

A few Income Bonds have a variable income. You would probably be better off with a Building Society account or an Offshore Bank account.

LIFE INSURANCE

Home Income Plan

A means by which people over age 70 can use part of the value of the home they own to borrow money which is used to buy an annuity to give them an income for life. You can get a cash lump sum too. The plans listed here have a fixed interest mortgage.

Who can use it Anyone over age 70 (69 at Carlyle Life) with an unmortgaged owner-occupied house or purpose-built flat (converted flats not always acceptable). If married, your joint ages must be at least 150 (145 at Carlyle Life).

How worthwhile Fair to good value for people not eligible for the State means tested Income Support, especially single people, widows or widowers and non-taxpayers. Better the older you are.

Minimum The value of your home must be at least £21,500 or £43,000 for you to borrow £15,000 or £30,000.

Maximum The maximum loan is usually £30,000; 70% to 75% of the value of your property. At Carlyle for older ages loans can be greater than £30,000 up to 60%.

Money back None unless you take a plan offering capital protection. When you die the loan plus any unpaid interest is taken from the proceeds of the sale of your home so your heirs get less. If you die within 5 years, your estate can get some of the money back but the income is lower if you take a 'capital protected' option.

Interest Fixed.

Interest paid Usually monthly. By cheque to you or direct to a bank or building society account.

Tax You get tax relief at 25% (if you are over 65) on the interest you pay on up to £30,000 of the money you have

borrowed. The tax relief will usually be given at source by MIRAS which means you pay a lower interest rate and don't have to reclaim the tax relief. The annuity payment is regarded as part income, part return of capital. The capital portion is not taxable but this amount depends on your age when you start the scheme. Basic rate tax is usually deducted from the income portion unless you are a non-taxpayer. If you are a 20% taxpayer, you can reclaim part of the tax deducted.

Fees to pay Valuation costs. The companies pay their own legal fees. Carlyle pays £150 plus VAT plus disbursements charged by your solicitors.

Passbook None. The lender will take a mortgage on your home and hold the deeds. You get an annuity contract from a life insurance company.

Children Not eligible.

Risk UK life companies are covered by a 90% compensation scheme less 'excessive' benefits.

How to use it Ask a specialist independent financial adviser like Hinton & Wild to get quotes from the companies or do it yourself.

Where from Allchurches Life, Carlyle Life (Mortgage Scheme).

Traditional Home Income Plans are of increasingly limited use because of the maximum loan of £30,000 which is eligible for tax relief. Another method most suited to the over 80s and valid for amounts over £30,000 is to sell your home (or part of it) to a reversion company which in exchange gives you an income for life as well as allowing you to remain in your home. Details also from Hinton & Wild.

LIFE INSURANCE

Equity Bond

Lump sum invested in a single premium life insurance policy linked to units in a fund of mainly UK shares. Some Equity Bonds are linked to a single unit trust or a fund of several trusts. The units reflect the value of the assets held in the fund plus the accumulated income. You can *switch* the investment link between equity, international, fixed-interest, money, property, mixed or any other type of fund offered by the same company without cashing the policy.

Who can invest Anyone.

How worthwhile Consider instead *Investment Trust Personal Equity Plan* or *Unit Trust Personal Equuity Plan* as they have the same type of investment but are tax free. Otherwise consider instead *Investment Trust Shares* or *Unit Trust Invested in UK Shares,* unless you regularly use up your annual capital gains tax exemption. Unsuitable for non-taxpayers or 20% taxpayers.

Minimum £500 to £5,000 usually £1,000.

Maximum None.

Suitable Lump sums.

Money back At any time or when you die. You get the current value of the units.

Interest Income is accumulated.

Interest paid When you cash the policy or die. You can choose to withdraw a certain amount each half-year; sometimes yearly, quarterly or monthly.

Tax The life company pays tax on income and capltal gains at a rate equal to the basic rate of tax which usually reflect in the price of the units. With bonds linked to individual unit trusts capital gains tax may be deducted from the proceeds of your policy before you get it, whereas had you invested directly it would usually fall within your individual annual exemption. The proceeds and all withdrawals come tax paid for basic rate taxpayers. Non-taxpayers and 20% taxpayers cannot reclaim the tax. Higher rate taxpayers have to pay extra tax, currently 15%, when they cash; and on withdrawals of over 5% a year of original investment or if they go on for more than 20 years.

Fees to pay Charges deducted from your investment are 5% to 10% (usually 5%) initially and usually ¾% to 1% yearly although trusts which the fund invests in may charge 1% to 1½% a year instead or in addition.

Passbook None. Insurance policy issued.

Children Convenient for a trust set up for children to avoid inheritance tax and probate.

Risk High. The value of the units goes down as well as up. UK life companies are covered by a 90% compensation scheme based on the current value of your units if the company fails. Do not invest in an overseas life company which is not authorised in the UK as your protection is less and your income or gain could be liable to UK basic as well as higher rate tax.

How to invest Fill in a proposal form from a life company.

Where from Many life companies.

It is better to invest in shares through a personal equity plan than through a life insurance policy.

LIFE INSURANCE

Fixed-Interest, Gilt or Money Bond

Lump sum invested in a single premium life insurance policy linked to a fund of fixed-interest securities (Fixed-Interest or Gilt) or to a fund invested in bank or other interest-bearing deposits (Money or Cash). The units reflect the value of the assets held in the fund plus the accumulated income. You can *switch* **the investment link between equity, international, fixed interest, money, property, mixed or any other type of fund offered by the same company without cashing the policy.**

Who can invest Anyone.

How worthwhile Consider instead of Fixed-Interest or Gilt Bond, *Stock Unit Trust Invested in Gilts* and *Stock Government Fixed-Interest.* Consider instead of Money or Cash Bond, *Unit Trust Cash Trust* and direct investment in building societies, banks and offshore banks. Unsuitable for non-taxpayers or 20% taxpayers.

Minimum £500 to £5,000 usually £1,000.

Maximum None.

Suitable Lump sums.

Money back At any time or when you die. You get the current value of the units.

Interest Income is accumulated.

Interest paid When you cash or die. You can choose to withdraw a certain amount each half-year; sometimes yearly, quarterly or monthly.

Tax The life company pays tax on the accumulated income at a rate equal to the basic rate of tax which usually reflects in the price of the units. The proceeds and all withdrawals are tax paid to basic rate taxpayers. Non-taxpayers and 20% taxpayers cannot reclaim the tax. Higher rate taxpayers pay extra tax, currently 15%, when they cash and on withdrawals of over 5% a year of the original amount or if they go on for more than 20 years.

Fees to pay Charges deducted from your investment are 3% to 10% (usually 5%) initially (sometimes less for 'Money' bonds); usually ¾% to 1% yearly.

Passbook None. Insurance policy issued.

Children Unsuitable.

Risk *Fixed-interest or Gilt:* Moderate as the value of the units can go down as well as up. *Money and Convertible:* None. UK life companies are covered by a 90% compensation scheme based on the current value of your units if the company fails. Do not invest in an overseas life company which is not authorised in the UK as your protection is less and your income or gain could be liable to UK basic as well as higher rate tax.

How to invest Fill in a proposal form from a life company.

Where from Many life companies.

Some companies have funds linked to Government Index Linked Stock. You should consider investing directly instead.

LIFE INSURANCE

International Bond

Lump sum invested in a single premium life insurance policy linked to units in a fund of stocks and shares mainly invested overseas. A few, called *Currency Bond*, invest in foreign currency bank accounts or fixed-interest stocks. Some bonds are linked to a single unit trust investing overseas. The units reflect the value of the assets held in the fund plus the accumulated income. You can *switch* the investment link to equity, fixed-interest, money, property, mixed or any other type of fund offered by the same company without cashing the policy.

Who can invest Anyone.

How worthwhile If you do not regularly use your capital gains exemption limit, consider instead *Unit Trust Invested in Overseas Shares* which give you the same investment opportunity but do not automatically deduct tax. Unsuitable for non-taxpayers and 20% taxpayers.

Minimum £500 to £5,000 usually £1,000.

Maximum None.

Suitable Lump sums.

Money back At any time or when you die. You get the current value of the units.

Interest Income is accumulated.

Interest paid When you cash the policy or die. You can choose to withdraw a certain amount each half-year; sometimes yearly, quarterly or monthly.

Tax The life company pays tax on income and capital gains at a rate equal to the basic rate of tax which usually reflects in the price of the units. With bonds linked to individual unit trusts capital gains tax may be deducted from the proceeds of your policy before you get it, whereas had you invested directly it would usually fall within your individual annual exemption. The proceeds and all withdrawals come tax paid for basic rate taxpayers. Non-taxpayers and 20% taxpayers cannot reclaim the tax. Higher rate taxpayers have to pay extra tax, currently 15%, when they cash the policy; and on withdrawals of over 5% a year or if they go on for more than 20 years

Fees to pay Charges deducted from your investment are 5% to 10% (usually 5%) initially and usually ¾% to 1% yearly although unit trusts which the fund invests in may charge 1½% a year instead or in addition.

Passbook None. Insurance policy issued.

Children Unsuitable.

Risk High. The value of the units goes down as well as up. UK life companies are covered by a 90% compensation scheme based on the current value of your units if the company fails. Do not invest in an overseas life company which is not authorised in the UK as your protection is less and your income or gain could be liable to UK basic as well as higher rate tax.

How to invest Fill in a proposal form from a life company.

Where from Many life companies

Some companies have higher charges on premiums under £5,000, say.

LIFE INSURANCE

Mixed Bond

(Also called Managed Bond, 3-Way Bond, Multiple Bond, Balanced Bond)

Lump sum invested in a single premium life insurance policy linked to units in a fund of shares, property and fixed interest stocks and/or bank deposits managed by professionals who seek to raise your return by choosing the right kind of investment at the right time. The units reflect the value of the assets held in the fund plus any accumulated income. You can *switch* the investment link to a property, equity, international, fixed-interest, money or any other type of fund offered by the same company without cashing the policy. Beware of 'managed' bonds which are really 'equity' bonds and have no property or fixed interest investments.

Who can invest Anyone.

How worthwhile Potentially good value for basic rate taxpayers who choose a company which does well. An alternative might be to split your investment between *Investment Trust Personal Equity Plan* or *Unit Trust Personal Equity Plan* or *Investment Trusts* or *Unit Trusts* and *Life Insurance Property Bond* and *Stock Personal Equity Plan* or *Stock Government Fixed Interest.* Unsuitable for non-taxpayers and 20% taxpayers.

Minimum £500 to £5,000 usually £1,000.

Maximum None.

Suitable Lump sums.

Money back At any time or when you die. You usually get the current value of the units.

Interest Income, dividends and rents are accumulated.

Interest paid When you cash the policy or die. You can choose to withdraw a certain amount each half-year; sometimes yearly, quarterly or monthly.

Tax The life company pays tax on income and capital gains at a rate equal to the basic rate of tax which usually reflects in the price of the units. The proceeds and all withdrawals are tax paid for basic rate tax payers. Non-taxpayers and 20% taxpayers cannot reclaim the tax. Higher rate taxpayers pay extra tax, currently 15%, when they cash; and on withdrawals of over 5% a year or if they go on for more than 20 years.

Fees to pay Charges deducted from your investment are 5% to 10% (usually 5%) and usually ¾% to 1 % yearly.

Passbook None. Insurance policy issued.

Children Convenient for a trust set up for children to avoid inheritance tax and probate.

Risk Moderate to high. The value of units goes down as well as up. UK authorised Insurance companies are covered by a 90% compensation scheme based on the current value of your units. Do not invest in an overseas life company which is not authorised in the UK as your protection is less and your income or gain could be liable to UK basic and higher rate tax.

How to invest Fill in a proposal form from a life company.

Where from Many life companies.

Some companies have higher charges on premiums under £5,000. Others give discounts for large amounts.

LIFE INSURANCE

Property Bond

Lump sum investment in a single premium life insurance policy linked to units in a fund of properties (eg shops, offices, warehouses, factories and property development). 'Property' funds which invest in property company shares are really 'equity' funds. The properties are valued regularly by independent valuers and their valuation plus rent income reflect in the price of the units. You can *switch* the investment link to a mixed, fixed-interest, money, equity, international or any other type of fund offered by the same company without cashing the policy.

Who can invest Anyone.

How worthwhile Fair to good value for taxpayers as a long term investment (over 5 years). Compare with *Property Commercial Direct Investment*. Unsuitable for non-taxpayers and 20% taxpayers.

Minimum £500 to £5,000 usually £1,000.

Maximum None.

Suitable Lump sums.

Money back At any time or when you die. You get the current value of the units (sometimes a bit more if you die). Most companies can defer payment for up to 6 months if they cannot sell a property

Interest Rents and other income are accumulated.

Interest paid When you cash the policy or die. You can choose to withdraw a certain amount each half-year; yearly, quarterly or monthly.

Tax The insurance company pays tax on Income and capital gains at the basic tax rate which reflects in the unit price. The proceeds and all withdrawals are tax paid for basic rate taxpayers. Non-taxpayers and 20% taxpayers cannot reclaim tax. Higher rate taxpayers pay extra, currently 15%, when they cash and on withdrawals over 5% a year or if they go on for more than 20 years.

Fees to pay Charges deducted from your investment are initially 5% to 10% (5% for companies listed below). ¾% to 1% yearly. Some companies can raise the yearly charge. Maintenance, legal, valuation and rent collection costs are also deducted.

Passbook None. Insurance policy issued.

Children Convenient for a trust set up for children to avoid inheritance tax and probate.

Risk Moderate to high. The value of units can go down as well as up. UK authorised life companies are covered by 90% compensation if the company fails.

How to invest Get details from some or all of the companies listed below and compare them or ask an independent financial adviser. 'Past performance' is published each month in magazines like *Money Management*.

Where from Abbey Life, Allied Dunbar, AXA Equity & Law, Barclays Life, Legal & General, Save & Prosper, Scottish Widows, Standard Life.

LIFE INSURANCE

School Fees Educational Trust

(Also called School Fees Capital Plan, School Fees Trust Plan)

A means of paying school fees in advance. You pay a lump sum into a trust for a child which pays part or all of the fees when they are needed. You have a choice of a fixed return, one linked to a unit fund or *with-profits*. The fees can be pre-paid for one term or up to 15 years, the payments last for 2 to 10 years. After you have joined the scheme you may be able to change your mind about when and to whom you want the fees paid.

Who can invest Anyone, eg parents, grandparents, godparents.

How worthwhile Good value for higher rate taxpaying parents who give the money themselves. Convenient for earmarking gifts from grandparents, etc, especially where the money is not needed for fees for a few years. Compare with the return you might get for paying fees in advance direct to a school and getting a discount (but check if any penalty on change of school). Unsuitable for non-taxpayers and 20% taxpayers.

Minimum £500 to £3,000 initial; £250 to £1,000 top up. Monthly scheme, £50 a month at Equitable Life.

Maximum None.

Suitable Lump sums. Regular savings at Equitable Life, School Fees Insurance Agency.

Money back Option for the person who gives the money to get it back before fees start to be paid (there can be a penalty). If the child dies, 90% to 100% of the money is returned plus interest. Fees can usually be paid for a second child, if the first no longer requires them. If the money is not used up for school fees, it can be used to support a child at University.

Interest Usually fixed, it is accumulated and then paid out together with capital to pay for school fees. Equitable Life (Plans A and B) offers with profits or unit-linked investments. School Fees Insurance Agency has a unit linked plan (Versatile Education Plan).

Interest paid Each term to pay school fees. Cheques usually sent to the parents payable to the chosen school. Parents must pay the balance and for any extras.

Tax The proceeds and all fee payments are tax paid. Payments to or from the scheme (other than by parents) may be liable to inheritance tax if they exceed the various exemptions, see Chapter 5. If you cash the scheme, any profit will be liable to higher rate tax (and basic rate tax if the investment is with an offshore life company which does not pay tax).

Fees to pay Charges included in the rate you get 5% initial (less for large amounts eg £10,000+); ½% to 1% yearly. If you change your plans, there may be extra charges.

Passbook Copy deed and statement.

Children Unsuitable for a child to invest in. He or she is the beneficiary of the school fees.

Risk UK life companies are covered by a 90% compensation scheme.

How to invest Get details from the companies listed below and compare what they have to offer.

Where from Equitable Life (School Fee Trust Plan), Save & Prosper (School Fees Capital Plan), School Fees Insurance Agency (Capital Payment Plans).

For other ways of saving for school fees turn to Chapter 11.

LIFE INSURANCE

Stock Market Guaranteed Bond

(Also known as Capital Guarantee Bond, Guaranteed Growth Account)

Lump sum invested in a single premium life insurance policy which rises in line with the growth in value of the FT-SE 100 Share Index for 5 years. You are guaranteed to get your money back over 5 years and schemes may also guarantee a minimum growth rate eg 2.5% a year too. If you want your money back early you get less growth but you usually still get all your capital back. Some schemes offer more complicated guarantees which offer you the chance of 'locking in' an existing gain. The bonds are issued for a limited time and different issues from the same company have different guarantees

Who can invest Anyone.

How worthwhile Compare with *Building Society Stock Market Guaranteed Bond* which may offer better guarantees and lower charges. If the stock market is in the doldrums by the time the bond matures you get a poor return although no loss of capital; if you stop early you also get a poor return. Higher rate taxpayers consider instead *Unit Trust Index Tracker*. Unsuitable for non-taxpayers and 20% taxpayers.

Minimum £1,000 to £5,000.

Maximum Varies.

Suitable Lump sums.

Money back After 5 years. Or earlier but with some penalty.

Interest Variable. Growth linked to the rise in the FT-SE 100 Share Index sometimes with a guaranteed minimum.

Interest paid After 5 years. Or when you cash if you cash early.

Tax The life company pays tax on income and capital gains at a rate equal to the basic rate of tax. The proceeds and any growth are basic rate tax paid for basic rate taxpayers. Non-taxpayers and 20% taxpayers cannot reclaim the tax. Higher rate taxpayers pay extra but only on the actual gain, currently 15%.

Fees to pay Charges deducted from your investment are usually 5% initial; 1.5% yearly.

Passbook Statement sent.

Children Unsuitable.

Risk Full value of original investment on withdrawal. 90% compensation scheme for UK authorised life companies. Do not invest in an overseas life company which is not authorised in the UK as your protection is less and your income or gain could be liable to UK basic and higher rate tax.

How to invest See surveys and adverts in the press. Ask for details and compare the guarantees and terms.

Where from Life insurance companies.

Building societies also offer this type of investment, generally with lower charges.

LIFE INSURANCE

Unit-Linked Savings Plan

A commitment to save a fixed amount, usually monthly or yearly, usually for 10 years or more. After deduction of the company's charges, the remainder of your money is linked to the price of units in a unit trust or other type of fund (eg property, mixed, fixed interest) run by the life company.

Who can invest Anyone in good health.

How worthwhile Poor to good value for basic and higher rate taxpayers for savings kept going for 10 years or more depending on the policy chosen. Very little basis for predicting in advance whether you will do well or badly 'Maximum Investment Plans' with lower charges may give potentially better value. Can be used to avoid inheritance tax if written *in trust*. Otherwise consider instead *Investment Trust Personal Equity Plan* or *Unit Trust Personal Equity Plan*. Also compare with *Life Insurance With-Profits Endowment Policy* and *Life Insurance With-Profits Flexible Policy*. Unsuitable for non-taxpayers and 20% taxpayers.

Minimum £10 to £100 a month.

Maximum None.

Suitable Regular savings.

Money back You get the value of the units allocated to you after 10 years, either when you choose or at an *option* or *maturity* date. Some plans allow you to withdraw a 'tax free' income after 10 years. On death there is usually a minimum guaranteed sum. You can stop saving at any time and take your money or leave it *paid-up* either way in the early years you lose out heavily.

Inerest Variable. Income from the investments is accumulated.

Interest paid When you cash the policy or when you die.

Tax The insurance company pays tax on income and capital gains at the basic tax rate which reflects in the price of the units; some deduct gains tax from the proceeds. There is no tax on the proceeds but there can be extra tax for higher rate taxpayers, currently 15%, if you cash a policy before 10 years or if it is a *non-qualifying* one.

Fees to pay Charges are made by the life company and deducted from your investment. Some companies charge less for higher premiums. It is impossible for a layman to compare charges because they are deducted in different ways.

Passbook None. Insurance policy issued. Unit valuation sent yearly.

Children Policies can be *in trust* for children to avoid probate and inheritance tax.

Risk Depends on the type of investment to which the policy is linked. The value of units can go down as well as up. UK authorised life companies are covered by a 90% compensation scheme based on the current value of your units.

How to invest Ask an independent financial adviser to recommend a few companies with the lowest charges and good investment managers. Also ask the companies which don't pay commission: Equitable Life, London Life, Professional Life for a quote.

Where from Many life companies

Policies issued on or before 13 March 1984 normally get tax relief (at a reduced rate) on the premiums. Keep them going.

LIFE INSURANCE

With Profits Bond

Lump sum invested in a single premium life insurance policy. Your life is insured for about the amount you invest to which profits or *bonuses* are added each year. On *unitised* contracts which are offered by many companies, the bonus is added to the unit price instead. The bonus rate can rise and fall but once a bonus is added to a policy it is guaranteed, but see *Risk* and *Money back*. The bonds are likely to be better value the longer you hold them. They are sometimes issued as limited offers.

Who can invest Anyone.

How worthwhile They have been described as a half-way house between a building society and the stockmarket. Compare with *Building Society Guaranteed Stock Market Bond*. Unsuitable for non-taxpayers and 20% taxpayers.

Minimum £500 to £5,000.

Maximum Varies.

Suitable Lump sums.

Money back The fixed sum insured plus bonuses plus possibly a *terminal bonus* is paid when you cash the policy or on earlier death. But may be subject to a deduction called *market value adjustment* other than on death. Equitable Life and Scottish Provident make no deduction on 5th anniversary and every next 5th anniversary. Friends Provident, MGM make no deduction on 5th anniversary. London & Manchester none on 6th, Prudential none on surrenders up to £25,000 or on 10th anniversary. Also not if you died or usually on 'income' withdrawals of up to 5% to 10% a year of the amount invested.

Interest Variable. Based on bonus rates at the discretion of the life company.

Interest paid When you cash or the person insured dies. You can withdraw a fixed amount each half-year; sometimes yearly, quarterly or monthly.

Tax The life company pays tax on income and capital gains at a rate usually equal to the basic rate of tax and this is reflected in the bonus rate. The proceeds and any profits are tax paid for basic rate taxpayers. Non-taxpayers and 20% taxpayers cannot reclaim tax. Higher rate taxpayers pay extra, currently 15%, when they cash and on withdrawals over 5% a year or if they go on for more than 20 years.

Fees to pay Charges deducted from your investment are usually 5% initial; yearly usually not explicit and at the discretion of the life company.

Passbook Statement sent.

Children Unsuitable.

Risk 90% compensation scheme for UK authorised life companies.

How to invest See surveys in the press. Ask for details from some of the companies below and compare them.

Where from AXA Equity & Law, Commercial Union, Equitable Life, Friends Provident, GA Life, London & Manchester, MGM Assurance, NPI, Prudential, Royal Life, Wesleyan. *The following only offer With Profits Bonds as part of a package with other investment links:* GA Life, Legal & General.

LIFE INSURANCE

With-Profits Endowment

A commitment to save a fixed amount, usually monthly or yearly, for a fixed term chosen by you at the outset of 10 to 25 years or more. In return a life (usually your own) is insured for a fixed amount to which profits called *reversionary bonuses* are added. The rate of bonus can rise and fall but once a bonus has been added to a policy, it is guaranteed. The fixed sum insured plus bonuses, plus with most companies a discretionary *terminal bonus* are paid when the term ends or on earlier death. On *unitised* contracts which are offered by many companies, the bonus is added to the unit price instead of ths sum insured.

Who can invest Anyone in good health. Better value the younger you are. The insured can be yourself or anyone in whom you have an insurable interest (eg. husband or wife). Joint policies available.

How worthwhile Poor to good value for taxpayers depending on the company chosen for savings kept going for 10 years or more. Poor value if you give up saving before you complete the term.

Minimum £10 to £20 a month.

Maximum None.

Suitable Regular savings.

Money back On maturity or death. You can stop saving at any time and take your money, the *surrender value*, or leave it *paid-up* in the policy. Iin the first few years you can lose most if not all your savings; even well into the policy there can be a heavy deduction with some companies.

Interest Variable. Based on bonus rate at the discretion of the life company.

Interest paid When policy matures or the person insured dies

Tax The insurance company pays tax on the income and capital gains it makes which reflects in your bonus rate. There is no tax on the proceeds but there can be extra tax for higher rate taxpayers, currently 15%, if you cash a policy before 10 years or if it is a *non-qualifying* one.

Fees to pay Premiums usually include a policy fee (eg £2 a month) which make a £100 a month policy better value than a £25 a month one.

Passbook None. Insurance policy.

Children Policies can be *in trust* to avoid probate and inheritance tax.

Risk The *terminal bonus* may account for over half the proceeds of a 25 year policy which makes *with-profits* a potentially risky investment as a terminal bonus can disappear overnight if the company decides to reduce or remove it. UK authorised insurance companies are covered by a 90% compensation scheme less 'excessive' benefits.

How to invest Ask an independent financial adviser to find the best company for your age and term based on past performance and the company's financial strength which is likely to be from one of the companies listed below.

Where from Clerical Medical, Commercial Union, Equitable Life, Friends Provident, Norwich Union, Royal London, Scottish Amicable, Scottish Life, Scottish Widows, Standard Life.

Policies issued on or before 13 March 1984 normally get tax relief (at a reduced rate). Keep them going. You can buy second-hand endowment policies - details from the Association of Policy Market Makers.

LIFE INSURANCE

With-Profits Flexible

A commitment to save a fixed monthly amount for at least 10 years. In return your life is insured for a fixed sum to which profits called *reversionary bonuses* are added every year. The bonus rate can can rise and fall but once a bonus has been added it is guaranteed. The fixed sum insured plus bonuses are paid (plus with some companies a *terminal bonus*) if you die or whenever you choose after 10 years. Some policies have to end after 20 to 25 years or when you reach age 65. On *unitised* contracts which are offered by many companies, the bonus is added to the unit price instead of ths sum insured.

Who can invest Anyone in good health usually up to age 50, 55, 60, 65 or 70.

How worthwhile Poor to good value depending on the company chosen, for savings you think you will need in 10 to 20 years time. Compare with a series of *Life Insurance With-Profits Endowment* which may be better value. Similar policies called *whole life* policies can be used *in trust* to avoid inheritance tax.

Minimum £10 to £25 a month.

Maximum None.

Suitable Regular savings.

Money back On death or at any time after 10 years. If you stop saving before 10 years, a heavy penalty is likely.

Interest Variable. Based on bonus rate.

Interest paid When you cash the policy after 10 years or when you die.

Tax The life company pays tax on the income and capital gains it makes which reflects in your bonus rate. There is extra tax for higher rate taxpayers if you cash a policy before 10 years or if it is a *non-qualifying* one. Make sure you are sold a *qualifying* policy.

Fees to pay The premiums may include a fixed policy fee (eg £2 a month) which make a £100 a month policy better value than a £25 a month one.

Passbook None. Insurance policy issued. Bonus statements normally issued yearly.

Children Policies can be *in trust* for children to avoid probate and inheritance tax.

Risk A cut in *terminal bonus* can seriously erode the return from your policy. UK authorised life insurance companies are covered by a 90% compensation scheme less 'excessive' benefits. For complete safety use an old established company.

How to invest Ask an independent financial adviser to get details of past performance and financial strength from the best companies for your age, and to advise you on which companies are the strongest financially.

Where from Consider the companies listed under *Life Insurance With Profits Endowment*. Some only issue *whole life* policies which are designed to pay out the best return on death, not if you cash them in.

With life insurance you get better value by choosing the company rather than letting the company choose you.

LOCAL AUTHORITY

Fixed Term Loan

(Also called Local Authority Bond)

Lump sum invested for a fixed term of 1 to 10 years at a fixed rate of interest. Some local authorities offer short-term loans for from 7 to 364 days but usually for amounts over £100,000. No additions or withdrawals allowed.

Who can invest Anyone 18 or over.

How worthwhile Good value for basic taxpayers, non-taxpayers and 20% taxpayers. Compare with *Co-operative Society Term Account, Stock Government Fixed Interest, Stock Debenture and Loan, National Savings Pensioners Bond, National Savings Capital Bond,* Taxpayers also compare with *Life Insurance Growth or Income Bond.* Terms over 5 years not recommended.

Minimum £500 to £1,000.

Maximum Varies.

Suitable Lump sums.

Money back At end of term.

Interest Fixed. Rates vary between different local authorities and depend on the length of term and minimum allowed.

Interest paid Usually half-yearly.

Tax Since 6 April 1991 (and before 6 April 1986) basic rate tax is deducted from the interest. Non-taxpayers can reclaim the tax from the Inland Revenue (or have interest paid with no deduction). 20% taxpayers can reclaim tax. Higher rate taxpayers pay extra.

Fees to pay None.

Passbook None. Certficate issued.

Children The investment must be held in an adult's name.

How to invest Subscribe to *Money£acts* which includes a table of rates updated each month. Phone the treasurer of the local authority you choose; check the rate and ask for an application form; or agree terms by phone and send a cheque with a letter confirming the details.

Where from Local authorities.

You can also invest in a local authority through Negotiable Yearling Bonds. These are issued by a number of local authorities every Tuesday for 1 year, 2 years or longer periods. The interest rate for all bonds issued on the same day is the same (eg 1 year 7%, 2 years 7¼%) and is fixed for the term of the bond. Bonds can also be bought and sold on the stock market. If you buy for less than the redemption value, you can make a capital gain which is exempt from capital gains tax; if you make a loss you can't get allowable loss relief.

NATIONAL SAVINGS

Capital Bond

A lump sum investment which accumulates interest at a fixed rate and should be held for the full 5 years. You can get your money back early but you will receive lower interest.

Who can invest Anyone.

How worthwhile Series I fair value, especially for non-taxpayers and 20% taxpayers who want to accumulate interest. The next new issue is likely to be at a higher interest rate. Non-taxpayers compare with *Co-operative Society Term Account, Building Society Term Account.* Taxpayers compare with *Life Insurance Growth Bond, Building Society Term Account, Local Authority Fixed Term Loan.* Higher rate taxpayers consider instead *National Savings Fixed Issue Certificates.*

Minimum £100.

Maximum £250,000 for Series B to I.

Money back About 2 weeks. If you only want to cash part, at least £100 must remain. There is always an interest penalty if you cash early. Ask for a repayment form and post paid envelope at a post office.

Interest Fixed for each series. Series I pays the equivalent of 7.75% a year. 5.15% in yr 1; 6.1% in yr 2; 7.6% in yr 3; 9% in yr 4; 11% in yr 5. For the current rate, phone a 24 hour recording on 01 71 605 9483 or 9484.

Interest paid Yearly, added to the bond on the anniversary of purchase.

Tax Not deducted. Taxpayers are liable to pay income tax on the interest which should be declared on a tax return. Interest is credited at a rising rate, so the tax bill grows year by year; it is twice as high in year 5 as in year 1.

Fees to pay None.

Passbook Certificate issued and you get a yearly interest statement in April.

Children Suitable, especially for money given by a parent which is intended to accumulate until the child is 18 (see Chapter 11). Money is repaid to parent or guardian designated at outset if bond matures when child under age 7. If you invest as a trustee, on the application write after your name 'as trustee for' and the name of the beneficiary, do the same after your signature. Maximum 2 trustees and 2 beneficiaries for each trust.

Risk None.

How to invest Ask for an application. Pay over the counter at a post office or by post to National Savings.

Where from Post offices or phone 0645 645 000.

If you give money to a child you don't have to put the money in the child's own name. It can be held by the parents, for instance, as trustees. Any tax advantages apply regardless of whose name the account is in. For more details see Chapters 4 and 11.

NATIONAL SAVINGS

✾ Children's Bonus Bond

A lump sum investment made for a child by a parent, grandparent or friend which accumulates interest at a fixed tax exempt rate and has a bonus after 5 years. The money can be held in the bond until the child is 21 under extension terms which are announced from time to time.

Who can invest Anyone aged over 16 for a child under 16.

How worthwhile Excellent value for taxpayer donors. Also suitable for non-taxpayers.

Minimum £25. And then in £25 units.

Maximum £1,000 for Issue G which can be held in addition to a previous issue for the same child.

Suitable Lump sums. Regular savings.

Money back About 2 weeks. You lose the bonus if you cash early. If cashed in first year, no interest paid. One calendar month's notice needed unless holder is 21 or over or cashed at a 5 year bonus date. Can be partially cashed in £25 units.

Interest 5% a year fixed plus, for *Issue G:* bonus of 18.28% of purchase price after 5 years equivalent to 7.85% a year. For the current rate, phone a 24 hour recording on 01 71 605 9483 or 9484. Bonuses for previous issues are as follows: *Issue A* 47.36%, equivalent to 11.84% a year; *Issue B* 40.12% equivalent to 10.9% a year; *Issue C* 34.16% equivalent to 10.1% a year; *Issue D* 26.96%, equivalent to 9.1% a year. *Issue E:* 18.28% equivalent to 7.85% a year. *Issue F:* 14.92% equivalent to 7.35% a year.

Interest paid Accumulated to increase its value at the end of each year.

Tax Interest and bonus are tax free and need not be entered on a tax return.

Fees to pay None.

Passbook None. Certificate provided.

Children Designed as a gift to the child.

Risk None.

How to invest Ask for an application. Pay over the counter at a post office or by post to National Savings.

Where from Post offices or phone 0645 645 000.

The only snag about this investment is that the child has complete control of the money invested from the age of 16 onward.

NATIONAL SAVINGS

FIRST Option Bond

A lump sum investment which accumulates interest at a fixed rate determined at the outset for 12 months. After 12 months you can withdraw or leave your money for another 12 months at the then current fixed rate plus a small bonus for sums over £20,000. If you want to withdraw before 12 months, you get no interest; if you want to withdraw at any other time, you get interest at half the agreed rate since the last anniversary date.

Who can invest Anyone over age 16. Joint accounts for 2 people are allowed.

How worthwhile Fair value for basic rate taxpayers and non-taxpayers who expect interest rates to remain the same or fall over the 12 month period. Better value for small amounts (ie. under £10,000). Compare with *Building Society Term Share, Co-operative Society Term Account, Stock Government Fixed Interest*. Higher rate taxpayers also compare with *Life Insurance Growth or Income Bond*.

Minimum £1,000.

Maximum £250,000.

Suitable Lump sums.

Money back About 2 weeks. A repayment form is on the back of the bond. There is no interest if you cash early in the first 12 months. Then if you cash other than at an anniversary, interest is paid at half the rate since the last anniversary with no extra interest for amounts over £20,000.

Interest Fixed. 0.4% year more interest paid for amounts over £20,000. For the current rate, phone a 24 hour recording on 0171 605 9483 or 9484.

Interest paid Added to your investment at the end of each 12 month period or when you withdraw.

Tax Basic rate tax is deducted from the interest. Non-taxpayers and 20% taxpayers can reclaim tax from the Inland Revenue. Higher rate taxpayers pay extra.

Fees to pay None but see *Money back*.

Passbook Statement sent with each transaction or yearly.

Children Over age 16 only or held in trust by up to 2 trustees for up to 2 beneficiaries of any age.

Risk Full value of original investment returned on withdrawal.

How to invest Ask for an application. Send your cheque by post to National Savings.

Where from Post offices or phone 0645 645 000.

Value for money on this investment depends on how the interest rate turns out compared to a variable interest rate at a building society.

NATIONAL SAVINGS

✹ Fixed Issue Certificates

A lump sum which accumulates interest at a fixed tax free rate and which should be held for 5 years to gain full interest.

Who can invest Anyone.

How worthwhile Good value for higher rate taxpayers. The next new issue is likely to be at a higher interest rate. Poor value for non-taxpayers and 20% taxpayers who should consider instead *National Savings Capital Bond*. Basic rate taxpayers compare with *Life Insurance Growth or Income Bond* or *Local Authority Fixed Term Loan*.

Minimum £100.

Maximum *42nd Issue:* £10,000 but you can also reinvest a further £20,000 from other fixed or index linked issues you hold which are more than 5 years old (see Appendix 3). You may hold more if you inherit them. Single maximum applies to joint holdings. Certificates may also be held in trust, thus doubling the maximum investment. You may buy these in addition to other issues of National Savings Certificates.

Suitable Lump sums.

Money back About 2 weeks. In cash at a post office or by cheque. Ask for a repayment form and post-paid envelope at a post office or bank.

Interest Fixed. For the *42nd Issue:* No interest until the end of year 1 when 4% is added. (If you have 'reinvestment certificates' interest is added every 3 months at 4% a year for the 1st year.) From year 2, it is added every 3 months at the following yearly rates: 2nd year 4.6%; 3rd 5.5%; 4th 6.75%; 5th 8.46%. This works out at 5.85% a year if certificates are held

for 5 years. For current rate phone a 24 hour recording on 01 71 605 9483.

Interest paid When certificates cashed. You can draw a yearly 'income' by cashing some of your units but it is better to spend capital, equivalent to the interest, from another investment eg a building society account.

Tax Interest is tax free. It need not be declared on a tax return.

Fees to pay None.

Passbook None. You get a certificate. If you don't have a holder's number card, you will be given one. This covers all issues of National Savings Certificates. The number should be quoted if you withdraw or buy more certificates. You should have a separate holder's card number for each trust holding.

Children Consider *National Savings Children's Bonus Bond* and *National Savings Capital Bond* instead. Certificates in the name of a child under 7 can normally be cashed by a parent or guardian.

Risk None. Full value of original investment returned on withdrawal.

How to invest Ask for an application. Pay over the counter at a post office or by post to National Savings.

Where from Post offices and most banks or phone 0645 645 000.

Many past issues of National Savings Certificates pay very poor interest even for higher rate taxpayers. If you hold them, you should re-invest elsewhere. To see whether other issues are worth keeping see Appendix 3.

NATIONAL SAVINGS

✹ Index-Linked Certificates

(Formerly known as Grannybonds)

A way of linking your investment to the Retail Prices Index. On top you get a fixed interest rate, which is lower if you stop before 5 years. Interest, once added, is index-linked too. For how the Retail Prices Index has risen in the past see Appendix 2.

Who can invest Anyone.

How worthwhile Good value for taxpayers, especially higher rate tax-payers. Poor value for non-taxpayers and 20% taxpayers who should consider instead *Stock Government Index-Linked.*

Minimum £100.

Maximum £10,000 and you can also reinvest a further £20,000 from other fixed or index linked issues which are more than 5 years old. You may hold more if you inherit them. Single maximum applies to joint holdings. Certificates may also be held in trust so doubling the maximum investment. You can buy these in addition to previous issues of Index Linked Certificates.

Suitable Lump sums. Regular savings.

Money back About 2 weeks. Ask for a repayment form and post-paid envelope at a post office or bank. Any number of units may be cashed. During the first year: your original investment returned. After 1st year (and in 1st year if 'reinvestment certificates'): index-linking and interest added.

Interest Variable. For the 8th *Issue:* If held for the full 5 years you get index-linking of your initial investment *and* 1¹/₄% in year 1; 1¾% in year 2; 2½% in year 3; 3½% in year 4; 6.07% in year 5. This is equivalent to 3% a year. For current rate phone a 24 hour recording on 0171 605 9483 or 9484.

Interest paid When certificates cashed.

Tax All increases in the value of the certificates are tax-free. Nothing need be declared on a tax return.

Fees to pay None.

Passbook None. You get a certificate. If you don't have a holder's number card, you will be given one. This covers all issues of National Savings Certificates. The number should be quoted if you withdraw or buy more certificates. You should have a separate holder's card for a trust holding.

Children Convenient for gifts. Certificates in the name of a child under 7 can normally be cashed by a parent or guardian.

Risk None. Full value of original investment returned on withdrawal.

How to invest Ask for an application. Pay over the counter at a post office or by post to National Savings.

Where from Post offices and most banks or phone 0645 645 000.

Previous issues of Index-Linked Certificates after they have matured now only pay 0.5% a year interest plus index-linking. They should be re-invested elsewhere although 2nd Issue Certificates pay a bonus of 4% on the 10th anniversary (the last bonus will be paid on 30 June 1995). For details of those which are not yet 5 years old, see Appendix 3.

NATIONAL SAVINGS

Income Bond

An investment which pays out monthly interest suitable for people who can tie up their money for at least a year. You can get your money back in full by giving 3 months' notice to expire after the end of the first 12 months you have held the bond. You can get your money back during the first 12 months but interest is paid at half the usual rate.

Who can invest Anyone.

How worthwhile Compare with *Building Society Monthly Income Account* or *Offshore Bank Notice Account* paying interest monthly. For a fixed interest rate compare with *National Savings Pensioners Guaranteed Income Bond.*

Minimum £2,000. Larger purchases and additions must be in multiples of £1,000.

Maximum £250,000 for individual or joint accounts.

Suitable Lump sums.

Money back At 3 months notice in multiples of £1,000 provided at least £2,000 remains; otherwise the whole investment must be cashed. If the end of the notice period is after the end of the first year there is no penalty; if it is during the first year, interest is reduced to half. Ask for a repayment form (DNS201) and post-paid envelope (DNS450) at a post office.

Interest Variable. Changes announced 6 weeks in advance. A higher rate is paid on holdings of £25,000 or more. For the current rate, phone a 24 hour recording on 01 71 605 9483 or 9484.

Interest paid Monthly on the 5th direct to a bank, building society or National Savings Investment Account. The first payment is made on the next interest date after you have held the bond 6 weeks and includes all interest from the date of purchase.

Tax Not deducted. Taxpayers are liable to pay income tax on the interest which should be declared on a tax return.

Fees to pay None.

Passbook Certificate issued.

Children Unsuitable. Consider *National Savings Capital Bond* or *National Savings Investment Account* instead. Income bonds are suitable for investment by the trustees of a formally constituted trust with children as the beneficiaries. Maximum 2 beneficiaries for each trust.

Risk None.

How to invest Ask for an application form. Send the application and cheque to National Savings by post.

Where from Post offices or phone 0645 645 000.

Always leave some of your money invested where you can get at it at once or within a few days without penalty. Only tie up money for as long as you are sure you will not need it.

NATIONAL SAVINGS

Investment Account

An account into which you can pay at any post office. To withdraw you must give 1 month's notice. A higher interest rate is paid for £500 or more and £25,000 or more.

Who can invest Anyone. Accounts can be held jointly.

How worthwhile Good value for small amounts. Compare with *Building Society 30 Day Notice Account* or *Offshore Bank Notice Account.*

Minimum £20 each time you make a deposit.

Maximum £100,000 including accumulated interest from all other National Savings Investment Accounts you hold.

Suitable Lump sums. Regular savings.

Money back Any amount at 1 month's notice from the day the withdrawal application reaches National Savings in Glasgow. Ask for a repayment form (DNS 32) and post-paid envelope at a post office. It can be paid in cash at a post office or by cheque.

Interest Variable More paid for £500 or more and £25,000 or more. For the current rates, phone a 24 hour recording on 01 71 605 9483 or 9484.

Interest paid Yearly added to account on 31 December.

Tax Not deducted. Taxpayers are liable to pay income tax on the interest which should be declared on a tax return.

Fees to pay None.

Passbook Yes.

Children Suitable. Under 7 a relative or friend can open an account in a child's name where withdrawals may be made by the child's parent or guardian. At age 7 the child can withdraw on his or her own signature; use application form DNS26B. An account can be opened by anyone as trustees for money belonging to a child; maximum 2 trustees and 2 beneficiaries for each trust account; to open such a trust account write to National Savings Glasgow G58 1SB .

Risk None. Full value of original investment returned on withdrawal.

How to invest Ask for an application. Pay over the counter at a post office or by post to National Savings.

Where from Post offices or phone 0645 645 000.

National Savings Ordinary Account allows you to pay in and withdraw up to £100 in cash at any post office (or up to £250 at one post office which you have used for at least 6 months if you have a Regular Customer Account). Interest is 3.75% (for 1995) if you have more than £500 in the account for the whole calendar year; otherwise it is 2%. No interest on deposit or withdrawal during the calendar month in which it is made. Interest up to £70 a year per person is tax exempt. Minimum £10 each deposit maximum £10,000 overall. Otherwise it is similar to National Savings Investment Account. From age 7, a child can operate the account itself. Poor value. An alternative to a bank current account for people on low pay or pensions who draw benefits from a post office. Compare with Building Society Instant Access Account.

NATIONAL SAVINGS

Pensioners Guaranteed Income Bond

An investment which pays out monthly interest at a fixed interest rate for 5 years. You can get your money back early by giving 60 days notice and you incur a penalty of 60 days interest on the amount withdrawn.

Who can invest Anyone age 65 or over. For joint accounts you must both be over age 65.

How worthwhile For a variable interest rate compare with *Building Society Monthly Income Account* or *Offshore Bank Notice Account* paying interest monthly. For a fixed interest rate compare with *Income Bonds*, see *Life Insurance Growth or Income Bond.*

Minimum £500.

Maximum £20,000 or £40,000 for a joint account. Bonds may also be held in trust so doubling the maximum investment. The beneficiaries must all be over age 65 but the trustees need not be.

Suitable Lump sums.

Money back At 60 days notice and 60 days loss of interest if before the 5 year term. Repaid without penalty on death. Fill in the form on the back of the bond and send it off. If you only want to cash part, you must cash at least £500 and at least £500 must remain.

Interest Fixed once you have invested for the full 5 years. Series 2 pays 7.5% a year. Series 1 paid 7% a year. For the current rate for new investments, phone a 24 hour recording on 01 71 605 9483 or 9484.

Interest paid Monthly on the 19th direct to a bank, building society or National Savings Investment Account. The first payment is made on the next interest date after you have held the bond 6 weeks and includes all interest from the date of purchase.

Tax Not deducted. Taxpayers are liable to pay income tax on the interest which should be declared on a tax return.

Fees to pay None.

Passbook Certificate issued.

Children Not allowed.

Risk None.

How to invest Ask for an application. Pay over the counter at a post office or by post to National Savings.

Where from Post offices or phone 0645 645 000.

This investment is restricted to the over 65's. It offers excelent value for money, especially for small amounts.

NATIONAL SAVINGS

Premium Bond

Once a month ERNIE (Electronic Random Number Indicator Equipment) selects £1 bond numbers at random to win prizes totalling about £19 million. **Monthly prizes range from £50 to £10,000, with 4 prizes of £25,000, 3 of £50,000, 2 of £100,000 and 1 prize of £1 million. Winning numbers of the big prizes are published in the newspapers but you will also be notified individually if you win. The names of the winners are never published.**

Who can invest Anyone. Joint holdings not allowed. Parents and grandparents can buy bonds for children.

How worthwhile If you are lucky and enjoy a gamble you may win a prize, but you may not. The odds on a £1 bond winning a prize are 15,000 to 1. Worth considering only if you are a higher rate taxpayer. On average you can expect to win a prize a year with £1,250 invested. With £20,000 you can expect 16 prizes a year though most will be £50 and you may win fewer or none at all. One of the £1 million winners in 1994, however, had £15,000 invested in Premium Bonds.

Minimum £100; then in multiples of £10. Each unit is still £1, so £100 gives 100 chances of winning. Bonds become eligible to win one clear calendar month after the month of purchase.

Maximum £20,000.

Suitable Lump sums.

Money back About 2 weeks. Ask for a repayment form (DNS350) and post-paid envelope at a post office. A partial withdrawal of a multiple bond is allowed. By cheque or in cash at a post office.

Interest None.

Tax Prizes are free of income tax and capital gains tax. They need not be declared on a tax return.

Fees to pay None.

Passbook None. You are issued with a bond which is individually numbered for each £1 unit and a holder's number card - this number should be quoted if you withdraw or buy more bonds.

Children Under age 16: bonds must be bought by a parent, guardian or grandparent. Any prize money will normally be paid to the parent or guardian. After age 16 the child takes over the bond.

Risk None. Full value of original investment returned on withdrawal.

How to invest Ask for an application. Pay over the counter at a post office or by post to National Savings.

Where from Post offices or phone 0645 645 000.

Always leave some of your money invested where you can get at it at once or within a few days without penalty. Only tie up money for as long as you are sure you will not need it.

OFFSHORE BANK

Foreign Currency Cheque Account

(Also called Multicurrency, Interbank, Offshore Reserve)

A bank account which holds money in foreign currencies eg US$, Yen, DM. With some you have a different cheque book for each currency. With others you have one cheque book with which you can issue cheques in any convertible currency. If the cheque clears through the UK (as opposed to the foreign) banking system, it may not be acceptable to an individual or company abroad.

Who can invest Anyone.

How worthwhile Useful if you receive payments in foreign currency or need to send cheques abroad in currencies outside the Eurocheque system (eg US $). Poor to fair value for taxpayers. Also consider *Offshore Single Currency Fund.*

Minimum Charterhouse, Guinness Mahon, Robert Fleming (with UK banking cheque book): US$5,000, DM 7,500, Yen 1 million (Yen 500,000 at Charterhouse), £2,500 and currency equivalent of £2,500 for 24 other currencies at Charterhouse; most major currencies (including FF and SwissF) at Guinness Mahon.

Maximum None.

Suitable Lump sums.

Money back A few days.

Interest Variable. No interest while balance below minimum.

Interest paid Added quarterly. Monthly at Charterhouse.

Tax *If account abroad, Isle of Man or Channel Islands:* No tax deducted but interest liable to income tax and should be declared on a tax return. *If account at UK bank:* Basic rate income tax deducted from interest for UK residents. Non-taxpayers and 20% taxpayers can reclaim

the tax from the Inland Revenue. Higher rate taxpayers pay extra. Gains on exchange rate changes on withdrawal liable to capital gains tax unless you spend the withdrawal (eg by paying a foreign currency credit card bill).

Fees to pay Robert Fleming: None. Charterhouse: 1st 15 cheques free per quarter, then £1.50 (or equivalent) per cheque; also payable when account falls below minimum investment plus £2.50 a month. Guinness Mahon US$200 a year per Amex card.

Passbook Statements quarterly.

Children Unsuitable.

Risk Full value of original investment in the foreign currency returned on withdrawal but if the currency has fallen against the £ sterling there will be a loss. Isle of Man banks only are covered by a compensation scheme: 75% on the foreign currency equivalent of the first £20,000 for each investor. From 1 July 1995 UK banks will be covered by 90% on the foreign currency equivalent of the first £20,000 for each investor but only for EU currencies (ie not US$, Yen, A$ etc). No compenstaion scheme in Guernsey.

How to invest Phone for details.

Where from *Isle of Man:* Robert Fleming (Offshore Reserve; US$, DM, Yen, £) *Guernsey:* Guinness Mahon (Private Interest Cheque Account; US$, DM, Yen, FF SwF and any major currency). *UK:* Charterhouse Bank (World Currency Account; choice of 25 currencies).

If you need to write occasional cheques in foreign currencies ask your bank for Eurocheques (unsuitable for US$, C$, A$) or a foreign currency bank draft (over the counter at Barclays for US$).

OFFSHORE BANK

✸ Instant Access Account

(Also called Gold Independent Reserve)

An account where you pay in by post and withdraw by post (or by immediate credit to a bank account for a charge). The account is held at a bank in the Isle of Man, Guernsey or Jersey. Higher rates of interest for larger sums. Some accounts not listed here, are exclusively for expatriates and may pay higher interest. Some pay interest on 6 to 30 April so delaying collection of income tax for a year.

Who can invest Anyone.

How worthwhile Good value for non-taxpayers and 20% taxpayers not eligible to have interest in a UK bank or building society paid with no tax deducted. Good value for higher rate taxpayers for accounts with interest paid in April. Taxpayers compare with *Building Society Postal Account.*

Minimum £500-£15,000. Minimum balance £5,000 at Yorkshire Guernsey.

Maximum £250,000 to £3million.

Suitable Lump sums.

Money back By post or for large amounts directly credited to a bank account for a charge.

Interest Variable. More interest paid over £5,000, £10,000, £25,000, £50,000, £100,000, £250,000.

Interest paid Usually yearly. By cheque to you; direct to a bank account; or left to accumulate. Derbyshire (Isle of Man), Yorkshire Guernsey, Woolwich Guernsey give you a choice of interest paid in March or April.

Tax Not deducted. Taxpayers are liable to pay income tax on the interest which should be declared on a tax return.

Fees to pay None.

Passbook Or statements sent.

Children Suitable for gifts from grandparents or ones which are expected to be accumulated.

Risk Full value of original investment returned on withdrawal. Subsidiaries of UK building societies are guaranteed by the parent. *Isle of Man:* 75% compensation scheme on the first £20,000 for each investor.

How to invest Phone or write to a company listed below which are all subsidiaries of building societies. Subscribe monthly to *Money£acts* or *Good Offshore Guide* for up-to-date rates.

Where from *Your minimum £500:* Woolwich Guernsey. *£5,000:* Portman Channel Islands. *£10,000+:* Derbyshire (IoM).

You can invest in this type of account held in US$ at C& G Guernsey and Woolwich Gurensey. Compare a US$ investment with Offshore Single Currency Fund.

OFFSHORE BANK

Notice Account

(Also called Investment Account, Extra Interest, Monthly Income)

An account with a bank, or a branch of a UK bank, or a subsidiary of a UK building society based in the Isle of Man, Guernsey or Jersey. It has a minimum investment which can be added to but notice of 60, 90 or 180 days must be given to withdraw. Some pay interest in the period 6-30 April so delaying collection of income tax for a year.

Who can invest Anyone.

How worthwhile Good value for non-taxpayers and 20% taxpayers not eligible to have interest in a UK bank or building society paid with no tax deducted. Good value for higher rate taxpayers for accounts with interest paid in April. Taxpayers compare with *Building Society 30, 60 or 90 Day Notice Accounts.* 180 days notice not recommended.

Minimum Usually £5,000. *£500:* Leeds Overseas; *£1,000:* Derbyshire IoM.

Maximum £500,000 to £5 million.

Suitable Lump sums.

Money back All or part at end of notice period. Abbey National Overseas, N&P Overseas, Portman Channel Islands, Yorkshire Guernsey allow early withdrawal with a loss of interest on the notice period. Britannia International and Leeds Permanent (IoM) allow balance over £10,000 at no notice with no penalty as in UK.

Interest Variable. More interest paid over £10,000, £25,000, £50,000, £100,000, £250,000.

Interest paid Usually yearly. Added to account or paid by cheque or direct to a bank account or UK account. Monthly income option at slightly lower nominal interest rate.

Tax Not deducted. Taxpayers are liable to pay income tax on the interest which should be declared on a tax return.

Fees to pay None .

Passbook Or statements sent.

Children Suitable for gifts from grandparents or ones which are expected to be accumulated.

Risk Full value of original investment returned on withdrawal. Subsidiaries of building societies are guaranteed by the parent. *Isle of Man:* 75% compensation scheme on the first £20,000 for each investor.

How to invest Phone or write to one of the companies listed below in the Isle of Man, Guernsey, Jersey and Alderney which are all subsidiaries of building societies. Rates surveyed monthly in the *Good Offshore Guide* and *Money£acts.*

Where from *For 90 day accounts with your minimum: £1,000-£5,000:* Instant access accounts pay better rates. *£5,000:* Portman Channel Islands. *£10,000:* Portman Channel Islands, Derbyshire IoM. *£25,000:* Derbyshire IoM; *£50,000+:* Derbyshire IoM.

Don't tie your money up for to long.

OFFSHORE

Investment Fund

You invest in units or shares which closely reflect the value of the shares or other assets held within the fund. Offshore funds are managed by professionals and although with many you are buying shares in a company, they work in a similar way to unit trusts but are partially outside the control of the UK authorities. They are usually based in places like Jersey, Guernsey, Isle of Man, Bermuda, Luxemburg or the Cayman Islands. Investment is often provided from London. The assets are sometimes held by a custodian which acts rather like a UK trustee.

Who can invest Anyone.

How worthwhile Suitable for people living abroad or thinking of doing so. For fixed interest funds see *Offshore Stock and Bond Fund.*

Minimum £100 to £4,000 or more.

Maximum None.

Suitable Lump sums.

Money back Usually immediately at the market price.

Interest Variable. Called *dividend* or *distribution.* Some funds don't pay interest. You hope to make a capital gain by selling for more than you buy; you may lose money.

Interest paid Often half-yearly by cheque to you or accumulated.

Tax Not deducted. If you are a UK resident and a taxpayer you are liable to pay tax on the income. If the fund accumulates more than 15% of its income UK residents are liable to income tax instead of capital gains tax on any gain

you make when you dispose of your units or shares, or if you make a gain when you switch to another sub-fund in an *umbrella fund.* Disposals and switches may be liable to capital gains tax for UK residents, but see Chapter 5.

Fees to pay Initial charge: Up to 6%. Yearly charge around 1% to 1½% deducted from your income.

Passbook None. Share certificate issued.

Children Unsuitable.

Risk High. The price of units fluctuates down as well as up. There is a chance that the managers will run off with your money but not if the fund is *recognised* in a territory with a compensation scheme, see page 43.

How to invest Phone the managers of the fund you are interested in, ask for a prospectus and read it carefully. You should be able to place your order by phone. Sales are also best made by phone so you know what price you get.

Where from *Money Management* and other magazines list funds and performance. See the *Financial Times* Offshore Funds page for prices, yields and *recognised* funds.

There are also offshore unit-linked life insurance policies, which are not recommended for reasons of safety and tax complications.

OFFSHORE

Managed Currency Fund

(Also called Multicurrency, International Reserves)

You buy shares in a fund of an investment company which invests in bank deposits in foreign currencies (including £ sterling). The choice of currencies is made by professionals and you hope to gain by their skill in investing in currencies which appreciate against the £, or staying in £ sterling if it appreciates against other currencies. These funds are generally one of a number of sub-funds of an *umbrella* investment company based in Guernsey. There is usually a choice of a US$ or £ denominated fund.

Who can invest Anyone except US permanent residents.

How worthwhile Suitable for taxpayers. Some managers are more skilful than others. Potential gains and losses are less than a *Unit Trust Invested in Shares*. If you want to choose the currencies and decide yourself when to move in and out consider instead *Offshore Single Foreign Currency Fund*.

Minimum *No minimum:* Five Arrows. *£2,000:* Hambros. *£5,000:* Guinness Flight. *US$10,000* Lloyds Bank.

Maximum None.

Suitable Lump sums. Five Arrows and Hambros have a regular savings plan.

Money back Up to 4 to 7 days. Shares in joint names avoids probate in Guernsey.

Interest Variable.

Interest paid Paid yearly or half-yearly. By cheque, direct to a bank account or accumulated in the fund.

Tax Not deducted. *If interest distributed:* eg Guinness Flight Global Strategy, Hambros (EMMA), taxpayers are liable to income tax; gains on shares sold are liable to capital gains tax (see Chapter 5). *If income accumulated:* eg Lloyds Bank, Five Arrows International Reserves, it need not be declared until you sell your shares (or *switch* to another fund) when gains as well as income are liable to income tax.

Fees to pay *Initial:* None at Lloyds Bank, Five Arrows; 4% Hambros; 5% Guinness Flight. *Yearly (including custodian fees):* Guinness Flight 0.88% (max 1.63%); Five Arrows 1.5%; Hambros 1.125% (max. 1.53%); Lloyds Bank 0.95% (max. 1.7%).

Passbook None. Statement usually issued with each transaction.

Children Under 18, shares must be held in an adult's name and can be *designated* with a child's name or initials.

Risk Moderate. The value of the fund can go down as well as up if the managers get the timing or choice of currencies wrong. There are compensation schemes for *recognised* funds - see page 44.

How to invest Get details from the *recognised* funds listed below and compare what they have to offer. Past performance of most funds is monitored in magazines like *Money Management*. Prices, yields and some recognised funds are listed in the *Financial Times* Offshore Funds page and others are listed in *Money Management* magazine.

Where from *Distributor:* Guinness Flight (Global Strategy), Hambros (EMMA). *Accumulation:* Lloyds Bank (International Money Market), Five Arrows International Reserves (Managed).

An Offshore Managed Currency Fund is an alternative to a unit trust and not to a bank or building society account.

OFFSHORE

❊ Single Foreign Currency Fund

(Also called International Reserves, Money Funds)

A sub-fund of an investment company where you pay in and withdraw like a building society postal account but technically you buy and sell its shares. Each sub-fund invests in one currency and the combined deposits from small investors are reinvested in bank and other deposits of less than 12 months. Currencies available from: USA, Germany, Japan, Switzerland, Singapore, Hong Kong, Canada, Australia, New Zealand, France, Belgian, Holland, Italy, Spain, Portugal, Norway, Sweden, Denmark, Finland, Austria, Eire, the ECU (European Currency Unit) and £. Shares can be switched between sub-funds on demand and withdrawn at up to 7 days notice. Money can be deposited and withdrawn in any currency but not in cash.

Who can invest Anyone except US permanent residents.

How worthwhile A convenient way to invest in foreign currency deposits. Taxpayers can use an *accumulation fund* to defer tax. For £ sterling see *Offshore Sterling Currency Fund.*

Minimum None at Fidelity, Five Arrows.

Maximum None.

Suitable Lump sums. Five Arrows has a regular savings plan.

Money back Up to 4 to 7 days. Switching on demand. Shares in joint names avoid probate abroad. You can't withdraw cash.

Interest Variable. Calculated daily.

Interest paid Interest is either *accumulated* to increase the value of the shares or *distributed.* If distributed it can be paid in the foreign currency, paid in £, or reinvested in extra shares.

Tax Not deducted. *If interest distributed:* Taxpayers liable to income tax on it; gains on shares sold, or switched to another currency, liable to capital gains tax (see Chapter 5). *If interest accumulated:* It need not be declared until you sell or switch to another currency, when gains (on exchange rate changes) as well as interest are liable to income tax.

Fees to pay *Initial:* None. *Yearly (including custodian fees):* Five Arrows 1%, Fidelity 1.03%.

Passbook None. Statement issued with each transaction.

Children Under 18 shares should be held in an adult's name and may be *designated* with the child's name or initials.

Risk Full value of original investment plus interest on withdrawal in currency chosen; if you convert to £ the value may have risen or fallen with the exchange rate. There are compensation schemes for *recognised funds,* see page 44.

How to invest Phone or write for details from the *recognised* funds listed below. Prices and yields are published in the *Financial Times* Offshore Funds page.

Where from *Distributor:* Fidelity (Money Funds, Bermuda), Five Arrows Currency Fund (Rothschild, Guernsey). *Accumulation:* Fidelity (Money Funds, Bermuda), Five Arrows International Reserves (Guernsey). Both Fidelity funds offer all currencies listed above. Both Five Arrows funds offer all except Portugal, Austria, Eire, Finland, Norway.

For large amounts in US$, you may be able to get a better interest rate from an Offshore Bank. Abbey National Jersey, C&G Guernsey and Woolwich Guernsey offer tiered interest rates in US$.

OFFSHORE

Sterling Currency Fund

(Also called International Reserves, Multicurrency Reserves)

A fund where you pay in and withdraw like a building society postal account but technically you buy and sell its shares. There are two main types which have different tax treatment. *Distributor* funds pay out interest half-yearly; no tax is deducted from the interest but it counts as your income in the tax year it is paid. *Accumulation funds* accumulate interest without deduction of tax. No tax is payable until you dispose of the shares (or switch to another fund). Then the 'gain' on the shares is liable to UK income tax in the tax year of the disposal or switch .

Who can invest Anyone except US permanent residents.

How worthwhile Interest rates are generally poor, especially for large amounts. Taxpayers can use an *Accumulation* fund to defer tax. Non-taxpayers compare *Distributor* funds with *National Savings Investment Account, Offshore Bank Instant Access Account.*

Minimum None at Fidelity, Five Arrows.

Maximum None.

Suitable Lump sums. Five Arrows has a regular savings plan.

Money back Up to 4 to 7 days. Switching to foreign currencies (see *Offshore Single Currency Fund)* on demand. If you leave the shares in your will, your executors will have to obtain probate abroad unless the shares are in joint names.

Interest Variable. Calculated daily.

Interest paid Interest is either accumulated to increase the value of the shares or distributed. If distributed it can be paid by cheque to you; to a bank account or reinvested in extra shares.

Tax Not deducted. See main description.

Fees to pay *Initially:* none. *Yearly* (including custodian fees): Five Arrows 1%; Fidelity 1.03%.

Passbook None. Statement issued with each transaction.

Children Under 18 shares should be held in an adult's name and may be *designated* with the child's name or initials.

Risk Full value of original investment plus interest returned on withdrawal. There are compensation schemes for *recognised* funds - see page 44.

How to invest Phone or write for details from the *recognised* funds listed below. Fund prices and yields are published on the *Financial Times* Offshore Funds page.

Where from *Distributor:* Fidelity (Money Funds, Bermuda), Five Arrows Currency Fund (Rothschild, Guernsey). *Accumulation:* Fidelity (Money Funds, Bermuda), Five Arrows International Reserves (Rothschild, Guernsey).

If you want to invest in foreign currencies. see Offshore Single Foreign Currency Fund on the previous page.

OFFSHORE

Stock and Bond Fund

(Also called International Bond Fund)

You invest in a sub-fund of an investment company in shares which reflect the value of foreign currency fixed interest stocks held by the fund. Some specialise in stocks in one area eg. North America, Europe, Australasia. Or alternatively the fund may invest worldwide. By using *derivatives* the managers may invest in a different currency profile from that indicated by the denomination of the bonds.

Who can invest Anyone.

How worthwhile Suitable for people who expect interest rates to fall in the country or area they choose to invest in thus boosting the capital value of the fund. Taxpayers should probably use *distributor* funds see Tax. Compare with *Unit Trust Stock and Bond Fund.*

Minimum £2,000: Hambros. £5,000: Guinness Flight.

Maximum None.

Suitable Lump sums.

Money back Usually 4-7 days at the market price.

Interest Variable. Called *dividend* or *distribution.* Some funds accumulate interest. You hope to make a capital gain by selling for more than you buy; you may lose money if bond prices fall with a general rise in interest rates.

Interest paid Half-yearly by cheque to you; direct to a bank account or accumulated within the fund.

Tax Not deducted. If you are a UK resident and a taxpayer you are liable to pay tax on the income. *Accumulation funds:* If the fund accumulates more than 15% of its income UK residents are liable to income tax instead of capital gains tax

on any gain you make when you dispose of your shares or switch to another sub-fund. *Distributor funds:* Capital gains on disposals or switches are liable to capital gains tax but see Chapter 5.

Fees to pay *Initial:* Emma 4%; Global Strategy 5%. *Yearly: (including custodian fees):* Emma .8125%; Global Strategy 0.925%-1.175% .

Passbook None. Statement issued with each transaction.

Children Under 18 shares must be held in an adult's name and may be *designated* with the child's initials.

Risk High. The price of units fluctuates down as well as up. Only invest in *recognised* funds - see page 44.

How to invest Phone or write for details; ask for a prospectus and read it carefully. If you are investing a large amount, say, £30,000 or more, ask for a reduced initial charge. You can buy and sell by phone. Magazines like *Money Management* list funds and performance. Also see the *Financial Times* Offshore Funds page for prices, yields and *recognised* funds.

Where from *Recognised Distributor:* Guinness Flight Global Strategy (Sub-funds: Global Bond, Global High Income Bond, European Bond, European High Income Bond, US$ Bond, Yen Bond, Asian Currency & Bond). Hambros Emma (Sub-funds: Continental European Bond, N. American Bond, Japanese Bond, Australasian Dollar Bond).

Offshore Stock and Bond Fund is a relatively risky investment because you can make or lose money from changes in exchange rates as well as changes in interest rates.

PENSION

Buy Out Bond

(Also called Transfer Plan 32, Job Changers Pension Fund , Early Leaver Bond)

If you leave your job for a new one or are made redundant, you can transfer the value of your pension rights from your job scheme to an individual fund where the money accumulates tax free until retirement, normally to the age when you would have retired at your former job. At retirement, when you start the pension, you can take part as a lump sum. Schemes have bonuses added (like *Life Insurance With-Profits Endowment*), are linked to a unit fund (like *Life Insurance Mixed Bond* or *Life Insurance Property Bond*) or give a fixed return.

Who can invest An employee who has left a job pension scheme. You can only put in money transferred from a previous job pension fund.

How worthwhile This depends on what terms you are offered as an alternative, either by the pension scheme you are leaving, or if you are joining a new scheme with a new job, what terms your new employer offers. If you want to transfer to your own individual scheme, consider instead *Pension Personal Pension* which gives you a choice of starting to receive the pension between age 50 and 75 whether or not you retire.

Maximum None.

Suitable Lump sums.

Money back As pension and lump sum starting on retirement until you die. Widows' or dependants' pensions are available and you can choose between a level pension or a (lower) rising pension. If you die before you start the pension, the value of your money then plus any interest may be returned .

Interest Variable (except non profit

schemes which say at the outset what you will get). Income is accumulated.

Interest paid When the scheme matures at retirement age, mostly as a pension. See also *Money back* in the previous column.

Tax There is no tax on the lump sum you receive nor on the interest or capital gains accumulated. The pension is taxed as earned income.

Fees to pay Charges are deducted from your investment. With schemes which add bonuses, the charges are hidden. With unit linked policies the charges may be disclosed, say ½% to 9% initially, usually ¾% to 1¼% yearly. You may be able to negotiate a reduction for a large investment.

Passbook None. Policy issued.

Children Not eligible.

Risk Depends on the investment to which the scheme is linked. Run by life insurance companies which are UK authorised and covered by a 90% compensation scheme.

How to invest Ask an independent financial adviser specialising in pensions to help you choose.

Where from Life insurance companies

Instead of transferring to a Buy Out Bond, you can usually transfer the money from a job pension to a Personal Pension. A Personal Pension will normally give better results than a Buy Out Bond for younger employees and is more flexible. Get advice before you decide. The Occupational Pensions Advisory Service is a charity which can advise job changers on problems related to pension transfers but it cannot give financial advice.

PENSION

❀ Director's Pension

(Also called Executive Pension, Top Hat Pension)

A means of saving towards a pension starting between ages 50 and 75 of up to 2/3rds of your salary at retirement after 20 years if you own and work for your own company. Also for senior executives to give them a special pension. You can take part of it as a lump sum at retirement. Schemes have bonuses added (like *Life Insurance With-Profits Endowment Policy*), are linked to a unit fund (like *Life Insurance Mixed Bond* or *Life Insurance Property Bond*) or give a fixed return.

Who can invest Company directors and senior executives. It is most tax efficient if the scheme is *non-contributory* ie the employer makes contributions not the director or executive.

How worthwhile Good value for taxpayers who want a pension and lump sum starting at age 50 to 75. Consider schemes as follows: 5 yrs or less to retirement, non-profit or cash fund; 6-10 yrs, with-profits or cash fund; 11+ yrs as for 6-10 yrs plus mixed, equity or property linked fund.

Minimum *Single stand alone:* £250 to £7,500 but some companies only allow a single premium as an add-on to a regular contract; *single add-on to regular:* None to £2,500. *Regular:* £20 to £100 a month.

Maximum How much an employer can contribute depends on your earnings and how much pension you have accumulated so far; it can range from nil to 51% of earnings. A director or employee can pay 15% of earnings up to £78,600 for 1995-96 tax year; the maximum pension is based on the same amount; this applies to new members of existing schemes or new schemes since 14 March 1989.

Suitable Lump sums. Regular savings.

Money back As a pension and lump sum between age 50 and 75 until you die (or with a minimum fixed period of, say, 5-10 years). Widows pensions also available. If you die before you start the pension, the value of fund or premiums with interest, depending on the company, is returned subject to certain restrictions.

Interest Variable (except non-profit schemes which say at the outset what you will get). Income is accumulated.

Interest paid When policy matures mostly as a pension. See *Money back* above.

Tax There is no tax on the lump sum you receive nor on the interest or capital gain accumulated. The pension is taxed as earnings. Contributions get full tax relief.

Fees to pay Charges deducted in many ways. Reductions for large amounts.

Passbook None. Pension document issued. Statements sent.

Children Not eligible.

Risk Depends on the investment to which the policy is linked. Run by life insurance companies which are UK authorised and covered by a 90% compensation scheme.

How to invest For detailed information on all plans, see *Executives' & Directors' Pensions* Financial Times Business Information. Ask an independent financial adviser specialising in pensions for help.

Where from *Regular premium with-profits:* A specialist independent adviser. *Regular premium unit-linked:* Equitable Life, Professional Life, Provident Life (through an adviser) plus other companies which offer low charges if low or no commission paid.

PENSION

Free Standing Top Up Plan

(Also called FSAVC, Free Standing Additional Voluntary Contributions)

A commitment to make extra contributions to raise the pension you get when you retire. You are only eligible if you already belong to a job pension scheme. The extra pension you get from *Pension Free Standing Top Up Plan* is based on how much you have paid and the interest and/or capital gains on the investments in which your contributions are placed. Schemes have bonuses added (like *Life Insurance With-Profits Endowment Policy*), are linked to a unit fund (like *Life Insurance Mixed Bond* or *Life Insurance Property Bond*) or to a unit trust or give a fixed return.

Who can invest Anyone in a job pension scheme.

How worthwhile Good value for taxpayers who want a larger pension than the one they will earn under their job scheme. Mainly of interest to people with up to 15 years to retirement age. Compare with *Pension In-house Top Up Plan* (if your employer offers one).

Minimum £10-£100 a month; usually £20 -£30. £250-£1,000 single. No minimum at Rothschild Asset Management.

Maximum The total amount of your normal and top up contributions to your job pension scheme must not be more than 15% of your pay from that job with a maximum normally of 15% of £78,600 for 1995-96 tax year. The top up contributions can either be a fixed amount (eg £50 a month) or a % of salary (so when your salary rises so do your contributions). Your pension on retirement from your job scheme and from your top up contributions can normally be up to two thirds of your salary just before you retire.

Suitable Regular savings.

Money back As a pension (*no* lump sum) starting at the retirement age for your job pension scheme and continuing until you die (or with a guaranteed period of say 5-10 years). Widows pensions also available. If you die before you start the pension, the value of the fund or your contributions, usually with interest, is returned. If you move to another job you can continue making contributions to the same *Pension Free Standing Top Up Plan*.

Interest paid When you reach pension age as a pension. See also *Money back* above.

Tax None on the interest or capital gain accumulated. The pension is taxed as earnings. Contributions get full tax relief

Fees to pay Life insurance companies: Charges are deducted in different ways and can be very high. Reductions for large contributions.

Passbook None. Statements sent.

Children Not eligible.

Risk Depends on the investment in which the contributions are placed.

How to invest For detailed information on all plans, see *Top Up Pension Plans* published by Financial Times Business Information.

Where from *Unit trust:* Rothschild Asset Management. *Life companies unit-linked:* Equitable Life, Professional Life, Provident Life (through an adviser). *With-profits:* Seek advice from an independent financial adviser.

For more advice on pension planning turn to Chapter 9.

PENSION

In-House Top Up Plan

(Also called Additional Voluntary Contributions, AVC, In-house AVC)

A commitment to make extra contributions to raise the pension you get from your job when you retire. Your main job pension usually depends on how many years you have been in the scheme and your salary at or near retirement; but the extra pension from *Pension In-house Top Up Plan* is usually based on how much you have paid and the interest and/or capital gains on the investments in which your contributions are placed. Schemes can be invested in a building society or with a life or unit trust company.

Who can invest Anyone in a job pension scheme.

How worthwhile Good value for taxpayers who want a larger pension than the one they have earned under their job scheme. Mainly of interest to people with 15 years or less to retirement age. Compare with *Pension Free Standing Top Up Plan.*

Minimum Around £10 a month.

Maximum The total amount of your normal and top up contributions to your job pension scheme must not be more than 15% of your pay from that job with a maximum normally of 15% of £78,600 for 1995-96 tax year. The top up contributions can either be a fixed amount (eg £50 a month) or a % of salary (so when your salary rises so do your contributions). Your pension on retirement from your job scheme and from your top up contributions can normally be up to two thirds of your salary just before you retire.

Suitable Regular savings.

Money back As a pension (*no* lump sum) starting at the retirement age for your job pension scheme and continuing until you die (or for a guaranteed period of say,

5-10 years) or until your surviving spouse dies. If you die before you start the pension, contributions returned, usually with interest. If you lose your job or move to another, you stop contributions and extra pension is based on what has accumulated so far plus interest; or you can transfer to a new employer or to a *Pension Personal Pension* or a *Pension Buy Out Bond*. With a life insurance scheme there may be a penalty for job changers.

Interest Variable or fixed.

Interest paid When you reach the pension age of your job. See also *Money back* in the previous column.

Tax None on the interest or capital gain accumulated. The pension is taxed as earnings. Contributions get full tax relief.

Fees to pay Building societies make no charges. Life insurance companies: Charges are deducted in different ways and can be very high.

Passbook None. Statements sent.

Children Not eligible.

Risk Depends on the investment in which the contributions are placed.

How to invest Your employer invests for you in a building society, life insurance company or unit trust.

Where from Ask your employer. Building society schemes often offer the best value if you only have a few years before retirement. You have to use a scheme offered by your employer. Employers wanting to set up a scheme, can get detailed information on all plans from *Top Up Pension Plans* published by Financial Times Business Information.

PENSION

❀ Personal Pension

(Also called Self-Employed Pension)

A means of saving towards a pension starting between ages 50 and 75 if you are self-employed or are not in a job pension scheme. You can take 25% of the accumulated pension fund as a lump sum when you start the pension. *Personal Pensions* have bonuses added (like *Life Insurance With-Profits Endowment Policy*), are linked to a unit fund (like *Life Insurance Mixed Bond* or *Life Insurance Property Bond*) or to a unit trust or give a fixed return.

Who can invest The self-employed or employees not in a job pension scheme or who wish to leave a job pension.

How worthwhile Good value for tax-payers who want a pension and lump sum starting at age 50 to 75. Consider schemes as follows: 5 yrs or less to retirement, non-profit or cash fund; 6-10 yrs, with-profits or cash fund; 11+ yrs as for 6-10 yrs plus mixed, equity or property linked fund.

Minimum None at Rothschild Asset Management. *Single stand alone:* £250-£2,000. *Single addition to a regular plan:* £100-£250. *Regular:* £20-£25+ a month.

Maximum Based on your earnings of up to £78,600 in 1995-96. Relief ranges from 17½% to 40% of earnings depending on age, see Table in Chapter 9.

Suitable Lump sums. Regular savings.

Money back As a lump sum and pension starting between ages 50 and 75 until you die (or with a guaranteed period of, say, 5-10 years). From a date in 1995, you will be able to cash part of the fund early but this will be taxed as income. Widows pensions available. If you die before you start the pension, the value of the fund or your contributions with interest, depending on the company, is returned.

Interest Variable except non-profit schemes where return fixed at the outset. Income is accumulated.

Interest paid When policy matures mostly as a pension. See also *Money back* in the previous column.

Tax No tax on the lump sum nor on the interest or capital gain accumulated. The pension is taxed as earnings. Contributions get full tax relief, see Chapter 9.

Fees to pay Charges are deducted in different ways and can be very high. Reductions for large contributions.

Passbook Pension contract. Statements.

Children Not usually eligible.

Risk Depends on the investment to which the policy is linked. UK life companies have The Policyholders Protection Act. Unit Trusts have The Investors Compensation Scheme, see Chapter 6.

How to invest Ask an independent financial adviser or the companies listed below for quotes. See also *Personal Pensions* published by *Financial Times*.

Where from *Investment trusts:* Foreign & Colonial *Unit trusts:* INVESCO, Rothschild Asset Management. *Life companies:* Equitable Life, Professional Life, Provident Life (through an adviser). Or ask an independent financial adviser.

If you hold a Retirement Annuity, which is like a Personal Pension, slightly different rules apply - see Chapter 9.

PROPERTY

Commercial Direct Investment

You buy commercial property (ie a shop, offices, warehouse, factory) which is already let on a lease to a tenant or tenants and you receive rent as an income. A commercial lease usually provides for rent reviews every 3, 4, 5 or 7 years depending on the lease, at which time you may be able to negotiate an increase. You can borrow all or part of the money you wish to invest and interest on the money borrowed is eligible for tax relief (from 6 April 1995 including property abroad) though only against rents from the property you buy and other property you own.

Who can invest Anyone 18 or over.

How worthwhile Potentially good value for taxpayers who don't want to sacrifice current income but want protection against inflation. In the past commercial rents have usually kept up with inflation and in some areas exceeded it. Commercial property within the means of most investors is called *secondary property;* it is located in less good locations, is often let to small businesses who may not always pay the rent and where there may be difficulty finding a new tenant if premises are vacated. To compensate *secondary property* shows a better return than *primary property.* Before tax rental returns of 10%-14% on the initial investment can be found. When you sell, if the rents have gone up, you can also expect to make a capital gain. Compare with *Property Enterprise Zone Trust.* Too expensive for non-taxpayers and 20% taxpayers.

Minimum £30,000 upwards. Less if you borrow to buy.

Maximum None.

Suitable Lump sums.

Money back You can sell your property when you wish but finding a buyer may be difficult. Sometimes a tenant or adjoining landlord will be interested or someone may approach you.

Interest You get an income from the rent. This can be paid by standing order or you can employ *managing agents* to collect it for 7%-15% of the rent; they will also act as a buffer between you and the tenants. Rent reviews usually provide increases.

Interest paid Usually quarterly or monthly. Best to get tenants to pay by monthly standing order.

Tax The rent after deduction of expenses (eg interest, agent's fees and repairs not paid for by tenants) is liable to income tax but no tax is deducted unless you live abroad. See also Chapter 4. When you sell or give the property away, the gain is liable to capital gains tax, see Chapter 5.

Fees to pay Legal costs when you buy or sell of £250-£700. 1% stamp duty when you buy. Estate agent's costs for negotiating rent review or new lease, 10% of rent. Agent's costs when you sell 1%-2%. VAT on all except stamp duty.

Children Normally unsuitable; property may be held by a trust.

Risk Moderate. The investment is not easily sold so you should only put in money you won't need for a long time. If tenants stop paying rent, you may have extra legal expenses.

How to invest Advice from commercial estate agents in the locality you want to invest in. Look for adverts in newspapers - and magazines like *Estates Gazette.*

PROPERTY

Enterprise Zone Trust

A means of investing in new commercial property (ie shops, offices, warehouses, factories) situated in designated areas called Enterprise Zones. You get a 100% Capital Allowance on your investment excluding land costs which means you get tax relief on about 95% of the money invested. The trust has a maximum 25 year life after which the assets are sold. You can borrow money to invest in the trust - and interest on money borrowed is also eligible for tax relief though only against rents from the trust and other rents.

Who can invest Anyone 18 or over.

How worthwhile Potentially good value for higher rate taxpayers. Compare with *Property Commercial Direct Investment*.

Minimum £5,000.

Maximum None.

Suitable Lump sums.

Money back After 25 years or sooner. You can sell your investment before then but there may be a tax *balancing charge* to pay. If you give away the investment or die, the balancing charge can be *rolled over* to the person who receives the investment. If the majority of investors agree, the property can be sold after 7 years without a tax *clawback*.

Interest The trust pays an income from the rents it receives on the properties. The rent should rise but may slow down later when the Enterprise Zones in which the property is situated cease to be Enterprise Zones and have their special concessions, like no rates for 10 years, withdrawn.

Interest paid Usually quarterly.

Tax You get full income tax relief on your investment but land costs are not tax allowable, so you normally get around 95% income tax relief. The rent you receive is liable to income tax but tax is not usually deducted. Taxpayers have to pay tax later, see Chapter 4. When you sell, any gain is liable to capital gains tax, see also Chapter 5.

Fees to pay Charges are around 5%-7% of the money you invest paid by the developer, plus up to around ¼% a year, paid by the trust.

Passbook None. Share certificate issued.

Children Normally unsuitable.

Risk Moderate. The investment is not easily sold so you should only put in money you won't need for a long time. A pre-let property to a good tenant like a Government department makes it much less risky.

How to invest Shares are offered for a limited period often in the period January to March. Notify a financial adviser that you are interested to ensure you hear of llaunches as advertising is restricted.

Where from Ask the Enterprise Zone Property Unit Trust Association for names of sponsors. Ask a financial adviser, solicitor or accountant to get details.

A higher rate taxpayer can make this investment with no cash outlay. You invest £10,000, get tax relief of £4,000 and borrow £6,000. You have an investment worth £9,000 (after charges) but you have a £6,000 loan so your net investment is £3,000 for which you have paid nothing. The interest, say £800 a year, should be largely covered by the trust income £600 a year.

PROPERTY

Ground Rents

You buy the *freehold* of residential property (ie houses and blocks of flats) or commercial property (ie shops, offices, warehouses, factories) which are already let on a long lease with many years still to run (usually 30 to 125 years). You usually receive a fixed low rent in relation to the value of the building. Tenants either occupy the property or let it to other tenants. You can either hold the ground rents for income or hope to sell to individual tenants or to a group of them at a profit. With residential property tenants have the right to extend their lease (flats) or buy the freehold (houses) at the market value. Sometimes you have the duty to organise the insurance and maintenance of the property.

Who can invest Anyone 18 or over.

How worthwhile Potentially good value for non-taxpayers, 20% taxpayers and basic taxpayers because the income is usually high in relation to the investment and does not fall when interest rates fall. No protection against inflation except for commercial property when your children or grandchildren inherit the *reversion,* the right to demand the market rent, when the lease expires. Compare with *Life Insurance Annuity.* Unsuitable for higher rate taxpayers; consider *Property Commercial Direct* instead.

Minimum £250 for a £50 year ground rent; £1,000 to £1,500 for a small block of 5 flats with ground rents of £50 a flat; £10,000 for a commercial property with a ground rent of £1,500 a year.

Maximum None.

Suitable Lump sums.

Money back Finding a buyer may not be easy. Often sold at auctions.

Interest You usually get a fixed income from the rent. This can be paid by standing order or you can employ *managing agents* to collect it and organise the insurance and maintenance, if applicable; they will charge around 10% of the rent and act as a buffer between you and the tenants.

Interest paid Usually yearly, half-yearly or quarterly in advance.

Tax Rent after deduction of expenses (eg agent's fees and repairs not paid for by tenants) is liable to income tax but no tax is normally deducted. Taxpayers have to pay tax later. You get full income tax relief on any interest paid on a loan to buy a property provided it is less than all your rents. See also Chapter 4. When you sell or give the property away, the gain may be liable to capital gains tax but see Chapter 5.

Fees to pay Legal costs when you buy would make most purchases not worthwhile: you would therefore have to do it yourself. Estate agent's costs of management about 10% of rent. Possible auctioneer's costs when you sell of up to 5%.

Children Children can eventually benefit from the *reversion.* See Chapter 11 for the different types of trust you can set up.

Risk Moderate. The investment is not easily sold so you should only put in money you will never need in a hurry. If tenants stop paying rent, you may have extra legal expense.

How to invest Look for auctions in the newspapers and magazines like *Estates Gazette.*

PROPERTY

Residential Direct Investment

You buy residential property (eg a house, flat or small block of flats) which you let to a tenant or tenants and you receive rent as an income. A residential lease usually lasts 1 to 5 years and can have rent reviews depending on what is agreed in the lease. Rents on new lettings are not regulated by the government; rents on some tenancies which started before are. However, if you don't follow the proper procedures you can find yourself with a tenant whom you are unable to get rid of which will lower the resale value of the property.

Who can invest Anyone 18 or over.

How worthwhile Good value for taxpayers if you don't mind the problems of being a residential landlord. The value of residential property is related to residential property in general, not to the rent which you can command. The return is generally lower than with *Property Commercial Direct Investment*. However the property is easier to sell vacant than commercial property.

Minimum £30,000 upwards. Less if you borrow to buy.

Maximum None.

Suitable Lump sums.

Money back You can sell your property. You will get a better price if it is vacant.

Interest You get an income from the rent. This can be paid by standing order or you can employ *managing agents* to collect it at around 10% of the rent; they will also at as a buffer between you and the tenants.

Interest paid Usually monthly.

Tax The rent after deduction of expenses

(eg agent's fees, repairs, utilities not paid for by tenants) is liable to income tax but no tax is deducted unless you live abroad. Taxpayers have to pay tax later. You get full income tax relief on any interest paid on a loan to buy a property provided it is less than all your rents. See also Chapter 4. When you sell or give the property away the gain is liable to capital gains tax see Chapter 5.

Fees to pay Legal costs when you buy or sell of £250-£700; 1% stamp duty when you buy. Estate agent's costs of management about 10% of rent. Estate agent's costs for finding new tenants 10% of rent. Estate agents will provide a standard lease or you can buy one from a legal stationers. Estate agents costs when you sell around 2%. VAT on all except stamp duty.

Children Unsuitable directly but property may be held by a trust.

Risk Moderate. The investment is not easily sold. If tenants stop paying rent, you may have extra legal expense.

How to invest Get advice from more than one firm of residential rental estate agents in the locality in which you want to invest. Certain types of properties which are less attractive to owner occupiers (eg on main roads) cost much less to buy but can still be rented. However such properties may be more difficult to sell and appreciate by less if house prices start to rise again.

Where from Estate agents.

SHARES

Enterprise Investment Scheme

A means of investing in the shares of businesses not listed by the Stock Exchange and obtaining tax relief at 20% (plus possibly up to 40% capital gains tax relief) on the money you invest. Your money buys new *unquoted* shares in companies which are usually recently formed and don't have to meet the conditions for those traded on the Stock Exchange. Only a few shares may be available to the public; the rest are kept by the people who run the company. You should choose individual shares in at least 7 to 10 companies to spread your risk. Your money is tied up for about 6 years.

Who can invest Anyone 18 or over not 'connected' with the businesses invested in by the fund.

How worthwhile There is a high chance of failure. The 20% income tax relief is probably insufficient to make this scheme attractive to most people. Consider instead *Shares Venture Capital Trust* which may be less risky.

Minimum £14,000-£20,000 for a portfolio of EIS shares bought for say £2,000 each in 7-10 companies. Lower amounts much riskier because of the lack of a diversified portfolio.

Maximum £100,000 for all investments in all schemes in each tax year.

Suitable Lump sums.

Money back You should be able to sell the shares after you have held them for 5 years; if you invest in a fund there may be a delay after you have invested but before the shares are bought of about 6 months.

Interest None. By the time the shares start to pay dividends, you will normally want to sell. You hope to make a capital gain by selling for more than you paid.

Tax You get income tax relief on your investment at 20%. If you have made a taxable capital gain on anything else after 29 November 1994 (a similar relief can apply after 30 November 1993) you can defer the gains tax on it if you invest the amount of the taxable gain in an Enterprise Investment Scheme. This can raise your tax relief to a maximum of 20% plus 40% equals 60%. When you sell the shares after 5 years, you are exempt from capital gains tax if you make a gain on the Enterprise Investment Scheme but any gain you deferred has to have tax paid on it at the then rate. If you make a loss, the loss can be set against either income tax or capital gains tax (eg the deferred gain) unless Enterprise Investment Scheme relief is withdrawn.

Fees to pay The launch costs are equivalent to an initial fee of 2% to 7%.

Passbook None. Share certificate.

Children Unsuitable.

Risk Very high. Some shares usually go bust. It is hoped that the rest more than make up for this. As there is no trustee to look after your money, only invest in a scheme sponsored by an established financial body. You may be unable to sell the shares when you want.

How to invest Get advice from a magazine, newspaper, stockbroker or independent financial adviser on which shares to choose. Shares tend to be limited issue.

Where from The Enterprise Investment & BES Association will send you a list of members.

SHARES

Open Ended Investment Fund

You invest in shares which closely reflect the value of the shares or other assets held within the fund. Open ended investment funds are managed by professionals. You are buying shares in a company, but they otherwise work in a similar way to unit trusts. They differ from *Investment Trust Shares* in that the number of shares in issue are increased or decreased at will by the managers in response to demand as they are with a *Unit Trust.* This is a new type of investment which will probably not become available before 1996. Unit trusts will be able to convert themselves into this type of investment.

Who can invest Anyone.

How worthwhile Potentially good value as a long-term investment for taxpayers if you buy and sell at the right time; poor value if you don't. High charges may make them unattractive. Consider instead *Investment Trust Shares, Unit Trust Index Tracker.*

Minimum Likely to be £500, £1,000 or £5,000.

Maximum None.

Suitable Lump sums.

Money back Usually up to 5 working days after you sell at the market price.

Interest Variable. Called *dividend* or *distribution.* Some funds don't pay interest. You hope to make a capital gain by selling for more than you buy; you may lose money.

Interest paid Often half-yearly by cheque to you or direct to a bank account or accumulated.

Tax 20% tax is deducted from the distribution (called a *tax credit)* whether or not you accumulate it. Non-taxpayers can reclaim the tax from the Inland Revenue Higher rate taxpayers have to pay extra; basic and 20% taxpayers don't. You can avoid this tax by investing through a *Personal Equity Plan.* Gains on shares are liable to capital gains tax (see Chapter 5) although the managers pay no capital gains tax if they make gains on shares held by the fund.

Fees to pay Initial charge: up to 6%. Yearly charge likely to be around 1½% deducted from your income.

Passbook None. Certificate issued.

Children Under 18 shares should be held in an adult's name and can be *designated* with the child's name or initials.

Risk High but not as risky as buying individual shares. The value of shares goes down as well as up.

How to invest There are likely to be lots of new offers advertised. Read press comment on them.

Where from See press advertisements. They will be marketed by existing unit trust and investment trust groups.

SHARES

Ordinary Quoted

Lump sum invested directly in the shares of a company which are *quoted*, **that is bought and sold in the Stock Exchange. You usually receive an income (which you hope will rise but can fall) and hope to make a capital gain by selling for more than you paid (but you may end up with a loss by selling for less). If the company you invest in goes bust, you will lose all your money which is why it is best to** *diversify* **and spread your money in a portfolio of 7 to 16 or more different shares. For more on investing in shares, see Chapter 8.**

Who can invest Anyone.

How worthwhile Potentially good value as a long-term investment for taxpayers if you choose the right shares and buy and sell at the right time; poor value if you don't. Alternatively you can invest through a *Shares Unit Trust* or *Shares Investment Trust* or (subject to the maximum) through *Shares Self Select Personal Equity Plan.*

Minimum £14,000-£20,000 for a portfolio of shares bought for say £2,000 each in 7-10 companies. Lower amounts not worthwhile because of minimum commission and lack of a diversified portfolio.

Maximum None.

Suitable Lump sums.

Money back 10 working days (5 days from 26 June 1995). You get the market price at the time you sell.

Interest Variable. Called *dividend.* The before-tax interest is called the *yield* which varies between different companies and different types of companies.

Interest paid Usually half-yearly by cheque to you or direct to a bank account.

About 5 weeks before the dividend date the shares go *ex-dividend,* this means the seller gets the next dividend, not the buyer.

Tax 20% tax is deducted from the dividend (called a tax *credit).* Non-taxpayers can reclaim the tax from the Inland Revenue. Higher rate taxpayers have to pay extra; basic and 20% taxpayers don't. Gains on shares are liable to capital gains tax, see Chapter 5.

Fees to pay When you buy, stockbrokers commission varies: 1% to 1.9% on first £5,000; then usually ½%; min. £15 to £30; stamp duty ½%. No commission or stamp duty on new issue. When you sell, commission only.

Passbook Share certificate issued.

Children Under 18 shares must be held in an adult's name but can be *designated* with a child's name or initials.

Risk High. The value of shares goes down as well as up.

How to invest You can choose shares by doing your own research or get advice from a stockbroker or the press. Stockbrokers or professional managers will make the choice for you. Buy and sell by phone to a stockbroker.

Where from A stockbroker. Your bank will introduce you to its own stockbrokers. For other brokers phone or write to the Pro-Share for a copy of the *Private Investors Directory.* Commission rates vary: choose one with the lowest commission rate at the value of shares you are likely to buy and sell at.

SHARES

Preference

Lump sum invested in a special type of share in a company quoted on the stock market at a fixed rate of interest. There is no fixed life for the shares which may be bought and sold at any time for the market price through a stockbroker. You may make or lose money when you sell. If the company you invest in goes bust, you will probably lose all your money. They are more like a Stock than a Share.

Who can invest Anyone aged 18 or over.

How worthwhile Good value for non-taxpayers, 20% and basic rate taxpayers either direct or through a Unit Trust specialising in Preference Shares provided interest rates don't rise after you buy in which case they may become poor value. Compare with *Stock Debenture and Loan* or *Stock Government Fixed-Interest.* Unsuitable for higher rate taxpayers.

Minimum £2,000. £500-£1,000 if you invest via a Unit Trust.

Maximum None but some shares are in short supply and a £10,000 maximum in any one share would be sensible.

Suitable Lump sums.

Money back 10 working days (5 days from 26 June 1995). You get the market price at the time you sell.

Interest High and fixed (variable through a unit trusts). Called *dividend.* If a company runs short of money, interest can be reduced or stopped. *Cumulative* preference shares must have their arrears paid later (but interest is not paid on arrears); non-cumulative ones need not. The *yield* of the shares varies according to the market price of the shares.

Interest paid Half-yearly by cheque to you or direct to a bank account. About 5 weeks before the dividend is paid, the shares go *ex-dividend* when the seller gets the next dividend, not the buyer.

Tax 20% rate tax is deducted from the dividend (called a *tax credit*). Non-taxpayers can reclaim the tax credit from the Inland Revenue. Higher rate tax-payers have to pay extra; basic and 20% taxpayers don't. Gains on shares are liable to capital gains tax, see Chapter 5.

Fees to pay *Through a unit trust:* 3% to 5¼% initial, ¾% to 1¼% yearly. *If you buy the shares direct:* Stockbrokers commission varies: 1% to 1.9%; stamp duty ½% Commission only when you sell.

Passbook No. Share certificate issued.

Children Under 18 shares or trusts are registered in an adult's name but can be *designated* with a child's initials or name.

Risk The company whose preference shares you own can stop paying interest or go bust so it is safer to invest in a Unit Trust which specialises in them. Possible capital loss if interest rates rise and the price of your shares or units falls.

How to invest Get advice from a stockbroker (your bank or accountant will introduce you to one)or contact a unit trust group.

Where from *Through a unit trust:* Edinburgh, Gartmore, Henderson Touche Remnant, Prolific, Thornton. *Direct:* A stockbroker.

The nominal interest on preference shares is quoted net of a 20% tax credit. Basic rate taxpayers and 20% taxpayers don't have to pay extra tax; higher rate taxpayers have to pay 20% extra. Non-taxpayers can reclaim the tax credit.

SHARES

❋ SAYE Share Option

(Also called Share Save, SAYE Series F)

A commitment to save a fixed monthly amount deducted from your pay by your employer for 5 years when you are paid a bonus. If you keep the money in for 2 more years, another bonus is added. When you join, you are given the option to buy a fixed number of shares in your company at the end of the 5 or 7 years. The number of shares is the amount your total savings, with or without the bonus depending on the rules of the company, could buy at the price (or 80% of it) when you started to save 5 or 7 years earlier. Up to 6 payments may be delayed: your contract is then extended by the same number of months. If you change employers, you lose the right to buy the shares but may continue saving.

Who can invest Anyone age 16 or over whose company runs a scheme and who has been an employee for long enough, eg. 2 to 5 years.

How worthwhile Good value. Possibly, excellent value if your company's shares go up over the 5 or 7 years you are saving.

Minimum £10 a month.

Maximum £250 a month.

Suitable Regular savings.

Money back In 2 to 3 weeks. No partial withdrawals. During the first year money back with no interest. During years 1-5: 3% interest. Completed savings withdrawn between years 5 to 7 receive the 5 year bonus plus 3% interest. If you retire, are made redundant, or become permanently disabled and leave, you can normally cash-in and buy some shares.

Interest Fixed. Series F which is currently under review: Equivalent to 5.53% a year over 5 years. If left another 2 years a further bonus is paid. The average return over 7 years is 5.87% a year. At the outset you choose to save for 5 or 7 years. Then you can either take the proceeds, buy the shares and immediately resell them at a gain if they have risen in value or you can hold the shares and sell later.

Interest paid When you withdraw. Possible gain on shares when you sell. Dividends on shares if you keep them.

Tax Interest on SAYE is tax free. Any gain on the difference between the option and the current price of the shares is free of income tax. If you hold the shares and sell later, there may be capital gains tax on the gain over the market price at the time you bought, see Chapter 5.

Fees to pay None.

Passbook SAYE certificate and share option document issued. Share certificate if you buy the shares.

Children Not eligible.

Risk None. Full value of original savings returned on withdrawal. Once you buy the shares, unless you sell at once, the risk is more than with *Shares Ordinary Quoted* if you only hold shares in one company.

How to invest Your employer must agree to run a scheme and have it approved by the Inland Revenue.

Where from Your employer. Most large building societies and some banks offer an identical SAYE contract (eg Halifax, Abbey National, Nationwide, Woolwich, Bradford & Bingley).

SHARES

❀ Self Select Personal Equity Plan

(Also called PEP, Share Purchase Plan, Blue Chip Portfolio, Equi-Plan)

A means of investing up to £6,000 a year in UK shares free of tax plus £3,000 each year in a single share (it can be a different share each year). You choose which shares to buy and sell and when (any share with most managers). You can hold money in cash while deciding where and when to invest.

Who can invest Anyone 18 or over. Joint plans are not allowed but husband and wife can have one each. In any one tax year you can only invest in one Personal Equity Plan from one manager plus a separate plan for a single share.

How worthwhile Good value for taxpayers, especially higher rate taxpayers. Best suited to a few shares. If you want someone else to choose the shares or you wish to invest less than the maximum, consider instead *Investment Trust Personal Equity Plan or Unit Trust Personal Equity Plan.* Poor value for non-taxpayers.

Minimum Usually £1,000 to £6,000 a year. Minimum in one share £1,500 to £3,000. None at Killik.

Maximum £6,000 plus £3,000 in a single share plus managers' charges. You have a choice of using your £6,000 limit instead on a fixed interest investment, see *Stock Personal Equity Plan.*

Suitable Lump sums.

Money back Any time. If you die the plan ends.

Interest Variable. Called *dividend.* The before tax interest is called the *yield* and shares which show the highest yield are most attractive as they make the most use of the tax exemption. Money on deposit awaiting investment is also tax free. The single share PEP must be invested within a few weeks but otherwise you can leave money on deposit indefinitely (you have to invest in shares before you cash, however).

Interest paid Your choice to accumulate within the plan or paid by cheque to you or to a bank account.

Tax Dividend income and capital gains are completely tax free and need not be entered on a tax return. Any tax deducted from dividends is reclaimed by the PEP manager on your behalf.

Fees to pay Initially none to 5% or £25 to £75; yearly nil to 1½% but not on those listed here. Commission on shares bought and sold 1%-1.85% (minimum nil to £40). Killik & Co charges commission on deals plus £7.50 for each dividend collected. Pilling has choice of fee of £6.75 for each dividend collected. or ½% a year fee (minimum £10). Alliance Trust has fee of £1 or £25 for each purchase or sale, £5-£10 for each withdrawal.

Passbook None. Statements sent.

Children Not allowed.

Risk High. You should have a balanced portfolio of at least 7-10 shares in and out of the PEP unless you buy investment trusts.

How to invest Contact a manager below.

Where from Alliance Trust Savings, Killik & Co, Pilling & Co. Also available from many banks and stockbrokers - but usually with a yearly charge as well as dealing costs.

If you don't want to choose your own shares, consider Investment Trust Personal Equity Plan or Unit Trust Personal Equity Plan instead.

SHARES

Traded Options

(Also called Options, Equity Options)

You invest in a contract which gives you the right to buy or sell a certain number of shares at a fixed price before the option *expires* in up to 3, 6 or 9 months time for options in shares and 12 months for options on a share index. A contract to buy shares is called a *call option*; a contract to sell shares is called a *put option*. With a call option you make money when the share price rises; with a put option you make money when the price falls. If you take a put and a call option at the same time it is called a *straddle*. You can buy options in 72 popular individual shares - like Allied Lyons, British Gas, HSBC, Marks & Spencer - and also in the FTSE 100 Share Index. You rarely *exercise* the option (ie. buy or sell the shares); to make money you sell the option at a higher price than you bought it for.

Who can invest Anyone 18 or over.

How worthwhile Potentially good value if you like to speculate. You can lose all of your investment very quickly if you predict share prices wrongly. If you are right you can double or treble your money in a short time too. Dealing in options needs regular attention and to deal effectively you probably need access to share and option prices on a screen. These are available on Ceefax and Teletext but may not be completely up to date.

Minimum One contract which is normally 1,000 shares at the option price: £30 to £750 depending on the share chosen. Before you start trading in options your stockbroker will usually expect you to send him a deposit or *margin* to cover some or all of your options.

Maximum None.

Suitable Lump sums.

Money back When you sell the option before its expiry date in up to 3, 6 or 9 months (12 months for an index option). You get the current option price which may be more or less than you paid.

Interest None.

Interest paid Not applicable.

Tax Any profits you make count as capital gains and are taxable - see Chapter 5. Any losses can be set against other capital gains.

Fees to pay Stockbrokers' commission 1½% to 2¾% of what you pay on the 1st £5,000 plus £1.50 to £2.25 per contract; minimum £17 to £40; same when you sell.

Passbook You receive a contract note from your stockbroker giving details of each transaction.

Children Unsuitable.

Risk High .

How to invest For a free booklet and a list of stockbrokers which specialise in traded options, phone or write to Publications Department, LIFFE.

Where from A stockbroker which specialises in options.

You have to be an active investor with options and follow the prices every day - more than once a day when share prices are moving quickly. If you don't have the time or are not prepared to do this, forget them. You can also invest in traded options in government stocks.

SHARES

Unquoted

(Also called Unlisted, Over The Counter ,OTC)

You invest a lump sum in the shares of an *unquoted* company. The shares are bought and sold by stockbrokers who make a market in the shares of their clients. Companies may be recently formed and do not have to meet the conditions for those traded in the Stock Exchange proper. Only a few shares may be available to the public; the rest are kept by the people who run the company. You don't usually receive an income and hope to make a capital gain by selling for more than you paid but you may end up with a loss by selling for less. It is best to invest in a portfolio consisting of shares from between 7 to 16 different companies to spread the risk.

Who can invest Anyone.

How worthwhile You are only likely to want to invest if you know the Directors of the company personally. Similar to *Shares Enterprise Investment Scheme* but without the tax relief. *Shares Ordinary Quoted* are much easier to sell and are less risky. Some investment trusts invest part of their portfolios in unquoted shares. Unsuitable for anyone other than higher rate taxpayers who like to gamble.

Minimum £14,000-£20,000 for a portfolio of unquoted and quoted shares: say £2,000 worth of shares in 7-10 companies. Lower amounts not worthwhile because of minimum commission and lack of diversified portfolio.

Maximum There are limited numbers of shares available to the public in some *unquoted* companies.

Suitable Lump sums.

Money back 10 working days if your stockbroker can find a buyer. You get the market price when you sell. Some shares turn out to be unsaleable.

Interest Variable. Called *dividend.* The before tax interest is called the *yield* which is generally nil.

Interest paid If there is any, usually half-yearly by cheque to you. About 5 weeks before the dividend date, the shares *go ex-dividend;* this means the seller gets the dividend, not the buyer.

Tax 20% tax deducted from the dividend (called a tax *credit).* Higher rate taxpayers have to pay extra; basic and 20% taxpayers don't. Gains on shares are liable to capital gains tax. If you buy *new* shares direct from an unquoted trading company and it later goes bust or the shares are sold realising a loss, you can normally set the loss against your income either in the tax year in which the loss occurred or the next tax year. Alternatively the loss can be set against your capital gains.

Fees to pay Commission when you buy 1%-1.9%, minimum £17 to £30; stamp duty ½%. Commission only when you sell.

Children Unsuitable.

Risk High. Safer to buy a new issue because of tax relief on losses - see *Tax* above.

How to invest These types of shares are best avoided by most people.

Where from A stockbroker.

SHARES

Venture Capital Trust

A means of investing in a special type of Investment Trust and obtaining tax relief at 20% (plus possibly up to 40% capital gains tax relief) on the money you invest. The Venture Capital Trust holds a portfolio of stocks and shares, of which (after 3 years) at least 70% must be in new shares and loan stocks of *unquoted* companies which are usually recently formed and don't have to meet the conditions for those *quoted* on the Stock Exchange. The least risky Trust can have a portfolio (after 3 years) with 50% invested in new ordinary shares of *unquoted* companies, 20% in new loan stocks of *unquoted* companies and 30% in loan stocks or shares in *quoted* companies. Your money is tied up for 5 years; if you sell earlier, you lose the tax relief.

Who can invest Anyone 18 or over.

How worthwhile This is a new form of investment with no track record. There is a high chance of failure of the unquoted companies which the Trust invests in although a Trust may invest in a reasonably large spread of such companies. However most people will only be eligible for 20% tax relief which may not be sufficient to counter the risk being taken.

Minimum Minimum£1,000.

Maximum £100,000 for all investments in all schemes in each tax year.

Suitable Lump sums.

Money back You should be able to sell the shares after you have held them for 5 years.

Interest This will be from the part of the portfolio of the Trust which is invested in *loan stocks* and *quoted* companies. You also hope to make a capital gain by selling for more than you paid.

Tax You get income tax relief on your investment at 20%. If you have made a taxable capital gain on anything else after 5 April 1995, you can generally defer the gains tax on it if you reinvest the amount of the gain in a Venture Capital Trust. This can raise your tax relief to a maximum 60% (20% income tax relief plus 40% capital gains tax relief). When you sell the shares after 5 years, you are exempt from capital gains tax on up to £100,000 a year of money invested in Venture Capital Trusts but any gain you deferred has to have tax paid on it at the then rate. Dividends are exempt from income tax.

Fees to pay The launch costs are equivalent to an initial fee of 2% to 7%.

Passbook None. Share certificate issued.

Children Unsuitable.

Risk Very high. Some shares in the Trust's portfolio are likely to go bust. It is hoped that the rest more than make up for this. As there is no trustee to look after your money, only invest in a scheme sponsored by an established financial body.

How to invest Get advice from a magazine, newspaper, stockbroker or independent financial adviser on which Trust to choose.

Where from Shares in Venture Capital Trusts will be in the form of limited offers.

STOCK

Convertible Loan

Lump sum invested in loan stock issued by a company for a fixed term at a fixed rate of interest where you have the right to convert the stock into *Ordinary Shares* of the company at a fixed price before or between fixed dates in the future. If the stock is not converted, it can continue to pay interest until it is repaid in full at the end of the term just like *Stock Loan and Debenture*. The stock value therefore tends to fluctuate in line with the value of ordinary shares of the company in which there are conversion rights but pays a higher yield. If the shares perform poorly, the value of the stock drops to what it would be if there were no conversion rights.

Who can invest Anyone.

How worthwhile Similar to *Shares Ordinary Quoted* but with a higher income which does not rise (or fall). Worth considering for basic taxpayers who think shares have too low an income. Higher rate taxpayers consider instead *Shares Ordinary Quoted*. Unsuitable for non-taxpayers and 20% taxpayers.

Minimum *Investing direct:* £7,000-£10,000 for a portfolio of stocks (and ordinary shares) bought for say £1,000 each in 7-10 companies. Lower amounts not worthwhile because of minimum commission and lack of a diversified portfolio. *Through a unit trust:* £500 to £1,000 with £50 to £250 additions.

Maximum None.

Suitable Lump sums.

Money back At end of term. Or 10 working days (5 days from June 1995) if you sell earlier when you get the market price; same if you have converted to ordinary shares except you sell the shares. Once converted, there is no longer any fixed term or higher inome.

Interest Fixed. The before tax income is called the *yield* which varies between different companies. It is normally quite a lot higher than the yield on the shares which you have the right to convert to. Once converted the yield is variable.

Interest paid Usually half-yearly by cheque to you or direct to a bank account.

Tax Basic rate tax is deducted from the interest. Non-taxpayers can reclaim the tax from the Inland Revenue. Higher rate taxpayers pay extra. Gains on convertible stocks are liable to capital gains tax but see Chapter 5.

Fees to pay *Investing direct:* when you buy: Stockbrokers commission varies: Around 1½%, min. £15 to £30; plus stamp duty ½%. Commission only when you sell. *Through a unit trust:* 3% to 5¼% initial for trusts listed here. 1% yearly.

Passbook None. Stock certificate issued. If you convert, it is replaced by a share certificate.

Children Under 18 stock should be held in an adult's name and can be designated with the child's name or initials.

Risk Not as high as Ordinary Shares but the value of convertible loan stocks go down as well as up.

How to invest You can invest through a unit trust which specialises in these types of stock or do your own research or get advice from a stockbroker. Buy and sell by phone to stockbroker if they know you.

Where from *Investing direct:* A stockbroker. *Through a unit trust:* Baillie Gifford, Barings, Edinburgh, Framlington, Prolific.

STOCK

Government Fixed Interest

(Also called Gilts, British Government Stock, British Funds)

Lump sum invested in a stock issued by the Government at a fixed interest rate. The stock usually has a fixed life at the end of which (the *redemption date*) the *nominal value* of 100 is repaid in full; it can be bought and sold at any time at the market price. The yearly return you get, called the *net redemption yield,* is the after tax interest you receive plus the averaged out gain (or loss) you expect. Many stocks will show no gain to redemption as they currently stand above the nominal value of 100.

Who can invest Anyone.

How worthwhile Different stocks are good for different rate taxpayers. Often good value for non-taxpayers and higher rate taxpayers. Can be good value for basic and 20% taxpayers, especially for small amounts. Stocks maturing in over 10 years or *undated* (eg. War Loan) not recommended. If you want to invest for longer or if you are a higher rate taxpayer, consider *Stock Government Index Linked.*

Minimum None through the National Savings Stock Register. Around £5,000 through a stockbroker because of minimum commission.

Maximum None. But each purchase bought through the National Savings Stock Register must not exceed £25,000 in any one stock in any one day. No maximum on sales.

Suitable Lump sums.

Money back At the redemption date. Or 2 working days if you sell before then; you get the market price at the time you sell (which may be more or less than you paid). You normally have to sell using the same type of intermediary eg stockbroker or National Savings, as you bought with. For National Savings you need a separate form for each stock you sell.

Interest Fixed. About 5 weeks before the interest (dividend) date, the stock goes *ex-dividend;* the seller gets the next interest payment. When you buy a stock (or if you sell before it matures) your *contract note,* giving details of the transaction, shows *accrued interest* as an addition or deduction from what you pay or receive. Whether it is an addition or deduction depends on when you buy or sell in relation to the next or last interest payment date and whether the stock is *ex-dividend* or not. There are special rules for taxing this, see *Tax* below.

Interest paid Usually half-yearly by cheque to you; or direct to a bank or building society account.

Tax Interest is liable to income tax. If the stock is bought through the National Savings Stock Register, no tax is deducted but taxpayers should declare it on a tax return. If the stock is bought through a stockbroker, tax is deducted at the basic rate. Non-taxpayers and 20% taxpayers can reclaim the tax from the Inland Revenue. Higher rate taxpayers have to pay extra. War Loan does not have tax deducted. Any *accrued interest added* to your *contract note* (see *Interest* above) is liable to income tax; if accrued interest is *deducted* from your contract note total, you can deduct it from other interest from the stock or claim a tax rebate if applicable. These rules don't apply if the *nominal* value of all your stocks is £5,000 or less; see Inland Revenue leaflet *IR68 Accrued Income Scheme.* Gains on stock are exempt from capital gains tax.

Fees to pay *If bought through the National Savings Stock Register:* Commission is 0.6% on the 1st £5,000 and 0.35% on the rest; minimum £5 for purchases. *If bought through a stockbroker:* Varies eg ½% (min. £18.50, max. £150) to around 1½% on first £7,000 (min. £10 to £30). Same when you sell. None if you buy a new issue direct or hold to redemption.

Passbook Stock certificate issued.

Children Under 18 stock must be held in an adult's name unless bought through the National Savings Stock Register.

Risk None if you hold until redemption although if you buy at a price of more than 100, you will only receive 100 at redemption. Possible capital loss if you want your money back early.

How to invest Phone a stockbroker. Ask which stock has the best *net redemption yield* for your tax rate and the period over which you want to invest. See list in next column for stocks available. Prices and before tax yields are published in the *Financial Times* under UK Gilt Prices in the Companies and Markets Section, and in other daily newspapers on the Share Price Page every day.

Where from Forms for National Savings Stock Register from post offices and by phone. Stockbrokers for very large amounts. All stocks are now available from National Savings.

Divide your money between stocks maturing say, every two years.

† Exempt from UK tax if held by non-residents. Some stocks have two dates eg. 1998-2001; this means the Government can repay the stock at any time between 1998 and 2001. Stocks standing at more than 100 are likely to be repaid earlier.

Government Fixed Interest Stocks

Stocks with up to 15 years to maturity	Interest dates (redemption month in black)	Life of stock from 1 June '95 Yrs	Mths
3% Gas 1990-95	1 **May** Nov	0	
10¼% Exchequer 1995	21 Jan **July**	2	
12¾% Treasury 1995†	15 Mar **Nov**	5	
14% Treasury 1996	22 **Jan** July	8	
15¼% Treasury 1996†	3 **May** Nov	11	
13¼% Exchequer 1996†	15 **May** Nov	11	½
10% Conversion 1996	15 May **Nov**	1	5 ½
13¼% Treasury 1997†	22 **Jan** July	1	8
10½% Exchequer 1997	21 **Feb** Aug	1	9
7% Treasury Cn. 1997	6 Feb **Aug**	2	2
8¾% Treasury 1997†	1 Mar **Sep**	2	3
15% Exchequer 1997	27 Apr **Oct**	2	5
9¾% Exchequer 1998	19 Jan **July**	2	8
7¼% Treasury 1998†	30 **Mar** Sep	2	10
6¾% Exchequer 1995-98†	1 **May** Nov	2	11
14% Treasury 1998-2001	22 **May** Nov	3	0
15½% Treasury 1998†	30 **Mar** Sep	3	4
12% Exchequer 1998	20 May **Nov**	3	6
9½% Treasury 1999†	15 Jan **July**	3	7 ½
12¼% Exchequer 1999	26 **Mar** Sep	3	10
6% Treasury 1999†	10 Feb **Aug**	4	2
10½% Treasury 1999	19 **May** Nov	4	5 ½
10¼% Conversion 1999	22 **May** Nov	4	6
9% Conversion 2000†	3 **Mar** Sep	4	9
13% Treasury 2000	14 **Jan** Jul	5	1 ½
8% Treasury 2000	7 Jun **Dec**	5	6
10% Treasury 2001	26 **Feb** Aug	5	9
7% Treasury 2001†	6 **May** Nov	6	4
9¾% Treasury 2002	27 **Feb** Aug	7	2
8% Treasury 2003†	10 Jun **Dec**	8	0
13¾% Treasury 2000-03	25 **Jan** Jul	8	1
10% Treasury 2003	8 **Mar** Sep	8	3
11½% Treasury 2001-04	19 **Mar** Sep	8	9 ½
3½% Funding 1999-2004	14 **Jan** Jul	9	1 ½
9½% Conversion 2004	25 **Apr** Oct	9	5
6¾% Treasury 2004†	26 **May** Nov	9	6
9½% Conversion 2005	18 **Apr** Oct	9	10 ½
12½% Treasury 2003-05	21 **May** Nov	10	6
8½% Treasury 2005	7 Jun **Dec**	10	7
7¾% Treasury 2006†	8 **Mar** Sep	11	3
8% Treasury 2002-06†	5 **Apr** Oct	11	4
11¾% Treasury 2003-07	22 **Jan** Jul	11	8
8½% Treasury 2007†	16 **Jan** Jul	12	1 ½
13½% Treasury 2004-08	26 **Mar** Sep	12	10
9% Treasury 2008†	13 **Apr** Oct	13	4 ½
8% Treasury 2009	25 **Mar** Sep	14	4

STOCK

❀ Government Index-Linked

(Also called Indexed Gilts)

Lump sum invested with the Government in return for an interest payment which rises in line with the Retail Prices Index. The stock has a fixed life at the end of which the Government guarantees to repay the *nominal value* of 100 in full plus the rise in the Retail Prices Index since the stock was issued. Both interest and capital are index-linked.

Who can invest Anyone.

How worthwhile Good value for taxpayers, especially higher rate taxpayers, who don't need a high income but wish to protect income and capital against inflation especially over periods of 10 years or more. The interest and re-payment value depends on the current and expected rate of inflation. The price fluctuates quite widely, especially the longer dated stocks. But if you hold the stock until it matures, it will grow by at least the rise in Retail Prices from date you bought. Unsuitable for non-taxpayers and 20% taxpayers. For amounts up to £10,000 consider instead *National Savings Index Linked Certificates.*

Minimum No minimum through National Savings Stock Register. Around £5,000 through a stockbroker because of minimum commission.

Maximum None. But each purchase bought through the National Savings Stock Register must not exceed £25,000 in any one stock in any one day. No maximum on sales.

Suitable Lump sums.

Money back At the redemption date. Or 2 working days if you sell before then; you can sell the stock at any time at the current market price. You normally have to sell using the same type of intermediary eg. stockbroker or National Savings, as you bought with. For National Savings you need a separate form for each stock you sell.

Interest Variable. Changes at each interest payment to reflect changes in the Retail Prices Index over a previous 6 month period with a lag of 8 months. About 5 weeks before the interest (dividend) date the stocks go *ex-dividend;* the seller gets the next interest payment, not the buyer. When you buy a stock (or if you sell before it matures) your *contract note* giving details of the transaction shows *accrued* Interest as an addition or deducton from what you pay or receive. Whether it is an addition or deduction depends on when you buy or sell in relation to the next or last interest payment date and whether the stock is *ex-dividend* or not. There are special rules for taxing this, see *Tax* below.

Interest paid Half-yearly by cheque to you or direct to bank account.

Tax Interest is liable to income tax. If the stock is bought through the National Savings Stock Register, no tax is deducted; taxpayers should declare it on a tax return. If stock is bought through a stockbroker, tax is deducted at the basic rate. Non-taxpayers and 20% taxpayers can reclaim the tax from the Inland Revenue. Higher rate taxpayers have to pay extra. Any *accrued interest* added to your *contract note* (see *Interest* above) is liable to income tax; if accrued interest is deducted, you can deduct it from other interest you receive from the stock and claim a tax rebate if applicable. These rules don't apply if the *nominal value* of all your stocks is £5,000 or less. Gains on stock are exempt from capital gains tax.

Fees to pay *If bought through National Savings Stock Register:* Commission is 0.6% on the 1st £5,000 and 0.35% on the rest; minimum £5 for purchases. *If bought through a stockbroker:* Varies eg. ½% (min. £18.50 - max. £150) to around 1½% on first £7,000 (min. £10 to £30). Same when you sell. None if you buy a new issue direct or hold to redemption.

Passbook Stock certificate issue.

Children Under age 18, stock must be held in an adult's name unless bought through the National Savings Stock Register.

Risk None if you hold until redemption. Some if sold before, but interest rate rises will not cause the price to fall as much as it does with stocks which have a fixed rate. Stocks with a longer period to redemption tend to fluctuate in price more than those with a shorter period.

How to invest Choose a stock from the list in the next column which matures close to the date you want your money back (eg expected retirement date) or invest in a number of different stocks so you have money maturing over a number of years.

Where from Forms for National Savings Stock Register from most post offices, banks and by phone. If you want to buy 5 stocks, you need 5 forms. Or from a stockbroker. If you buy through the National Savings Stock Register, you have to sell through it - and vice-versa.

Government Index-Linked Stocks

Index-Linked Treasury Stock	Notional value on 1 June 1995‡	Interest dates (redemption month in black)	Life of stock from 1 June '95 Yrs Mths	
2% 1996	213	16 Mar **Sep**	1	3 ½
4¹/₈% 1998†	107	27 Apr **Oct**	2	11
2½% 2001	185	24 Mar *Sep*	6	4
2½% 2003	184	20 May **Nov**	7	11½
4³/₈% 2004†	107	21 Apr **Oct**	9	4½
2% 2006	208	19 Jan **July**	11	1½
2½% 2009	184	20 May **Nov**	13	11 ½
2½% 2011	194	23 Feb **Aug**	16	3
2½% 2013	162	16 Feb **Aug**	18	2 ½
2½% 2016	177	26 Jan **July**	21	2
2½% 2020	174	16 Apr **Oct**	24	10 ½
2 ½% 2024†	148	17 Jan **July**	29	1 ½
4¹/₈% 2030†	107	22 Jan **July**	35	2

‡ The 'notional value' is the 'nominal' value, 100, plus index-linking added so far. Index-linked additions are made to the 'notional' value. † Tax exempt to non-residents.

In the table above, the column 'notional value on 1 June 1995' gives you an idea as to the value for money of each stock. This figure is the amount of index-linking added so far to the initial issue price of the stock. When you compare it to the actual market price which the stock is offered at, the market price is usually less. However in the case of stocks which pay higher interest, the market price may actually be more than the 'notional value'. Your choice depends on whether you want income now, in the form of higher interest each year, or in the future, in the form of a higher 'redemption' value. Government Index-Linked Stock is an excellent long term investment even if high rates of inflation don't return.

STOCK

Loan and Debenture

(Also called Unsecured Loan Stock, Fixed Interest)

Lump sum invested in a stock issued by a company for a fixed term at a fixed interest rate. At the end of the term (the *redemption date*), the original value is repaid in full; meanwhile the stock can be bought and sold at any time at the market price. The yearly return you get, called the *net redemption yield* is the after tax interest you receive plus the averaged out gain (or loss) you expect. The *running yield* is the return ignoring any gain or loss. Some stocks will show no gain to redemption as they currently stand above the *nominal value* of 100. Sometimes a re-organisation can result in the interest rate being raised, the stock being repaid early or a loan stock being converted to a debenture (see *Risk* below).

Who can invest Anyone.

How worthwhile Different stocks are good for different rate taxpayers. Compare with *Stock Government Fixed Interest*. Stock maturing in 10+ years not recommended although these generally have a higher *running yield*. See also *Stock Convertible Loan*.

Minimum A portfolio of 7 stocks worth £2,000-£5,000 each. Lower amounts not worthwhile because of minimum commission and lack of a diversified portfolio.

Maximum None but some stocks are in short supply.

Suitable Lump sums.

Money back At end of term. Or 10 working days (5 days from June 1995) if you sell earlier when you get the market price.

Interest Fixed. About 5 weeks before the interest is paid the stocks go *ex-dividend*. The seller gets the next interest payment. When you buy a stock (or if you sell before it matures) your *contract note* giving details of the transaction shows *accrued interest* as an addition or deduction from what you pay or receive.

Interest paid Half-yearly by cheque or direct to a bank account.

Tax Basic rate tax is deducted from the interest. Non-taxpayers can reclaim the tax from the Inland Revenue. Higher rate taxpayers pay extra. Any *accrued interest* added to your *contract note* (see *Interest* above) is liable to income tax. If accrued interest is deducted, you can deduct it from other interest from the stock or claim a tax rebate if applicable. These accrued interest rules don't apply if the *nominal value* of all your stocks is £5,000 or less, see Inland Revenue leaflet IR68 *Accrued Income Scheme*. Gains are exempt from capital gains tax.

Fees to pay Stockbrokers commission when you buy varies from ¾% to 1½%; min. £10 to £30. Same when you sell. None if you buy a new issue direct or hold to redemption.

Passbook Stock certificate issued.

Children Under 18 stock must be held in an adult's name but can be *designated* with the child's initials or name.

Risk If a company goes bust, debenture holders have the right to be paid in full before other creditors get anything; loan stock holders don't but are paid before ordinary shareholders. Possible capital loss if you sell early.

How to invest Ask a stockbroker which stock has the best *net redemption yield* for your tax rate and the time you want to invest. With loan stocks check they think the company is likely to stay in business until your stock matures.

Where from A stockbroker.

STOCK

❀ Personal Equity Plan

A means of investing up to £6,000 a year from 6 April 1995 in UK and/or EU commercial stocks and/or preference shares in addition or instead of UK or EU ordinary shares free of all tax. Up to £1,500 can be in 'non-qualifying' trusts where at least 50% of the assets must be in such stocks or shares, but not necessarily in the UK or EU. Some plans will invest exclusively in stocks, others will have a mixture of stocks and shares. To consider the investment merits of a plan invested exclusively in stocks or preference shares, see *Stock Convertible Loan, Stock Debenture and Loan, Offshore Stock and Bond Fund, Shares Preference, Unit Trust Stock and Bond Fund.*

Who can invest Anyone 18 or over. Joint plans are not allowed but husband and wife can have one each. In any one tax year you can only invest in one Personal Equity Plan from one manager.

How worthwhile Potentially good value for tax-payers, especially higher rate tax payers. You have a choice of using your £6,000 limit instead on an equity investment, see *Investment Trust Personal Equity Plan* and *Unit Trust Personal Equity Plan.* Higher rate taxpayers also consider *Shares Self Select Personal Equity Plan.*

Minimum £30 - £100 a month.

Maximum £6,000 a year, £500 a month plus managers' charges. These maximums apply to al types of PEPS except single share ones.

Suitable Lump sums. Regular savings.

Money back You can normally sell the stocks or units when you like. If you die the plan ends.

Interest Variable. The before tax interest is called the *yield* and plans which show the highest yield are most attractive as they make the most use of the tax exemptions.

Interest paid Interest may be accumulated; or paid by cheque to a bank account, yearly or half-yearly.

Tax Income and capital gains are tax free and need not be entered on a tax return. Tax deducted from the distribution is reclaimed for you by the managers. Most of these stocks are already except from Capital Gains Tax, so you are only gaining from income tax exemption.

Fees to pay Same as for *Shares Personal Equity Plan* or *Unit Trust Personal Equity Plan.* Look for plans with low fees and 'no front end load'.

Passbook None. Receipt provided. Statements sent.

Children Not allowed.

Risk The value of the stocks and units can go down as well as up.

How to invest Phone or write to a plan manager, ask for details and compare them. Choose their highest yielding fund or unit trust. Monthly investment will normally have to be by direct debit or standing order from a bank account.

Where from Many investment managers. The plans will become available from April 1995 and are likely to be advertised extensively.

STOCK

Private Index-Linked

Lump sum invested with a loan stock in a building society or private company in return for an interest payment which increases in line with the Retail Prices Index. The stock has a fixed life at the end of which the company guarantees to repay the *nominal value* in full plus the rise in the Retail Prices Index since the stock was issued. Both interest and capital are index-linked.

Who can invest Anyone.

How worthwhile Good value for tax-payers who don't need a high income but wish to protect income and capital against inflation. There is more choice of stock with *Stock Government Index-Linked.* For up to £10,000 for periods of 5 years, consider instead *National Savings Index Linked Certificates.*

Minimum £2,000-£5,000. Less not worthwhile because of minimum commission.

Maximum None.

Suitable Lump sums.

Money back A few days. You can sell the stock at any time at the current market price. The interest and repayment value depends on the current and expected rate of inflation. The price does not match changes in the Retail Prices Index.

Interest Variable. Changes at each interest payment to reflect changes in the Retail Prices Index over a previous 6 month period. About 5 weeks before the interest (dividend) date, the stocks go *ex-dividend*. The seller gets the next interest. When you buy a stock (or if you sell before it matures) your *contract note* giving details of the transaction, shows *accrued interest* as an addition or deduction from what you pay or receive. There are special rules for taxing this - see *Tax* below.

Interest paid Half-yearly by cheque to you or direct to bank account.

Tax Tax is deducted from interest at the basic rate. Non-taxpayers and 20% taxpayers can reclaim tax from the Inland Revenue. Higher rate taxpayers have to pay extra. Any *accrued interest* added to your *contract note* (see *Interest* above) is liable to income tax; if accrued interest is deducted you can deduct it from other interest you receive from the stock and claim a tax rebate if applicable. These accrued interest rules don't apply if the nominal value of all your stocks is £5,000 or less, see Inland Revenue leaflet *IR68 Accrued Interest Scheme*. Gains on stock are exempt from capital gains tax.

Fees to pay Stockbrokers charges vary: Around ¾% to 1½%; minimum £10 - £30. Same when you sell. None if you buy a new issue direct or on redemption.

Passbook Stock certificate issued.

Children Under 18 stock must be held in an adult's name.

Risk Low if you hold until redemption. Some if sold before but interest rate rises will not cause the price to fall as much as they do with stocks which have a fixed rate.

How to invest Ask a stockbroker about Nationwide 3⅞% Index-Linked 2021, 4¼% Index-Linked 2024 and any other issues.

Where from A stockbroker.

STOCK

Unit Trust Invested in Gilts

You invest in a fund of Government fixed interest stocks managed by professionals. The units closely reflect the value of the stocks held within the trust. The aim of some Gilt unit trusts is to achieve capital growth, these trusts have a low yield. 'Income' trusts have a higher yield. Gilt trusts rise in value when interest rates fall (or are expected to fall); when interest rates rise (or are expected to rise) the trusts tend to fall in value but see note at the end of this page.

Who can invest Anyone.

How worthwhile Poor value for large amounts or higher rate tax or capital gains tax payers. Consider investing directly in gilts yourself, see *Stock Government Fixed Interest*. If you want this type of investment in a foreign currency, basic taxpayers see *Unit Trust Stock and Bond Fund*. Higher rate taxpayers and non-taxpayers see *Offshore Stock and Bond Fund*. Non-taxpayers also consider *Shares Preference*.

Minimum £500 to £1,000.

Maximum None.

Suitable Lump sums.

Money back Usually a few days, at most 10 working days.

Interest Variable. Called *distribution*. The before tax interest is called *yield*. The yield is usually calculated after deduction of the yearly fund charge. Some trusts calculate the yield without deducting the charge which gives the impression of a higher yield. These are marked with a 'C' in the *Financial Times* unit trust prices page.

Interest paid Half-yearly or quarterly by cheque to you or direct to a bank account.

Tax Tax is deducted from the interest. Non-taxpayers can reclaim the tax from the Inland Revenue. Higher rate taxpayers have to pay extra, basic taxpayers and 20% taxpayers don't. Gains on units are liable to capital gains tax (see Chapter 5) even though direct investments in Government stock is exempt from capital gains tax. The managers pay no capital gains tax when they make gains on stock held within the trust.

Fees to pay Initial charge 1%-5% included in difference between buying and selling price of 1½%-5%. Yearly charge ¾%-1% deducted from your income.

Passbook None. Statement or certificate sent with each transaction. Report and distribution voucher usually half-yearly.

Children Under 18 units should be held in an adult's name and can be designated with the child's name or initials.

Risk Some. The value of units goes down as well as up as interest rates are expected to change. The stocks in the trust are held by a Government approved trustee to ensure the managers invest in what they say they do.

How to invest Get advice from an independent financial adviser on the best time to buy (and sell) and which trust to choose. Purchases and sales can be made by phone so you know what price you get.

Where from Around 50 trusts from many unit trust groups.

It's better to invest in Gilts direct rather than through a unit trust - see Stock Government Fixed Interest.

UNIT TRUST

Cash Trust

(Also called Money Market, Reserve, Sterling Deposit, Maximum Income)

A fund where you pay in and withdraw like a *Building Society Postal Account* but technically you buy and sell units in a unit trust. The units only rise and fall slightly to reflect accumulating income and distributions (see *Interest paid*). Cash trusts generally only invest in bank and building society accounts but they are allowed to invest in a number of other types of short term investments including *treasury bills*, *certificates of deposit* and short dated *Stock Government Fixed Interest*.

Who can invest Anyone.

How worthwhile Compare with *Building Society Postal Account* and *Building Society Instant Access Account*. Likely to be most worthwhile for small amounts eg £500-£10,000 as the same interest rate is paid for all sizes of investment whereas building societies usually pay more for larger amounts.

Minimum Usually £1,000. Baring £500. Smith & Williamson £2,500.

Maximum None.

Suitable Lump sums. You can only deposit by cheque not cash.

Money back Usually a few days.

Interest Variable. Called *distribution*. The before tax interest (after deduction of the yearly charge - see *Fees to pay*) is called the *yield*. This is similar to the before tax interest rate on building society accounts.

Interest paid Half yearly, quarterly or monthly depending on the trust; by cheque to you or direct to a bank account. Around half the trusts only have accumulation units which accumulate income; with others your income can automatically buy extra units or there is a choice of units.

Tax Tax is deducted from the distribution (called *tax credit*). Non-taxpayers can reclaim the tax credit from the Inland Revenue. Higher rate taxpayers pay extra; basic taxpayers and 20% taxpayers don't. The first distribution you receive after buying the units consists partly of interest and partly of an *equalisation payment*. This equalisation payment counts as a return of capital and is not taxable.

Fees to pay Initial charge nil to 2%. Yearly ½% 1% deducted from the interest. Trusts listed below all nil initial, ½% yearly.

Passbook None. Statement or certificate sent with each transaction. Report and distribution voucher usually half-yearly.

Children Under 18, units must be held in an adult's name but can be designated with a child's name or initials.

Risk None.

How to invest Phone the managers below and ask what their current yield and minimum investment are.

Where from A number of unit trust groups. Money Management runs a list.

Unit Trust Cash Trust is suited for relatively small sums eg £500 to £10,000.

UNIT TRUST

Index Tracker

(Also known as Index Trust)

A unit trust which aims to duplicate the growth of a stock exchange index, usually an index of ordinary shares. It may also have a similar income to the index. This way the trust is always invested in shares so the trust will not underperform the market because part is in cash on deposit. Charges are generally less than for other unit trusts. There are tracker trusts for stock markets in the UK, USA, Europe, Japan and the Far East.

Who can invest Anyone.

How worthwhile Potentially good value as a long term investment for taxpayers if you buy and sell at the right time; poor value if you don't. Compare with *Investment Trust Shares* which generally don't have an initial charge.

Minimum Usually £1,000. £5,000 Gartmore UK Index.

Maximum Phone deals of £15,000 or more per trust may be delayed until the next valuation.

Suitable Lump sums. Regular savings, see *Unit Trust Savings Plan.*

Money back A few days at the market price. You can usually buy and sell by phone.

Interest Variable. Called *distribution.* The before tax interest is called *yield.* Trusts which track overseas markets tend to have a low yield or none at all.

Interest paid Usually yearly or half-yearly by cheque to you or direct to a bank account. Some trusts have accumulation units which accumulate income; with others your income can automatically buy extra units (at a charge).

Tax 20% tax is deducted from the distribution (called a *tax credit*) whether or not you accumulate income. Non-taxpayers can reclaim the tax from the Inland Revenue. Higher rate taxpayers pay extra; basic taxpayers and 20% taxpayers don't. Gains on units are liable to capital gains tax, see Chapter 5, though the managers pay no tax on gains on shares held by the trust.

Fees to pay Initial charge 4%-6% (maximum 5¼% for trusts listed here; nil Gartmore UK Index) included in spread between buy (offer) and sell (bid) price of 5½%-7½% (1.9% Gartmore). Yearly ½%-1% (maximum ¾% for trusts listed here).

Children Under 18, units should be held in an adult's name and can be *designated* with the child's name or initials.

Passbook None. Statement or certificate sent with each transaction. Report and distribution voucher usually half-yearly.

How to invest Phone the managers of the trusts listed below and ask for literature. You can buy by phone too.

Where from HSBC (Footsie, Trixsie, UK, US, Eurotrack 100, Japan, Tiger), Morgan Grenfell (UK, US, Japan), Legal & General (UK, US, European, Japan).

These funds are linked to an index of share prices, not retail prices. So they can go down as well as up. If you buy direct, try and negotiate a reduced intial charge as the managers are not paying commission. Or buy through an accountant, solicitor or some independent financial advisers, who will give you back some or all of the commission.

UNIT TRUST

Invested in Shares

You invest in a fund of shares managed by professionals. The units closely reflect the value of the shares held within the trust. You may receive an income and hope to make a capital gain by selling for more than you paid, but you may end up with a loss by selling for less. Some trusts specialise in particular types of shares. See lists on the next two pages.

Who can invest Anyone.

How worthwhile Potentially good value as a long-term investment for taxpayers if you buy and sell at the right time; poor value if you don't. High charges make most trusts unattractive. Consider instead *Investment Trust Shares* or *Unit Trust Index Tracker*.

Minimum Usually £250, £500 or £1,000.

Maximum None.

Suitable Lump sums.

Money back At the market price; usually a few days, at most 10 working days.

Interest Variable. Called *distribution*. The before tax interest is called *yield;* different types of trusts have different yields. The yield is usually calculated after deduction of the yearly fund charge. Some trusts calculate the yield without deducting the charge which gives the impression of a higher yield. These are marked with a 'C' in the *Financial Times* unit trust prices page.

Interest paid Usually half-yearly. Some managers can arrange a monthly income. By cheque to you or direct to a bank account. Some trusts have accumulation units which accumulate income, with others your income automatically buys extra units at an extra charge.

Tax 20% tax is deducted from the distribution (called a *tax credit)* whether or not you accumulate it. Non-taxpayers can reclaim the tax from the Inland Revenue Higher rate taxpayers have to pay extra; basic and 20% taxpayers don't. You can avoid this tax by investing through a *Unit Trust Personal Equity Plan.* Gains on units are liable to capital gains tax (see Chapter 5) though the managers pay no capital gains tax if they make gains on shares held by the trust.

Fees to pay Initial charge usually 5%-6% included in difference between buying and selling price of 5½%-7%. Yearly charge 1%-1½% deducted from income or capital.

Passbook None. Statement or certificate sent with each transaction. Report and distribution voucher usually half-yearly.

Children Under 18, units should be held in an adult's name and are *designated with* the child's name or initials.

Risk High but not as risky as buying individual shares. The value of units goes down as well as up. The shares owned by the trust are held by a Government approved trustee.

How to invest Phone the managers of the trust you are interested in and ask for their literature; you can buy by phone too. They will send you a contract note and you then send your money. Sales can also be made by phone. Watch what the newspapers say or follow a hunch.

Where from Around 170 trust managers.

Fleming Private (minimum £10,000) and Lazard and Dimensional (each minimum £5,000) don't have an initial charge. Murray Johnstone (minimum £500) has a 1% initial charge. The yearly charge is 1.5% a year for all three.

UNIT TRUST

Invested in UK Shares

The best performing trusts change frequently. Most monthly financial magazines publish performance for all trusts each month. Some also publish lists of the *Standard Deviation* of each trust's performance. This is a guide to a trust's *volatility* - a trust with a high volatility goes up by more than other trusts when it rises, but also falls by a greater amount when it falls. A volatile trust is a riskier form of investment. The average *standard deviation* for each sector published below are from Money Management February 1995 which also publishes a figure for each individual trust each month. The higher the figure the greater gain (and loss) you can expect from investing in a trust or sector.

UK Equity Growth Trusts which invest at least 80% of their assets in UK shares. Their main aim is capital growth. 144 trusts. Sector average standard deviation: 3.9.

UK Equity General Trusts which invest at least 80% in UK shares. Their aim is to produce a combination of income and growth with an income yield of between 80% and 110% of the yield of the FT All Share Index. 104 trusts. Sector average standard deviation: 3.9.

UK Equity Income Trusts which invest at least 80% in UK shares. Their income yield is over 110% of the yield of the FT All Share Index. 112 trusts. Sector average standard deviation: 3.9.

UK Balanced Trusts where at least 80% is invested In UK shares UK government stocks and other UK fixed interest stocks. 54 trusts. Sector average standard deviation: 3.5.

Financial and Property Trusts which invest at least 80% in financial and property shares (usually in the UK) but some investments may be abroad. 11 trusts. Sector average standard deviation: 4.1.

UK Smaller Companies Trusts which invest at least 80% of their assets in UK equities which form part of the Hoare Govett UK Smaller Companies Extended Index This index includes 10% of the smallest companies by market capitalisation in the main UK stockmarket plus all £ sterling denominated companies on the USM. 74 trusts. Sector average standard deviation: 4.2.

Investment Trust Units Invest direct. See *Investment Trust Shares*. 14 trusts. Sector average standard deviation: 4.5.

Convertibles Trusts where at least 60% is invested in convertible loan stocks in the UK or overseas. See *Stock Convertible Loan*. 9 trusts. Sector average standard deviation: 3.3.

Fund of Funds Trusts which invest in other unit trusts. Not recommened because of excessive charges.

For pessimists If you think shares are going to crash, make money by investing in Govett MIS Bear Funds. These go up when the stock market goes down!

Trusts which avoid investments in arms companies, tobacco companies, etc are called ethical unit trusts. Some also try to invest in companies which have a positive attitude to the environment. A guide 'Choosing an Ethical Investment Fund' is available from EIRIS. Ethical trusts include: Allchurches Amity, Credit Suisse Fellowship, Friends Provident Stewardship, Stewardship Income and North American Stewardship, Jupiter Ecology.

UNIT TRUST

Invested in Overseas Shares

(Also called International Unit Trust, Worldwide Unit Trust)

The best performing trusts change frequently. Most trusts invested abroad in ordinary shares have a low income yield or none at all. The sector average *standard deviations* published below are from Money Management February 1995 which also publishes a figure for each individual trust each month. The higher the figure the greater gain (or loss) you can expect from investing in a trust or sector. Trusts investing in the Far East are most *volatile*.

International Equity Growth Trusts which invest at least 80% of their assets in overseas shares and whose main aim is capital growth. 175 trusts. Sector average standard deviation: 3.9.

International Equity Income At least 80% in overseas shares whose income yield is more than 110% of the FT Worldwide Index. 10 trusts. Sector average standard deviation: 3.6.

International Fixed Interest See *Unit Trust Stock & Bond Fund.* 34 trusts. Sector average standard deviation: 2.5.

International Balanced At least 80% in overseas shares and or foreign currency or overseas government fixed interest stocks. 30 trusts. Sector average standard deviation: 3.0.

North America At least 80% in North American stocks and shares and 20% to 100% in North American shares. 119 trusts. Sector average standard deviation: 3.7.

Europe At least 80% in European stocks and shares (including the UK) and 20% to 100% in European shares (excluding the UK). 120 trusts. Sector average standard deviation: 3.9.

Japan At least 80% in Japanese stocks and shares and 20% to 100% in Japanese shares. 82 trusts. Sector average standard deviation: 6.3.

Far East including Japan At least 80% in the Far East including Japan and Australia where 20% to 100% is in Far Eastern shares, and 20% to 100% in countries other than Japan and 20% to 100% in countries other than Australia and New Zealand. 43 trusts. Sector average standard deviation: 5.6.

Far East excluding Japan At least 80% in the Far East excluding Japan where 20% to 100% is in Far Eastern shares, and 20% to 100% is in countries other than Australia and New Zealand and none in Japan. 69 trusts. Sector average standard deviation: 8.0.

Australasia At least 80% in Australia and New Zealand and 20% to 100% in shares. 4 trusts. Sector average standard deviation: 6.6.

Commodity and Energy Trusts At least 80% in commodity shares (including gold mining company shares) and energy shares in abroad and in the UK. 14 trusts. Sector average standard deviation: 8.2.

If you buy direct, try and negotiate a reduced intial charge as the managers are not paying commission. Or buy through an accountant, solicitor who will give you credit for the commission against their fees.

UNIT TRUST

✿ Personal Equity Plan

(Also called Unit Trust PEP Tax Break, Stratagem Tax Free Portfolio)

A means of investing up to £6,000 a year in unit trusts with at least 50% of their assets in UK or EU stocks and/or shares free of all tax. Up to £1,500 can be in *non-qualifying* trusts where at least 50% of the assets must be in shares, but not necessarily in the UK or EU. It's easiest to invest monthly. You usually have a choice of trusts and should choose one with a higher income to benefit from the tax exemption. See *Unit Trust Invested in UK Shares*, *Unit Trust Invested in Overseas Shares* and *Unit Trust Index Tracker* to help decide which trust to invest in.

Who can invest Anyone 18 or over. Joint plans are not allowed but husband and wife can have one each. In any one tax year you can only invest in one Personal Equity Plan from one manager although a *Self Select Personal Equity Plan* can be with a separate manager.

How worthwhile Good value for tax-payers, especially higher rate tax payers. Compare with *Investment Trust Personal Equity Plan*. Higher rate taxpayers also consider *Shares Self Select Personal Equity Plan*. You have a choice of using your £6,000 limit instead in full or part on a fixed interest investment, see *Stock Personal Equity Plan*.

Minimum *£40 a month:* Equitable Life, Friends Provident. *£50 a month:* Barclays Unicorn, GT, Mercury Asset, M&G. *£100 a month:* Murray Johnstone.

Maximum £6,000 a year, £500 a month.

Suitable Lump sums. Regular savings.

Money back You can normally sell the units when you like. If you die the plan ends. Only a few groups allow you to go liquid once you have invested.

Interest Variable. Called *distribution*. The before tax interest is called the *yield* and plans which show the highest yield are most attractive as they make the most use of the tax exemptions. The yield is usually calculated after deduction of the yearly fund charge. Some trusts calculate the yield without deducting the charge which gives the impression of a higher yield. These are marked with a 'C' in the *Financial Times* unit trust prices page.

Interest paid Dividends and interest may be accumulated; or paid by cheque to you or to a bank account, usually half-yearly You usually have a choice of whether interest is paid out or accumulated.

Tax Income and capital gains are tax free and need not be entered on a tax return. Tax deducted from the distribution is reclaimed for you by the managers.

Fees to pay Usually same as for unit trusts: Initial 1% to 6%; yearly 1% to 1½%. Some managers, not listed here, charge you twice: once for the personal equity plan and again within the Unit Trust. Some managers listed below don't have an initial charge, or have a low one.

Passbook Statements sent.

Children Not allowed

Risk High but not as risky as buying individual shares.

How to invest Phone a manager, ask for details and compare them. Monthly investment by direct debit from a bank account.

Where from Equitable Life, Fidelity, Friends Provident, INVESCO, M&G, Murray Johnstone.

UNIT TRUST

Savings Plan

A commitment to save a fixed minimum amount regularly, usually monthly, which is invested in units of a unit trust (a fund of stocks and shares managed by professionals). The units closely reflect the value of the stocks and shares held within the trust. You can make additional savings in any month. The plan can be stopped at any time; you either sell the units back to the managers at the current market price or continue holding the units as an ordinary unit trust. See *Unit Trust Invested in UK Shares*, *Unit Trust Invested in Overseas Shares* and *Unit Trust Index Tracker* to help decide which trust to invest in.

Who can invest Anyone.

How worthwhile Flexible and potentially good value for taxpayers who want to link their regular savings to the value of a fund of stocks and shares provided you avoid trusts with high charges. If you have less than £6,000 a year (£500 a month) consider instead *Unit Trust Personal Equity Plan*. Compare with *Investment Trust Savings Plan* and *Investment Trust Personal Equity Plan*. Unsuitable for non-taxpayers and 20% taxpayers.

Minimum £20 to £100 a month. You can buy more when you feel like.

Maximum None.

Money back Within 1-2 weeks. Units are sold at the current market price. Some companies allow partial withdrawals.

Interest Variable. Called *distribution*. The before tax interest is called *yield;* different types of trusts have different yields. The yield is usually calculated after deduction of the yearly fund charge. Some trusts calculate the yield without deducting the charge which gives the impression of a higher yield. These are marked with a 'C' in the *Financial Times* unit trust prices page.

Interest paid Accumulated within the trust or to buy extra units at a charge.

Tax 20% tax is deducted from the interest called a *tax credit*. Non-taxpayers can reclaim the tax credit from the Inland Revenue. Higher rate taxpayers have to pay extra; basic and 20% taxpayers don't. Gains on units are liable to capital gains tax (see Chapter 5) although the managers pay no capital gains tax on gains on shares held within the trust.

Fees to pay Initial charge usually 5%-6% included in difference between buying and selling price usually of between 5½% and 7%. Yearly charge ¾%-1½%. Some trusts give regular savers a discount or a loyalty bonus.

Passbook None. Statements of units and distributions sent half-yearly.

Children Under 18 units should be in an adult's name and can be *designated* with the child's name or initials.

Risk By buying regularly you even out fluctuations in the market price eg you buy when prices are low as well as high. You still need to choose the right time to sell. Otherwise the same as *Unit Trust Invested in Shares*.

How to invest Phone the managers, ask for their literature. Choose a trust.

Where from The following managers give discounts or loyalty bonuses: Abtrust, Allchurches, Commercial Union, Edinburgh, Fidelity, Framlington, Friends Provident, Scottish Widows.

UNIT TRUST

Stock and Bond Fund

(Also called International Fixed Interest, Currency Bond, Global Bond, EMU)

You invest in a fund of foreign currency fixed interest stocks. Most funds invest in a mixture of stocks in different foreign currencies including £. Others invest in certain areas eg Europe, North America. By using *derivatives* the managers may invest in a different currency profile from that indicated by the denomination of the stocks.

Who can invest Anyone.

How worthwhile Suitable for people who expect interest rates to fall in the country or areas the managers choose to invest in thus boosting the capital value of the fund. You may be able to make this investment tax free through *Stock Personal Equity Plan.* Unsuitable for non-taxpayers or 20% taxpayers unless the fund has a high yield. If you want to invest in stocks in a single foreign currency, see *Offshore Stock and Bond Fund.* If you want a similar investment confined to the UK see *Shares Preference* and *Stock Unit Trust Invested in Gilts.*

Minimum Around £1,000 initially.

Maximum None.

Suitable Lump sums. Regular savings.

Money back A few days.

Interest Variable. Called *distribution.* The before tax interest is called the *yield;* trusts specialising in different countries have different yields. Invest in trusts with a relatively high yield. The yield is usually calculated after deduction of the yearly fund charge. Some trusts calculate the yield without deducting the charge which gives the impression of a higher yield. These are marked with a 'C' in the *Financial Times* unit trust prices page.

Interest paid Half-yearly or quarterly by cheque to you or direct to a bank account.

Tax Variable Tax is deducted from the interest. Non-taxpayers can reclaim the tax from the Inland Revenue. Higher rate taxpayers have to pay extra; basic and 20% taxpayers don't. Gains on units are liable to capital gains tax, see Chapter 5.

Fees to pay Initial charge: 1%-6% included in difference between buying and selling price of 4%-7%. Yearly 1%-1½% deducted from your income.

Passbook None. Statement or certificate sent with each transaction. Report and distribution voucher usually half-yearly.

Children Under 18, units should be held in an adult's name and can be *designated* with the child's name or initials.

Risk Reasonably high. The value of the units goes down as well as up in line with changes in exchange rates as well as interest rates in the relevant countries. Some funds are *hedged* to avoid the currency risk. The stocks in the trust are held by a Government approved trustee to ensure managers invest in what they say they do.

How to invest Phone the managers for details or get advice from an independent financial adviser on the best time to buy (and sell) and which trust to choose.

Where from Highest yielding trusts include Guinness Flight Global High Income, Barclays European Bond, Guinness Flight EMU, Murray Global Bond. These yields can change rapidly. For a list of the 34 trusts available, see the section International Fixed Interest in the unit trust statistics section of *Money Management* magazine.

Appendix 1

Useful Addresses

Calls to numbers which start with 0800 and 0500 are free and those with 0345 are at local call rates. If you phone from abroad, omit the 01 and dial your international dialing code for the UK instead eg 0044 plus the rest of the number. If you are in the area, use just the last 5, 6 or 7 figures.

Abbey Life plc
100 Holdenhurst Road. Bournemouth, BH8 8AL. Tel: 01 202 292 373.

Abbey National plc
Abbey House, Baker Street, London NW1 6XL. Tel: 01 71 612 4000.

Abbey National (Overseas) Ltd
PO Box 545, St Helier, Jersey JE4 8XG. Tel: 01 534 58 815.

Abtrust Unit Trusts
10 Queens Terrace, Aberdeen, AB5 IQJ. Tel: 01 224 633 070.

AIB Bank
Bank Centre Britain, Belmont Road, Uxbridge UB8 1SA. Tel: 01 895 272 222. Subsidiary of Allied Irish Banks, Eire.

Allchurches
Beaufort House, Brunswick Road, Gloucester GL1 1JZ. Tel: *Life:* 01 452 526 265. *Unit trusts:* 01 452 305 958.

Alliance & Leicester Building Society
Administration Centre, Hove Park, Hove, BN3 7AZ. Tel: 01 273 775 454.

Alliance Trust Savings
PO Box 64, Meadow House, 64 Reform Street, Dundee DD1 9YP. Tel: 01 382 201 700. Investment trust and personal equity plan managers.

Allied Dunbar Group
Allied Dunbar Centre, Swindon SN1 IEL. Tel: 01 793 514 514. Life and unit trust company.

American Express
International Dollar Card, Prestamex House. 171-173 Preston Road, Brighton BN2 1YX. Tel: 01 273 693 555.

Association of Investment Trust Companies
Park House, (6th Floor), 16 Finsbury Circus, London EC2M 7JJ. Tel: 01 71 588 5347.

Association of Policy Market Makers
The Holywell Centre, 1 Phipp Street, London EC2A 4PS. Te: 01 71 739 3949.

Association of Private Client Investment Managers & Stockbrokers
112 Midldlesex Street, London E1 7HY. Tel: 01 71 247 7080. Has a free booklet with member's names and specialities.

AXA Equity & Law
Amersham Road, High Wycombe, Bucks HPI3 5AL. Tel: 01 494 463 463. Life company and unit trust managers.

Baillie Gifford & Co
1 Rutland Count, Edinburgh EH3 8EY. Tel: 01 31 222 4000. Dealers: 01 31 222 4242. Unit trust managers.

Bank of Scotland
Uberior House, 61 Grass Market, Edinburgh EH1 2JF.Tel: 01 31 442 7777.

Banking Ombudsman
70 Gray's Inn Road, London WC1X 8NB. Tel: 01 71 404 9944.

Barclays Bank
1 Royal Mint Court, London EC3N 4HJ. Tel: 01 71 626 1567.

Baring Fund Managers Ltd
155 Bishopsgate, London EC2M 3XY. Tel: 01 71 628 6000.

Birmingham Midshires Building Society
PO Box 81, 35-49 Lichfield Street, Wolverhampton WVI IEL. Tel: 01 902 302 832 or 710 710.

Bradford & Bingley Building Society
PO Box 2, Bingley, W Yorkshire BD16 2LW. Tel: 01 274 555 555.

Bristol & West Building Society
PO Box 27, Broad Quay, Bristol BS99 7AX. Tel: 01 17 929 4271.

Britannia International Ltd
8 Victoria Street, Douglas, Isle of Man IM99
1SD. Tel: 01 624 628 512. Offshore bank,
subsidiary of UK building society.

Building Society Choice
Riverside House, Rattlesden, Bury St
Edmunds 1P30 0SF. Tel: 01 449 736 287. A
monthly newsletter. Also publishes Good
Savings Guide, Good Offshore Guide, Good
Tessa Guide, Expats and Charities Choice.

Capital Ventures plc
Rutherford Way, Cheltenham GL51 9TR.
Tel: 01 242 584 380. Property enterprise
zone trust and enterprise investment
scheme managers.

Carlyle Life
21 Windsor Place, Cardiff CF1 38Y. Tel: 01
222 371 726.

**Chartered Accountants Compensa-
tion Scheme**
PO Box 433, Moorgate Place, London EC2P
2BJ. Tel: 01 71 828 7060.

Charterhouse Bank
1 Paternoster Row, St Pauls, London EC4M
7DH. Tel: 01 71 248 4000.

Chelsea Building Society
Thirlestaine Hall, Cheltenham, Glos GL53
7AL. Tel: 01 242 521 391.

**Cheltenham & Gloucester Building
Society**
Chief Office, Barnett Way, Gloucester GL4
7RL. Tel: 01 452 372 372.

Chesham Building Society
12 Market Square, Chesham, Bucks HP5
1ER. Tel: 01 494 782 575.

Cheshire Building Society
Castle Street, Macclesfeld, Cheshire SK11
6AH. Tel: 01 625 613 612.

Citibank
St Martins House, 1 Hammersmith Grove,
London W6 0NY. Tel: 01 81 846 8311

City & Metropolitan Building Society
219 High Street, Bromley, Kent BR1 1PR.
Tel: 01 81 464 0814.

Clerical Medical
Narrow Plain, Bristol BS2 0JH. Tel: 01 71
930 5474 or 01 17 929 0566. Life company
and unit trust managers.

Clydesdale Bank
PO Box 43, 150 Buchanan Street, Glasgow
G1 2HL. Tel: 01 41 248 7070.

Commercial Union Assurance
3 Bedford Park, Croydon CR0 2AQ. Tel: 01
71 283 7500 or 01 81 681 2222. Life
company and unit trust managers.

Coventry Building Society
PO Box 105, West Orchard House, 28
Corporation Street, Coventry CV1 1QR. Tel:
01 203 252 277 or 01 203 555 255.

Credit Suisse Investment Funds
Beaufort House, 15 St Botolph Street,
London EC3A 7JJ. Tel: 01 71 247 7474. Unit
trust managers.

CRS Co-operative Retail Services
National Investment Office, 29 Dantzic
Street, Manchester M4 4BA. Tel: 01 61 832
8152.

Darlington Bilding Society
8-10 Tubwell Row, Darlington, Co Durham
DL1 1NX. Tel: 01 325 487 171.

Derbyshire Building Society
PO Box 1, Duffield Hall, Duffield, Derby
DE56 1AG. Tel: 01 332 841 791.

Derbyshire (Isle of Man) Ltd
PO Box 136, Celtic House, 39 Victoria
Street, Douglas, Isle of Man IM99 1LR. Tel:
01 624 663 432. Offshore bank, subsidiary
of UK building society.

Dudley Building Society
Stone Street, Dudley W Midlands DY1 1NP.
Tel: 01 384 231 414.

Dunedin Fund Managers
25 Ravelston Terrace, Edinburgh EH4 3EX.
Tel: 0800 838 993 or 01 31 315 2500.
Investment trust and unit trust managers.

Dunfermline Building Society
Caledonia House, Carneghie Avenue,
Dunfermline KY11 5PJ. Tel: 01 383 627 727

Earl Shilton Building Society
22 The Hollow, Earl Shilton, Leicester LE9
7NB. Tel: 01 455 844 422.

Edinburgh Fund Managers
Donaldson House, 97 Haymarket Terrace,
Edinburgh EH12 5HD. Tel: 01 31 313 1000.
Dealers: 0345 090 526. Unit trust managers.

**Enterprise Investment & BES
Association**
The Holywell Centre, 1 Phipp Street, London
EC2A 4PS. Tel: 01 71 613 0032.

**Enterprise Zone Property Unit Trust
Association** 45 Conduit Street, London
W1R 9FB. Tel: 01 71 437 4132. Can provide
names of sponsors.

Equitable Life
Walton Street, Aylesbury HP21 7QW. Tel:
01 71 606 6611 or 01 296 391 000. Life
company, unit trust and personal equity plan
managers.

F&C Foreign & Colonial
8th Floor, Exchange House, Primrose
Street, London EC2A 2NY. Tel: 01 71 628
8000.

Fidelity Investment Services
Oakhill House, 130 Tonbridge Road, Tonbridge, Kent TN11 9DZ. Tel: 01 732 361 144. Dealers: 0800 414 161. Unit trust and personal equity plan managers.

Financial Times Business Publishing
Subscription Department: Tel: 01 81 402 8485. *Editorial:* Tel: 01 71 405 6969. Publishers of Personal Pensions, Top Up Pension Plans, Executives' & Directors' Pensions, The Unit Trust Year Book, Money Management Magazine, Investors Chronicle, Pensions Management Magazine.

First Direct
Arlington Business Centre, Milshaw Park Lane, Leeds LS11 OLT. Tel: 0345 100 100 (open 7 days, 24 hours). A bank, part of Midland Bank Group.

Five Arrows Funds (CI)
Rothschild Asset Management (CI), PO Box 242, St Julian's Count, St Peter Port. Guernsey GY1 3PH. Tel: 01 481 713 713. Offshore funds.

Fleming Investment Management
25 Copthall Avenue, London EC2R 7DR. Tel: 01 71 920 0539. Unit trust managers.

Fleming Private Investment Fund Management Ltd
20 Finsbury Street, London EC2Y 9AQ. Tel: 01 71 814 2700.

Framlington Unit Management
155 Bishopsgate, London EC2M 3ST. Tel: 01 71 374 4100.

Friends' Provident
UK House, 72-122 Castle Street, Salisbury SP1 3SH. Tel: 01 722 413 366. Life company and unit trust managers.

Furness Building Society
51-55 Duke Street, Barrow-in-Furness, Cumbria LA14 1RT. Tel: 01 229 824 560.

GA Life
2 Rougier Street, York YO1 1HR. Tel: 01 904 628 982. Life company and unit trust managers.

Gartmore Investment Management
PO Box 65, Gartmore House, 16-18 Monument Street, London EC3R 8AJ. Tel: 01 71 623 1212. Dealers: 01 277 264 421.

General Portfolio Life
General Portfolio House, Station Approach, Harlow, Essex CM20 2EW. Tel: 01 279 626 262.

Good Savings Guide
See Building Society Choice.

Govett
See John Govett.

Greenwich Building Society
279 Greenwich High Street, London SE10 8NL. Tel: 01 81 558 8212.

Guinness Flight (CI)
PO Box 250, La Plaiderie, St Peter Port, Guernsey. Tel: 01 481 710 404.

Guinness Flight Unit Trusts
Lighterman's Court, 5 Gainsford Street, London SE1 2NE. Tel: 01 71 522 2100.

Guinness Mahon Guernsey
PO Box 188, La Veieille Court, St. Peter Pont, Guernsey. Tel: 01 481 723 506. Offshore bank.

Halifax Building Society
Trinity Road, Halifax HX1 2RG. Tel: 01 422 333 333.

Hambros Fund Managers (CI)
PO Box 255, Barfield House, St Julian's Avenue, St Peter Port, Guernsey GY1 3QL. Tel: 01 481 715 454. Offshore fund.

Harpenden Building Society
14 Station Road, Harpenden, Herts AL5 4SE. Tel: 01 582 765 411.

Henderson Touche Remnant
3 Finsbury Avenue, London EC2M 2PA Tel: 01 71 638 5757. Unit trust managers.

Henry Cooke Lumsden
24 Chiswell Street, London ECIY 4TY. Tel: 01 71 814 8700. Booklet on shareholder perks. Phone for price.

HFC Bank
North Street, Winkfield, Windsor, Berks SL4 4TD. Tel: 01 344 890 000.

Hinton & Wild (Insurance)
374 Ewell Road, Surbiton, Surrey KT6 7BB. Tel: 01 81 390 8166. Financial adviser specialising in home income plans.

Homeowners Friendly Society
PO Box 94, Harrogate HG2 8XE. Tel: 0800 373 010.

HSBC Unit Trust Managers
6 Bevis Marks, London EC3A 7QS. Tel: 01 71 955 5050.

IMRO (Investment Managers Regulatory Organisation)
Broadwalk House, Appold Street, London EC2A 2AA. Tel: 01 71 628 6022. Regulatory organisation for investment managers including unit trusts.

Independent Schools Information Service (ISIS)
56 Buckingham Gate, London SW1E 6AG. Tel: 01 71 630 8793.

Inland Revenue PAYE Enquiry Offices
Public Enquiry Room, Somerset House, London WC2R 1LB. Tel: 01 71 438 6622. Supplies list of local enquiry offices. Will provide leaflets listed on page 29 if you can't get them from a local office.

IBRC Insurance Brokers Registration Council
15 St Helen's Place, London EC3A 8OS. Tel: 01 71 588 4387.

Insurance Ombudsman Bureau
135 Park Street, London SE1 9PA. Tel: 01 71 928 7600. 10am-noon and 2pm-4pm.

Investment Ombudsman
6 Frederick's Place, London EC2R 8BT. Tel: 01 71 796 3065.

Investors Chronicle
A weekly magazine. See Financial Times Business Publishing.

INVESCO
11 Devonshire Square, London EC2M 4YR. Tel: 01 71 626 3434. Unit trust and personal equity plan managers.

Ipswich Building Society
44 Upper Brook Street, Ipswich, Suffolk IP4 1DP. Tel: 01 473 211 021.

Ivory & Sime
PO Box 189, Edinburgh EH2 4DZ. Tel: 01 506 441 234 or 01 31 225 1357. Investment trust and personal equity plan managers.

John Govett Unit Management
Shackleton House, 4 Battle Bridge Lane, London SE1 2HR. Tel: 01 71 378 7979. Dealers: 01 71 407 7888.

Johnson Fry
Dorland House, 20 Regent Street, London SW1Y 4PZ. Tel: 01 71 321 0220.

Jupiter Fund Managers Ltd
197 Knightsbridge, London SW7 1RB. Tel: 01 71 581 8015.

Killik & Co
24 Royal Exchange, Threadneedle Street, London EC3V 3LP. Tel: 01 71 928 1331. Stockbrokers and PEP managers.

Lambeth Building Society
118 Westminster Bridge Road, London SEI 7XE. Tel: 01 71 928 1331.

Law Society Compensation Fund
Victoria Court, 8 Dormer Place, Leamington Spa CV32 5FE. Tel: 01 926 820 082.

Lazard Unit Trust Managers Ltd
21 Moorfields, London EC2P 2HT. Tel: 01 71 588 2721. *Dealers:* 01 71 374 0916.

Leeds & Holbeck Building Society
105 Albion Street, Leeds LS1 5AS. Tel: 01 13 245 9511.

Leeds Permanent Building Society
Permanent House, The Headrow, Leeds LS1 1NS. Tel: 01 13 243 8181.

Leeds Permanent Overseas Ltd
61 Strand Street, Douglas, Isle of Man. Tel: 01 624 626 266. Offshore bank, subsidiary of building society.

Leek United & Midllands Building Society
50 St Edward Street, Leek, Staffs ST13 5DH. Tel: 01 538 384 151.

Legal & General Assurance
Kingswood, Tadworth, Surrey KT20 6EU. Tel: 01 737 370 370. Life and pensions company.

Legal & General Unit Trust Managers
Bucklesbury House, 3 Queen Victoria Street, London EC4N 4EL. Tel: 01 71 528 6793.

LIFFE. London International Financial Futures and Options Exchange
Equity Products Dept, Cannon Bridge, London EC4R 3XX. Tel: 01 71 379 2486.

Lloyds Bank
71 Lombard Street, London EC3P 3BS. Tel: 01 71 626 1500.

London & Manchester
Winslade Park, Exeter, Devon EX5 1DS. Tel: 01 392 444 888.

London Life
100 Temple Street, Bristol BS1 6EA.Tel: 01 17 927 9179.

Loughborough Building Society
6 High Street, Loughborough LE11 2QB. Tel: 01 509 610 707.

M & G Group
Three Quays, Tower Hill, London EC3R 6BQ. Tel: 01 71 626 4588. Unit trust and personal equity plan managers and life company.

Manchester Building Society
18 Bridge Street, Manchester M3 3BU. Tel: 061 834 9465.

Mansfield Building Society
53 Portland Square, Sutton-in-Ashfield, Notts NG17 1AZ. Tel: 01 623 554 265.

Market Harborough Building Societ
The Square, Market Harborough, Leic shire LE16 7PD. Tel: 01 858 463 24

Marsden Building Societv
6-20 Russell Street, Nels 7NJ. Tel: 01 282 692 82

Midland Bank plc
Poultry, London EC2P 2BX. Tel: 01 71 260 8000.

Money Management
Editorial: 01 71 405 6969. See Financial Times Business Publishing. A useful monthly magazine.

Money Observer
4th Floor, 75 Farringdon Road, London EC1M 3JY. *Editorial:* 01 71 278 2332. *Subscriptions:* 01 424 755 755. A useful monthly magazine.

Money£acts
Laundry Lokes, Near Walsham, Norfolk NR2B 0BD. Tel: 01 692 500 765. A useful monthly newsletter.

Moneywise Magazine
10 Old Bailey, London EC4M 7NB. *Editorial:* 01 71 409 5273. *Subscriptions:* 01 793 552 663. A useful monthly magazine.

Monmouthshire Building Society
John Frost Square, Newport, Gwent NP9 1PX. Tel: 01 633 840 454.

Moorgate Investment Management
49 Hay's Mews, London W1X 7RT. Tel: 01 71 409 3419. Investment trust managers.

Morgan Grenfell & Co
20 Finsbury Circus, London EC2M IUT. Tel: 01 71 256 7500. *Dealers:* 01 71 826 0826. Unit trust managers.

Murray Johnstone
7 West Nile Street, Glasgow G1 2PX. Tel: 0345 090 933 or 01 41 226 3131. Investment and unit trust managers.

National & Provincial Building Society
Provincial House, Bradford, West Yorkshire BD1 1NL. Tel: 01 274 733 444.

N & P (Overseas) Ltd
56 Strand Street, Douglas, Isle of Man. Tel: 01 624 662 828. Offshore bank, subsidiary of UK building society.

National Counties Building Society
147 High Street, Epsom, Surrey KT19 BEN. Tel: 01 372 742 211.

National Savings
Charles ... 375 Kensington High Street, ... General enquiries: 01 71 ... For latest interest rates ... ssage) phone 01 71 ... kpool 01 253 723 ...

... nital Bond
... 555.

National Savings Certificate and SAYE Office
Durham DH99 INS. Tel: 01 91 386 4900. Deals with Savings Certificates, Index-Linked Certificates, Yearly Plan and SAYE.

National Savings Stock Register
Blackpool FY3 9YP. Tel: 01 253 766 151. Deals with Government Stock and Income Bonds.

National Westminster Bank plc
41 Lothbury, London EC2P 2BP. Tel: 01 71 726 1000 or 0800 200 400.

Nationwide Building Society
Nationwide House, Pipers Way, Swindon SN38 1NW. Tel: 01 793 456 800 or 01 71 242 8822.

Newcastle Building Society
Hood Street, Newcastle-upon-Tyne NE1 6JP. Tel: 01 91 232 6676.

Northern Bank
PO Box 183, Donegal Square West, Belfast BT1 6JS. Tel. 01 232 245 277.

Northern Rock Building Society
Northern Rock House, Gosforth, Newcastle-upon-Tyne NE3 4PL. Tel: 01 91 285 7191.

Norwich & Peterborough Building Society
Peterborough Business Park, Lynch Wood. Peterborough PE2 6WZ. Tel: 01 733 371 371.

Norwich Union
PO Box 4, Surrey Street, Norwich NR1 3NG. Tel: 01 603 62 22 00. Life company and unit trust managers.

Nottingham Building Society
5-13 Upper Parliament Street, Nottingham NG1 2BX. Tel: 01 15 948 1444.

NPI
55 Caverley Road, Tunbridge Wells, Kent TH1 2UE. Tel: 01 892 51 51 51.

OPAS Occupational Pensions Advisory Service
11 Belgrave Road, London SW1V IRB. Tel: 01 71 233 8080.

Occupational Pensions Board
PO Box 2EE, Newcastle-upon-Tyne NE99 2EE. Tel: 01 91 225 6414 or 6417. Operates the Registry of Occupational Pensions.

Pensions Ombudsman
11 Belgrave Road, London SW1V 1RB. Tel: 01 71 834 9144.

PIA Personal Investment Authority
Complaints Department, 2-6 Sydenham Road, Croydon CR0 OXE. Tel: 01 81 688 8350. Regulatory organisation for life companies, unit trusts and financial advisers.

Personal Investment Authority Ombudsman Bureau Ltd
6th Floor, No 1 London Wall, London EC2Y 5EA. Tel: 01 71 600 3838.

Pilling & Co
12 St Ann's Square, Manchester M2 7HT. Tel: 01 61 832 6581. Stockbrokers and peronal equity plan managers.

Planned Savings
33-39 Bowling Green Lane, London EC1R 0DA. Tel: 01 71 837 1212. A useful monthly magazine.

Portman Building Society
Portman House, Richmond Hill, Bournemouth BH2 6EP. Tel: 01 202 292 444.

Portman Channel Islands
Olivier Court, Olivier Street, St Anne Alderney, Cl. Tel: 01 481 822 747. Offshore bank, subsidiary of building society.

Professional Life
PO Box 26, Skandia House, Portland Terrace, Southampton S09 7RS. Tel: 01 703 23 23 23.

Progresive Building Society
33-37 Wellington Place, Belfast BT1 6HH. Tel: 01 232 244 926.

Prolific Unit Trusts
Walbrook House, 23 Walbrook, London EC4N 8LD. Tel: 01 71 280 3700. Dealing: 0800 262 443.

Provident Life
Provident Way, Basingstoke, Hants RG21 2SZ. Tel: 01 256 470 707.

Prudential Unit Trust Managers
Valentine House, 51-69 Ilford Hill, Ilford, Essex IG1 2DL. Tel: 01 71 911 4490.

Robert Fleming (Isle of Man)
5 Mount Pleasant, Douglas, Isle of Man. Tel: 01 624 661 880. Offshore bank, subsidiary of UK bank.

Rothschild Asset Management
Five Arrows House, St Swithin's Lane, London EC4N 8NR. Tel: 01 71 280 5000. Operates Five Arrows Funds and unit trusts.

Royal Bank of Scotland
42 St Andrew Square, Edinburgh EH2 2YE. Tel: 01 31 556 8555 or London 01 71 623 4356.

Royal Life
PO Box 30, New Hall Place, Liverpool L69 3HS. Tel: 01 51 239 5000.

Royal London Group
Royal London House, 27 Middleborough, Colchester, Essex COI 1RA. Tel: 01 206 761 761. Life company.

Royal Mint Coin Club
PO Box 500, Cardiff CF1 1HA. Tel: 01 443 223 880 or 01 443 222 111.

Save & Prosper Group
1 Finsbury Avenue, London EC2M 2QY. Tel: 01 71 588 1717 or 0800 282 101. Admin Centre: 16-22 Western Road, Romford RMl 1TZ. Life company, unit trust managers, personal equity plan managers, bankers (as agents for Robert Fleming & Co Ltd).

Scarborough Building Society
Prospect House, PO Box 6, 442 Scalby Road, Scarborough, YO12 6EO. Tel: 01 723 368 155.

School Fees Insurance Agency
15 Forlease Road, Maidenhead, Berkshire SL6 1JA. Tel: 01 628 50 20 20.

Scottish Amicable
PO Box 132, 150 St Vincent Street, Glasgow G2 5NQ. Tel: 01 41 248 2323.

Scottish Life
19 St Andrew Square, Edinburgh EH2 IYE. Tel: 01 31 225 2211. Life company and unit trust managers.

Scottish Provident
6 St Andrew Square, Edinburgh EH2 2YA. Tal: 0131 556 9181. Life company and unit trust managers.

Scottish Widows
15 Dalkeith Road, Edinburgh EH16 5BU. Tel: 01 31 655 6000. Life company and unit trust managers.

Securities & Investment Board (SIB)
Gavrelle House, 2-14 Bunhill Row, London EC1Y 8RA. Tel: 01 71 638 1240. Regulatory body.

Skipton Building Society
The Bailey, Skipton, North Yorkshire BD23 1DN. Tel: *Customer services:* 01 756 700 511. *General:* 01 756 700 500.

Smith & Williamson Fund Managers
No 1 Riding House Street, London W1A 3AS. Tel: 01 71 637 5377.

Spink & Son
5 King Street, St James, London SW1Y 60S. Tel: 01 71 930 7888.

Standard Life
PO Box 141, Tanfield House, 1 Tanfield Edinburgh EH2 2LJ. Tel: 01 31 225 2 Life company and unit trust managers.

Stock Exchange
Old Broad Street, London EC2 01 71 797 1000. Will provi brokers willing to take Also from Birmingham Manchester (01 61 232 321 094)

Or write to Proshare, Library Chambers, 13-14 Basinghall Street, London EC2.

Stroud & Swindon Building Society
Rowcroft, Stroud, Gloucestershire GL5 3BG. Tel: 01 453 757 011.

Thornton Unit Trust Managers
33 Queen Street, London EC4R 1AX. Tel: 071 246 3000.

Tipton & Cosely Building Society
70 Owen Street. Tipton, W Midlands DY4 8HG. Tel: 01 21 577 2551.

TSB Bank
Victoria House, Victoria Square, Birmingham B1 18Z. Tel: 01 21 600 6000.

UDT
PO Box 92, Holbrook House, 116 Cockfosters Road, Barnet, Herts EN4 ODY. Tel: 01 81 447 2438. A bank.

Unit Trust Year Book
See Financial Times Business Publishing.

Vernon Building Society
19 St Petersgate, Stockport, Cheshire SK1 1HF. Tel: 01 61 429 6262.

Wesleyan Assurance Society
Colmore Circus, Birmingham B4 6AR. Tel: 01 21 200 3003.

West Bromwich Building Society
374 High Street, West Bromwich, West Midlands B70 8LR. Tel: 01 21 525 7070.

Western Trust & Savings
The Moneycentre, Plymouth PL1 1SE. Tel: 01 752 224 141. A bank.

Woolwich Building Society
Watling Street, Bexleyheath, Kent DA6 7RR. Tel: 01 81 298 5000.

Woolwich Guernsey Ltd
PO Box 341, St Peter Port, Gurnsey GY1 3UW. Tel: 01 481 715 735.

Yorkshire Building Society
Yorkshire Drive, Bradford BD5 8LJ. Tel: 01 274 734 822.

Yorkshire Guernsey Ltd
PO Box 304, Canada Court, St. Peter Port. Guernsey GY1 3SF. Tel: 01 481 719 898. Offshore bank, subsidiary of UK building society.

Appendix 2

The Retail Prices Index

The Retail Prices Index is the official measure of inflation. It is calculated once a month by the Central Statistical Office which sends people round the country to record the price of many different types of goods and services. These are averaged out according to a typical family's expenditure and summarised as an index number which is announced on the second or third Wednesday of the month following the month to which the index relates. All the available index numbers are listed opposite or overleaf; up to 1961 there are yearly figures; since 1962 they are monthly.

Working out how much prices have gone up by Suppose you had £1,000 in November 1968 and want to know what it should be worth today to have kept pace with inflation. Check the latest price index, say 145.3 for November 1994. Divide by the index number for November 1968, 16.8 which gives 8.6488. Then multiply 8.6488 by £1,000 which gives the answer £8,649. The percentage increase in prices over that period would be 765% (not 865%). To work out percentage rise in prices over the last 12 months divide the latest index number by the one 12 months before. For instance November 1994, 145.3 divided by November 1993, 141.6 comes to 1.0261299. That means prices have risen by 2.6% over 12 months.

Index-Linked Savings Certificates The index number relating to investment is the one for two months earlier. If you invest in June, it is the April index number which counts as the starting index. The April index is published in May. The same applies when you cash. The final value of your certificates relates to the index for two months earlier, published the month before.

Retail Prices Index 1914 to 1985

Figures based on 100 at January 1987.

	1920	1921	1922	1923	1924	1925
Average	7.0	6.4	5.2	4.9	4.9	5.0

	1932	1933	1934	1935	1936	1937
Average	4.1	4.0	4.0	4.0	4.2	4.4

	1950	1951	1952	1953	1954	1955
Average	9.0	9.8	10.4	10.6	10.8	11.2

	1962	1963	1964	1965	1966	1967
Average	13.4	13.7	14.1	14.8	15.4	15.8
Jan	13.2	13.6	13.8	14.5	15.1	15.7
Feb	13.2	13.7	13.8	14.5	15.1	15.7
March	13.3	13.7	13.9	14.5	15.1	15.7
April	13.5	13.7	14.0	14.8	15.3	15.8
May	13.5	13.7	14.1	14.9	15.4	15.8
June	13.6	13.7	14.2	14.9	15.5	15.8
July	13.5	13.7	14.2	14.9	15.4	15.7
Aug	13.4	13.6	14.2	14.9	15.5	15.7
Sept	13.4	13.7	14.2	14.9	15.5	15.7
Oct	13.4	13.7	14.3	15.0	15.5	15.8
Nov	13.5	13.7	14.4	15.0	15.6	15.9
Dec	13.5	13.8	14.4	15.1	15.6	16.0

	1974	1975	1976	1977	1978	1979
Average	27.5	34.2	39.8	46.1	50.0	56.7
Jan	25.3	30.4	37.5	43.7	48.0	52.5
Feb	25.8	30.9	38.0	44.1	48.3	53.0
March	26.0	31.5	38.2	44.6	48.6	53.4
April	26.9	32.7	38.9	45.7	49.3	54.3
May	27.3	34.1	39.3	46.1	49.6	54.7
June	27.6	34.8	39.5	46.5	50.0	55.7
July	27.8	35.1	39.6	46.6	50.2	58.1
Aug	27.8	35.3	40.2	46.8	50.5	58.5
Sept	28.1	35.6	40.7	47.1	50.7	59.1
Oct	28.7	36.1	41.4	47.3	51.0	59.7
Nov	29.2	36.6	42.0	47.5	51.3	60.3
Dec	29.6	37.0	42.6	47.8	51.8	60.7

	1914	1915	1916	1917	1918	1919
Average	2.8	3.5	4.1	5.0	5.7	6.1

	1926	1927	1928	1929	1930	1931
Average	4.8	4.7	4.7	4.6	4.5	4.2

	1938	1939–45	1946	1947	1948	1949
Average	44.0	na	7.5	8.0	8.6	8.8

	1956	1957	1958	1959	1960	1961
Average	11.7	12.0	12.4	12.4	12.6	12.9

	1968	1969	1970	1971	1972	1973
Average	16.5	17.4	18.5	20.3	21.7	23.7
Jan	16.1	17.1	17.9	19.4	21.0	22.6
Feb	16.1	17.2	18.0	19.5	21.1	22.8
March	16.2	17.2	18.1	19.7	21.2	22.9
April	16.5	17.4	18.4	20.1	21.4	23.3
May	16.5	17.4	18.4	20.3	21.5	23.5
June	16.6	17.5	18.5	20.4	21.6	23.7
July	16.6	17.5	18.6	20.5	21.7	23.8
Aug	16.6	17.4	18.6	20.5	21.9	23.8
Sept	16.6	17.5	18.7	20.6	22.0	24.0
Oct	16.7	17.6	18.9	20.7	22.3	24.5
Nov	16.8	17.6	19.0	20.8	22.4	24.7
Dec	17.0	17.8	19.2	20.9	22.5	24.9

	1980	1981	1982	1983	1984	1985
Average	66.8	74.8	81.2	84.9	89.2	94.6
Jan	62.2	70.3	78.7	82.6	86.8	91.2
Feb	63.1	70.9	78.8	83.0	87.2	91.9
March	63.9	72.0	79.4	83.1	87.5	92.8
April	66.1	74.1	81.0	84.3	88.6	94.8
May	66.7	74.6	81.6	84.6	89.0	95.2
June	67.4	75.0	81.9	84.8	89.2	95.4
July	67.9	75.3	81.9	85.3	89.1	95.2
Aug	68.1	75.9	81.9	85.7	89.9	95.5
Sept	68.5	76.3	81.9	86.1	90.1	95.4
Oct	68.9	77.0	82.3	86.4	90.7	95.6
Nov	69.5	77.8	82.7	86.7	91.0	95.9
Dec	69.9	78.3	82.5	86.9	90.9	96.0

Retail Prices Index 1986-1995

	1986	1987	1988	1989	1990	1991
Average	97.8	101.9	106.8	115.2	126.1	133.5
Jan	96.2	100.0	103.3	111.0	119.5	130.2
Feb	96.6	100.4	103.7	111.8	120.2	130.9
March	96.7	100.6	104.1	112.3	121.4	131.4
April	97.7	101.8	105.8	114.3	125.1	133.1
May	97.8	101.9	106.2	115.0	126.2	133.5
June	97.8	101.9	106.6	115.4	126.7	134.1
July	97.5	101.8	106.7	115.5	126.8	133.8
Aug	97.8	102.1	107.9	115.8	128.1	134.1
Sept	98.3	102.4	108.4	116.6	129.3	134.6
Oct	98.5	102.9	109.5	117.5	130.3	135.1
Nov	99.3	103.4	110.0	118.5	130.0	135.6
Dec	99.6	103.3	110.3	118.8	129.9	135.7

	1992	1993	1994	1995
Average	138.5	140.7	144.1	
Jan	135.6	137.9	141.3	146.0
Feb	136.3	138.8	142.1	
March	136.7	139.3	142.5	
April	138.8	140.6	144.2	
May	139.3	141.1	144.7	
June	139.3	141.0	144.7	
July	138.8	140.7	144.0	
Aug	138.9	141.3	144.7	
Sept	139.4	141.9	145.0	
Oct	139.9	141.8	145.2	
Nov	139.7	141.6	145.3	
Dec	139.2	141.9	146.0	

For later numbers phone 0171 217 4310 or 0171 270 6363 or 6364 or
0171 217 4905 (24 hour recording of the latest index number).

Appendix 3

Past issues of National Savings Certificates

If you hold any of these issues you can find out what they are yielding from the following tables. If you can do better elsewhere for your tax rate, cash them in; if not hold on. Interest on all issues is tax-free.

The tables show the interest for the year and the average compound yearly interest you get by holding on from now until the end of the fixed term. By comparing the rate in the table with the rate on competitive investments eg building societies, you can decide whether to cash or stay put. After the end of the periods listed in these tables, all certificates will receive interest at a common rate which is variable; for rates turn to the table at the end of this Appendix entitled *General Extension Rate: Variable Interest*. If you hold certificates in the 1st to 6th issues, sold between 1916 and 1939, cash them at once; they yield less than 1.75% a year.

£1, 7th, 8th, 9th, 10th, 11th, Decimal, 14th, 16th, 18th, 19th, 21st, 23rd, 24th, 25th, 26th, 27th, 28th, 29th, 30th, 31st, 32nd, 33rd Issue Savings Certificates

Interest is variable and added every 3 months, see tables on page 207.

34th Issue Savings Certificates
£100 investment made 22 July 1988 to 16 June 1990

Year	Value at start £	Value up each 3 months by £	Value at end £	Yield for year %	Yield if held [1] to year 6 %
4	120.79	2.57	131.08	8.51	9.01
5	131.08	3.12	145.56	9.52	9.52

[1] Original yield for 5 years 7.5% a year

35th Issue Savings Certificates
£100 investment made 18 June 1990 to 30 March 1991

Year	Value at start £	Value up each 3 months by £	Value at end £	Yield for year %	Yield if held [1] to year 6 %
4	125.10	2.44[2]	138.59	10.78	12.18
5	138.59	2.92[3]	157.42	13.59	13.59

[1] Original yield for 5 years 9.5% a year. [2] Plus £3.76 on anniversary. [3] Plus £7.16 on maturity.

36th Issue Savings Certificates

£100 investment made 2 April 1991 to 2 May 1992

Year	Value at start £	Value up each 3 months by £	Value at end £	Yield for year %	Yield if held [1] to year 6 %
3	112.36	2.32	121.64	8.26	10.20
4	121.64	2.98	133.56	9.80	11.18
5	133.56	4.20	150.36	12.58	12.58

[1] Original yield for 5 years 8.5% a year

37th Issue Savings Certificates

£100 investment made 13 May 1992 to 5 August 1992

Year	Value at start £	Value up each 3 months by £	Value at end £	Yield for year %	Yield if held [1] to year 6 %
3	112.04	2.24	121.00	8.00	9.47
4	121.00	2.84	132.36	9.39	10.21
5	132.36	3.65	146.96	11.03	11.03

[1] Original yield for 5 years 8% a year

38th Issue Savings Certificates

£100 investment made 6 August 1992 to 4 October 1992

Year	Value at start £	Value up each 3 months by £	Value at end £	Yield for year %	Yield if held [1] to year 6 %
3	111.76	2.01	119.80	7.19	8.70
4	119.80	2.52	129.88	8.41	9.47
5	129.88	3.42	143.56	10.53	10.53

[1] Original yield for 5 years 7.5% a year

39th Issue Savings Certificates

£100 investment made 5 October 1992 to 12 November 1992

Year	Value at start £	Value up each 3 months by £	Value at end £	Yield for year %	Yield if held [1] to year 6 %
3	110.09	1.86	117.51	6.74	7.99
4	117.51	2.32	126.81	7.91	8.61
5	126.81	2.95	138.63	9.32	9.32

[1] Original yield for 5 years 6.75% a year

40th Issue Savings Certificates

£100 investment made 13 November 1992 to 16 December 1993

Year	Value at start £	Value up each 3 months by £	Value at end £	Yield for year %	Yield if held [1] to year 6 %
3	108.58	1.56	114.82	5.75	6.79
4	114.82	1.94	122.57	6.75	7.32
5	122.57	2.42	132.25	7.90	7.90

[1] Original yield for 5 years 5.75% a year

41st Issue Savings Certificates

£100 investment made 17 December 1993 to 19 September 1994

Year	Value at start £	Value up each 3 months by £	Value at end £	Yield for year %	Yield if held [1] to year 6 %
1	100.00	0.91	103.65	3.65	5.40
2	103.65	1.05	107.85	4.05	5.84
3	107.85	1.46	113.67	5.40	6.45
4	113.67	1.82	120.95	6.40	6.98
5	120.95	2.28	130.08	7.55	7.55

[1] Original yield for 5 years 5.4% a year

42nd Issue Savings Certificates

£100 investment made since 20 September 1994

Year	Value at start £	Value up each 3 months by £	Value at end £	Yield for year %	Yield if held [1] to year 6 %
1	100.00	1.00	104.00	4.00	5.85
2	104.00	1.20	108.78	4.60	6.32
3	108.78	1.50	114.77	5.50	6.90
4	114.77	1.94	122.51	6.75	7.60
5	122.51	2.59	132.88	8.46	8.47

[1] Original yield for 5 years 5.85% a year

3rd Index Linked Issue Savings Certificates

£100 investment made 30 June 1985 to 31 July 1986

After 5 years ½% of previous anniversary value added each year plus the rise in the Retail Prices Index each month.

4th Index Linked Issue Savings Certificates

£100 investment made 1 August 1986 to 30 June 1990

Year	Value at start [1] £	Value at end [1] £	Yield for year [1] %	Yield if held [1,2] to year 6 %
5	115.03	121.92	6.00	6.00

[1] Plus rise in retail prices index over the period. [2] Original yield for 5 years 4.04% a year plus index linking.

5th Index Linked Issue Savings Certificates

£100 investment made 2 July 1990 to 4 October 1992

Year	Value at start [1] £	Value at end [1] £	Yield for year [1] %	Yield if held [1,2] to year 6 %
3	101.00	103.03	2.01	7.26
4	103.03	108.24	2.72	10.00
5	108.24	124.62	15.13	15.13

[1] Plus rise in retail prices index. [2] Original yield for 5 years 4.5% a year plus indexing.

6th Index Linked Issue Savings Certificates

£100 investment made 13 November 1992 to 16 December 1993

Year	Value at start [1] £	Value at end [1] £	Yield for year [1] %	Yield if held [1,2] to year 6 %
3	103.53	106.38	2.75	4.27
4	106.38	110.37	3.75	5.03
5	110.37	117.35	6.32	6.32

[1] Plus rise in retail prices index over the period. [2] Original yield for 5 years 3.25% a year plus index linking.

7th Index Linked Issue Savings Certificates

£100 investment 17 December 1993 to 19 September 1994

Year	Value at start [1] £	Value at end [1] £	Yield for year [1] %	Yield if held [1,2] to year 6 %
1	100.00	101.25	1.25	3.00
2	101.25	103.02	1.75	3.45
3	103.02	105.60	2.50	4.02
4	105.60	109.29	3.50	4.79
5	109.29	115.93	6.07	6.08

[1] Plus rise in retail prices index over the period. [2] Original yield for 5 years 3% a year plus index linking.

8th Index Linked Issue Savings Certificates

£100 investment made since 20 September 1994

Year	Value at start [1] £	Value at end [1] £	Yield for year [1] %	Yield if held [1,2] to year 6 %
1	100.00	101.25	1.25	3.00
2	101.25	103.02	1.75	3.45
3	103.02	105.60	2.50	4.02
4	105.60	109.29	3.50	4.79
5	109.29	115.93	6.07	6.08

[1] Plus rise in retail prices index over the period. [2] Original yield for 5 years 3% a year plus index linking.

Issues past the end of fixed interest extensions

Issue	Dates when purchased	Years after purchase date	Value at end of fixed interest term £
£1	11 Jan 1943 to 3 March 1947	42	361 50
7th	22 Nov 1939 to 31 March 1947	45	558.67
8th	1 April 1947 to 31 Jan 1951	38	464.00
9th	1 Feb 1951 to 31 July 1956	34	434.67
10th	1 Aug 1956 to 12 March 1963	28	381 33
11th	13 May 1963 to 26 March 1966	20	290.00
12th	28 March 1966 to 3 Oct 1970	18	270.50
Decimal	5 Oct 1970 to 15 June 1974	13	226.50
14th	17June 1974 to 11Dec1976	8	185.00
	1 April 1977 to 27 Jan 1979	8	185.00
16th	13 Dec 1976 to 31 March 1977	6	170.30
18th	29 Jan 1979 to 2 Feb 1980	5	150.00
19th	4 Feb 1980 to 9 May 1981	5	163.50
21st	11 May 1981 to 7 Nov 1981	5	154.00
23rd	9 Nov 1981 to 10 March 1982	5	164.80
24th	9 April 1982 to 4 Nov 1982	5	138.08
25th	17 Nov 1982 to 13Aug 1983	5	143.60
26th	14 Aug 1983 to 19 March 1984	5	134.40
27th	5 April to 7Aug 1984	5	141.92
28th	8 Aug to 11 Sept 1984	5	153.88
29th	15 Oct 1984 to 12 Feb 1985	5	146.96
30th	13 Feb to 9 Sept 1985	5	152.84
31st	26 Sept 1985 to11 Nov 1986	5	145.92
32nd	12 Nov 1986 to 10 March 1987	5	152.12
33rd	1 May 1987 to 21 July 1988	5	140.26

Since these dates the General extension interest rate has been applied as listed below.

General extension rate: variable interest

Added every 3 months after fixed rate term ends. The rates are % a year.

17 June 1982 to 30 November 1982 8.4%
1 December 1982 to 31 August 1983 7.08%
1 September 1983 to 31 March 1984 7.68%
1 April 1984 to 31 July 1984 6.84%
1 August 1984 to 30 November 1984 8.52%
1 December 1984 to 31 January 1985 8.28%
1 February 1985 to 31 March 1985 9%
1 April 1985 to 31 September 1985 9.51%
1 October 1985 to 31 May 1986 8.52%
1 June 1986 to 31 October 1986 8.01%
1 November 1986 to 31 March 1987 8.7%
1 April 1987 to 30 April 1987 7.5%
1 May 1987 to 30 September 1987 7.02%
1 October 1987 to 29 February 1988 6.51%
1 March 1988 to 30 April 1988 5.76%
1 May 1988 to 30 November 1992 5.01%
1 December 1992 to December 31 1993 3.75%
1 January 1994 3.51%

The current rate can be obtained by phoning London 0171 605 9483 or 9484 or on Glasgow 0141 632 2766.

Appendix 4

How Money Grows
and Falls in Value

This appendix contains four sets of compound interest tables which can be used for different kinds of investment arithmetic. They are as follows:
- Table 1 How lump sums grow.
- Table 2 How money invested yearly grows.
- Table 3 How much you need now to accumulate for the future or how inflation reduces the value of your money.
- Table 4 How much you need to save each year.

Example 1A Suppose you have £1,000 and you reckon it will grow at 8% a year. How much will you have accumulated after 20 years. Look up Table 1 for 8% and 20 years and the answer is £4,661. If you are actually investing £5,000 then multiply the answer by five which gives £23,305.

Example 1B Suppose you want to know how much you will need in 10 years to buy something which costs £1,000 now and you expect prices to rise by 3% a year. Look up Table 1 for 3% and 10 years; the answer is £1,344. If what you intend to buy costs £4,500 now multiply the answer £1,344 by 4.5 which comes to just over £6,048.

Example 2 Suppose you want to invest £1,000 a year. How much will you accumulate after saving for 25 years with a return of 7% a year? Look up Table 2 for 7% and 25 years; the answer is £67,676. If you are actually investing £100 a month, an approximate estimate of what you will get is to divide the answer by ten which gives £6,768 and then multiply by 12 which gives £81,216.

Example 3A Suppose you want to accumulate £1,000 in six years' time? How much do you need now? Assume you get 6% a year interest. Look up Table 3 for 6% a year and six years; the answer is £705. If you want £3,000 in six years time at the same rate of interest, multiply the answer £705 by three which comes to £2,115.

But what about inflation? Suppose you expect inflation to average 3% a year over the next six years. Deduct from your interest rate, 6% a year, the expected rate of inflation, 3% a year, and you have the rate at which your money is accumulating in *real* terms, 3% a year. So instead look up Table 3 for 3% a year and six years; the answer is £837. So if you wanted £3,000 in today's money in six years time, taking into account inflation, you need to invest three times £837 which is £2,511.

Example 3B Suppose you reckon inflation is going to average 5% a year for the next ten years. And you reckon you will have £10,000 accumulated by then. How much in today's money will that £10,000 be worth. Look up 5% a year and 10 years in Table 3 and the answer is £614. That is the answer for £1,000. So for £10,000 multiply by ten which gives £6,140.

Example 4 Suppose you want to save regularly to accumulate £100,000 when you retire in 15 years time and you reckon you can get a return of 7% a year on your money in a personal pension, say. Look up Table 4 for 7% a year and 15 years and you get £37.19. This is the amount you need to save each year to accumulate £1,000. So to accumulate £100,000 you multiply by 100 which gives you £3,719. If you save monthly, divide by 12 which is approximately £310 a month.

But over 15 years inflation will take its toll. Suppose you expect inflation to average 5% a year over the next 15 years. That £100,000 will not buy the same amount as £100,000 in today's money. You need to calculate how much you will need in 15 years time to have the same purchasing power as £100,000 today. Look up Table 1 for 5% and 15 years and the answer is £2,079. Multiply by 100 to get the answer for £100,000 instead of £1,000; you get £207,900. Now that's a real shame because you've got to save over twice as much with inflation at only 5% a year.

So multiply £37.19 by 207.9 and you get £7,732 which is how much you need to save a year to accumulate £100,000 in today's money value in 15 years time. If you save monthly the amount is approximately £7,732 divided by 12 which is £644 a month.

If that's too much for you now, try another strategy.

• Be more optimistic about inflation. Assume it averages only 3% a year - about the rate at the time of writing. Look up 3% instead of 5% and in Table 1 for 15 years and you get £1,558 and multiply by 100 and you get £155,800 instead of £207,900.

• Then you only need to save £37.19 times 155.8 which is £5,794 a year which is £482 monthly.

• If inflation rises, then you can review your monthly savings, say, once a year and raise them, in line with it. So long as inflation stays at your original estimate, you won't have to raise the amount.

Table 1 How lump sums grow

This table shows how much £1,000 will grow to at 2% a year to 7% a year over different time periods.

Years	Interest or growth rate					
	2%	3%	4%	5%	6%	7%
	£	£	£	£	£	£
1	1,020	1,030	1,040	1,050	1,060	1,070
2	1,040	1,061	1,082	1,103	1,124	1,145
3	1,061	1,093	1,125	1,158	1,191	1,225
4	1,082	1,126	1,170	1,216	1,262	1,311
5	1,104	1,159	1,217	1,276	1,338	1,403
6	1,126	1,194	1,265	1,340	1,419	1,501
7	1,149	1,230	1,316	1,407	1,504	1,606
8	1,172	1,267	1,369	1,477	1,594	1,718
9	1,195	1,305	1,423	1,551	1,689	1,838
10	1,219	1,344	1,480	1,629	1,791	1,967
11	1,243	1,384	1,539	1,710	1,898	2,105
12	1,268	1,426	1,601	1,796	2,012	2,252
13	1,294	1,469	1,665	1,886	2,133	2,410
14	1,319	1,513	1,732	1,980	2,261	2,579
15	1,346	1,558	1,801	2,079	2,397	2,759
16	1,373	1,605	1,873	2,183	2,540	2,952
17	1,400	1,653	1,948	2,292	2,693	3,159
18	1,428	1,702	2,026	2,407	2,854	3,380
19	1,457	1,754	2,107	2,527	3,026	3,617
20	1,486	1,806	2,191	2,653	3,207	3,870
21	1,516	1,860	2,279	2,786	3,400	4,141
22	1,546	1,916	2,370	2,925	3,604	4,430
23	1,577	1,974	2,465	3,072	3,820	4,741
24	1,608	2,033	2,563	3,225	4,049	5,072
25	1,641	2,094	2,666	3,386	4,292	5,427
30	1,811	2,427	3,243	4,322	5,743	7,612
35	2,000	2,814	3,946	5,516	7,686	10,677
40	2,208	3,262	4,801	7,040	10,286	14,974
45	2,438	3,782	5,841	8,985	13,765	21,002
50	2,692	4,384	7,107	11,467	18,420	29,457

This table shows how much £1,000 will grow to at 8% a year to 13% a year over different time periods.

Interest or growth rate						Years
8%	9%	10%	11%	12%	13%	
£	£	£	£	£	£	
1,080	1,090	1,100	1,110	1,120	1,130	1
1,166	1,188	1,210	1,232	1,254	1,277	2
1,260	1,295	1,331	1,368	1,405	1,443	3
1,360	1,412	1,464	1,518	1,574	1,630	4
1,469	1,539	1,611	1,685	1,762	1,842	5
1,587	1,677	1,772	1,870	1,974	2,082	6
1,714	1,828	1,949	2,076	2,211	2,353	7
1,851	1,993	2,144	2,305	2,476	2,658	8
1,999	2,172	2,358	2,558	2,773	3,004	9
2,159	2,367	2,594	2,839	3,106	3,395	10
2,332	2,580	2,853	3,152	3,479	3,836	11
2,518	2,813	3,138	3,498	3,896	4,335	12
2,720	3,066	3,452	3,883	4,363	4,898	13
2,937	3,342	3,797	4,310	4,887	5,535	14
3,172	3,642	4,177	4,785	5,474	6,254	15
3,426	3,970	4,595	5,311	6,130	7,067	16
3,700	4,328	5,054	5,895	6,866	7,986	17
3,996	4,717	5,560	6,544	7,690	9,024	18
4,316	5,142	6,116	7,263	8,613	10,197	19
4,661	5,604	6,727	8,062	9,646	11,523	20
5,034	6,109	7,400	8,949	10,804	13,021	21
5,437	6,659	8,140	9,934	12,100	14,714	22
5,871	7,258	8,954	11,026	13,552	16,627	23
6,341	7,911	9,850	12,239	15,179	18,788	24
6,848	8,623	10,835	13,585	17,000	21,231	25
10,063	13,268	17,449	22,892	29,960	39,116	30
14,785	20,414	28,102	38,575	52,800	72,069	35
21,725	31,409	45,259	65,001	93,051	132,782	40
31,920	48,327	72,890	109,530	163,988	244,641	45
46,902	74,358	117,391	184,565	289,002	450,736	50

Table 2 How money invested yearly grows

This table shows how much £1,000 invested each year grows to at 2% a year to 7% a year over different time periods.

Years	Interest or growth rate					
	2%	3%	4%	5%	6%	7%
	£	£	£	£	£	£
1	1,020	1,030	1,040	1,050	1,060	1,070
2	2,060	2,091	2,122	2,153	2,184	2,215
3	3,122	3,184	3,246	3,310	3,375	3,440
4	4,204	4,309	4,416	4,526	4,637	4,751
5	5,308	5,468	5,633	5,802	5,975	6,153
6	6,434	6,662	6,898	7,142	7,394	7,654
7	7,583	7,892	8,214	8,549	8,897	9,260
8	8,755	9,159	9,583	10,027	10,491	10,978
9	9,950	10,464	11,006	11,578	12,181	12,816
10	11,169	11,808	12,486	13,207	13,972	14,784
11	12,412	13,192	14,026	14,917	15,870	16,888
12	13,680	14,618	15,627	16,713	17,882	19,141
13	14,974	16,086	17,292	18,599	20,015	21,550
14	16,293	17,599	19,024	20,579	22,276	24,129
15	17,639	19,157	20,825	22,657	24,673	26,888
16	19,012	20,762	22,698	24,840	27,213	29,840
17	20,412	22,414	24,645	27,132	29,906	32,999
18	21,841	24,117	26,671	29,539	32,760	36,379
19	23,297	25,870	28,778	32,066	35,786	39,995
20	24,783	27,676	30,969	34,719	38,993	43,865
21	26,299	29,537	33,248	37,505	42,392	48,006
22	27,845	31,453	35,618	40,430	45,996	52,436
23	29,422	33,426	38,083	43,502	49,816	57,177
24	31,030	35,459	40,646	46,727	53,865	62,249
25	32,671	37,553	43,312	50,113	58,156	67,676
30	41,379	49,003	58,328	69,761	83,802	101,073
35	50,994	62,276	76,598	94,836	118,121	147,913
40	61,610	77,663	98,827	126,840	164,048	213,610
45	73,331	95,501	125,871	167,685	225,508	305,752
50	86,271	116,181	158,774	219,815	307,756	434,986

This table shows how much £1,000 invested each year grows to at 8% a year to 13% a year over different time periods.

Interest or growth rate						Years
8%	9%	10%	11%	12%	13%	
£	£	£	£	£	£	
1,080	1,090	1,100	1,110	1,120	1,130	1
2,246	2,278	2,310	2,342	2,374	2,407	2
3,506	3,573	3,641	3,710	3,779	3,850	3
4,867	4,985	5,105	5,228	5,353	5,480	4
6,336	6,523	6,716	6,913	7,115	7,323	5
7,923	8,200	8,487	8,783	9,089	9,405	6
9,637	10,028	10,436	10,859	11,300	11,757	7
11,488	12,021	12,579	13,164	13,776	14,416	8
13,487	14,193	14,937	15,722	16,549	17,420	9
15,645	16,560	17,531	18,561	19,655	20,814	10
17,977	19,141	20,384	21,713	23,133	24,650	11
20,495	21,953	23,523	25,212	27,029	28,985	12
23,215	25,019	26,975	29,095	31,393	33,883	13
26,152	28,361	30,772	33,405	36,280	39,417	14
29,324	32,003	34,950	38,190	41,753	45,672	15
32,750	35,974	39,545	43,501	47,884	52,739	16
36,450	40,301	44,599	49,396	54,750	60,725	17
40,446	45,018	50,159	55,939	62,440	69,749	18
44,762	50,160	56,275	63,203	71,052	79,947	19
49,423	55,765	63,002	71,265	80,699	91,470	20
54,457	61,873	70,403	80,214	91,503	104,491	21
59,893	68,532	78,543	90,148	103,603	119,205	22
65,765	75,790	87,497	101,174	117,155	135,831	23
72,106	83,701	97,347	113,413	132,334	154,620	24
78,954	92,324	108,182	126,999	149,334	175,850	25
122,346	148,575	180,943	220,913	270,293	331,315	30
186,102	235,125	298,127	379,164	483,463	617,749	35
279,781	368,292	486,852	645,827	859,142	1,145,486	40
417,426	573,186	790,795	1,095,169	1,521,218	2,117,806	45
619,672	888,441	1,280,299	1,852,336	2,688,020	3,909,243	50

Table 3 How much you need to accumulate for the future

This table shows the lump sum you need now to accumulate £1,000 at
2% to 7% a year growth over different time periods. It also shows
how much £1,000 at the end of the different periods of time is worth in
today's money at 2% to 7% a year inflation.

Years	Interest or growth rate or inflation rate					
	2%	3%	4%	5%	6%	7%
	£	£	£	£	£	£
1	980	971	962	952	943	935
2	961	943	925	907	890	873
3	942	915	889	864	840	816
4	924	888	855	823	792	763
5	906	863	822	784	747	713
6	888	837	790	746	705	666
7	871	813	760	711	665	623
8	853	789	731	677	627	582
9	837	766	703	645	592	544
10	820	744	676	614	558	508
11	804	722	650	585	527	475
12	788	701	625	557	497	444
13	773	681	601	530	469	415
14	758	661	577	505	442	388
15	743	642	555	481	417	362
16	728	623	534	458	394	339
17	714	605	513	436	371	317
18	700	587	494	416	350	296
19	686	570	475	396	331	277
20	673	554	456	377	312	258
21	660	538	439	359	294	242
22	647	522	422	342	278	226
23	634	507	406	326	262	211
24	622	492	390	310	247	197
25	610	478	375	295	233	184
30	552	412	308	231	174	131
35	500	355	253	181	130	94
40	453	307	208	142	97	67
45	410	264	171	111	73	48
50	372	228	141	87	54	34

or how inflation reduces the value of your money

This table shows the lump sum you need now to accumulate £1,000 at
8% to 13% a year growth over different time periods. It also shows
how much £1,000 at the end of the different periods of time is worth in
today's money at 8% to 13% a year inflation.

Interest or growth rate or inflation rate						Years
8%	9%	10%	11%	12%	13%	
£	£	£	£	£	£	
926	917	909	901	893	885	1
857	842	826	812	797	783	2
794	772	751	731	712	693	3
735	708	683	659	636	613	4
681	650	621	593	567	543	5
630	596	564	535	507	480	6
583	547	513	482	452	425	7
540	502	467	434	404	376	8
500	460	424	391	361	333	9
463	422	386	352	322	295	10
429	388	350	317	287	261	11
397	356	319	286	257	231	12
368	326	290	258	229	204	13
340	299	263	232	205	181	14
315	275	239	209	183	160	15
292	252	218	188	163	141	16
270	231	198	170	146	125	17
250	212	180	153	130	111	18
232	194	164	138	116	98	19
215	178	149	124	104	87	20
199	164	135	112	93	77	21
184	150	123	101	83	68	22
170	138	112	91	74	60	23
158	126	102	82	66	53	24
146	116	92	74	59	47	25
99	75	57	44	33	26	30
68	49	36	26	19	14	35
46	32	22	15	11	8	40
31	21	14	9	6	4	45
21	13	9	5	3	2	50

Table 4 How much you need to invest each year

This table shows how much you need to invest each year to accumulate £1,000 if your money grows from 2% to 7% a year over different time periods.

Years	Interest or growth rate					
	2%	3%	4%	5%	6%	7%
	£	£	£	£	£	£
1	980.39	970.87	961.54	952.38	943.40	934.58
2	485.34	478.26	471.34	464.58	457.96	451.49
3	320.35	314.11	308.03	302.10	296.33	290.70
4	237.87	232.07	226.43	220.96	215.65	210.49
5	188.39	182.87	177.53	172.36	167.36	162.51
6	155.42	150.09	144.96	140.02	135.25	130.65
7	131.87	126.71	121.74	116.97	112.39	107.99
8	114.23	109.18	104.35	99.74	95.32	91.09
9	100.51	95.57	90.86	86.37	82.10	78.02
10	89.54	84.69	80.09	75.72	71.57	67.64
11	80.57	75.80	71.30	67.04	63.01	59.21
12	73.10	68.41	63.99	59.83	55.92	52.24
13	66.78	62.16	57.83	53.77	49.96	46.40
14	61.37	56.82	52.57	48.59	44.89	41.44
15	56.69	52.20	48.02	44.14	40.53	37.19
16	52.60	48.17	44.06	40.26	36.75	33.51
17	48.99	44.61	40.58	36.86	33.44	30.30
18	45.79	41.46	37.49	33.85	30.53	27.49
19	42.92	38.65	34.75	31.19	27.94	25.00
20	40.35	36.13	32.29	28.80	25.65	22.80
21	38.02	33.86	30.08	26.66	23.59	20.83
22	35.91	31.79	28.08	24.73	21.74	19.07
23	33.99	29.92	26.26	22.99	20.07	17.49
24	32.23	28.20	24.60	21.40	18.57	16.06
25	30.61	26.63	23.09	19.95	17.20	14.78
30	24.17	20.41	17.14	14.33	11.93	9.89
35	19.61	16.06	13.06	10.54	8.47	6.76
40	16.23	12.88	10.12	7.88	6.10	4.68
45	13.64	10.47	7.94	5.96	4.43	3.27
50	11.59	8.61	6.30	4.55	3.25	2.30

This table shows how much you need to invest each year to accumulate £1,000 if your money grows from 8% to 13% a year over different time periods.

Interest or growth rate						Years
8%	9%	10%	11%	12%	13%	
£	£	£	£	£	£	
925.93	917.43	909.09	900.90	892.86	884.96	1
445.16	438.96	432.90	426.97	421.16	415.47	2
285.22	279.87	274.65	269.56	264.60	259.75	3
205.48	200.61	195.88	191.29	186.82	182.47	4
157.83	153.30	148.91	144.66	140.54	136.56	5
126.22	121.94	117.82	113.85	110.02	106.33	6
103.77	99.72	95.82	92.09	88.50	85.05	7
87.05	83.19	79.49	75.96	72.59	69.37	8
74.15	70.46	66.95	63.61	60.43	57.41	9
63.92	60.39	57.04	53.88	50.88	48.04	10
55.63	52.24	49.06	46.05	43.23	40.57	11
48.79	45.55	42.51	39.66	37.00	34.50	12
43.08	39.97	37.07	34.37	31.85	29.51	13
38.24	35.26	32.50	29.94	27.56	25.37	14
34.10	31.25	28.61	26.18	23.95	21.90	15
30.53	27.80	25.29	22.99	20.88	18.96	16
27.43	24.81	22.42	20.24	18.26	16.47	17
24.72	22.21	19.94	17.88	16.02	14.34	18
22.34	19.94	17.77	15.82	14.07	12.51	19
20.23	17.93	15.87	14.03	12.39	10.93	20
18.36	16.16	14.20	12.47	10.93	9.57	21
16.70	14.59	12.73	11.09	9.65	8.39	22
15.21	13.19	11.43	9.88	8.54	7.36	23
13.87	11.95	10.27	8.82	7.56	6.47	24
12.67	10.83	9.24	7.87	6.70	5.69	25
8.17	6.73	5.53	4.53	3.70	3.02	30
5.37	4.25	3.35	2.64	2.07	1.62	35
3.57	2.72	2.05	1.55	1.16	0.87	40
2.40	1.74	1.26	0.91	0.66	0.47	45
1.61	1.13	0.78	0.54	0.37	0.26	50

Index